APOCALYPTIC AI

ROBERT M. GERACI

APOCALYPTIC AI

VISIONS OF HEAVEN IN ROBOTICS, ARTIFICIAL INTELLIGENCE, AND VIRTUAL REALITY

OXFORD
UNIVERSITY PRESS

OXFORD
UNIVERSITY PRESS

Oxford University Press is a department of the University of Oxford.
It furthers the University's objective of excellence in research, scholarship,
and education by publishing worldwide.

Oxford   New York
Auckland   Cape Town   Dar es Salaam   Hong Kong   Karachi
Kuala Lumpur   Madrid   Melbourne   Mexico City   Nairobi
New Delhi   Shanghai   Taipei   Toronto

With offices in
Argentina   Austria   Brazil   Chile   Czech Republic   France   Greece
Guatemala   Hungary   Italy   Japan   Poland   Portugal   Singapore
South Korea   Switzerland   Thailand   Turkey   Ukraine   Vietnam

Oxford is a registered trade mark of Oxford University Press
in the UK and certain other countries.

Published in the United States of America by
Oxford University Press
198 Madison Avenue, New York, NY 10016

Library of Congress Cataloging-in-Publication Data
Geraci, Robert M.
Apocalyptic AI : visions of heaven in robotics, artificial intelligence,
and virtual reality / Robert M. Geraci.
p. cm.
Includes bibliographical references and index.
ISBN 978-0-19-539302-6 (hardcover); 978-0-19-996400-0 (paperback)
1. Religion and science. 2. Robotics. 3. Artificial intelligence.
4. Virtual reality. I. Title.
BL255.5.G47 2010
201'.6006—dc22
2009025891

Printed in the United States of America
on acid-free paper

To my brothers
(in order of appearance: Vinny, Cody, Randy, Frank, and Kenn)
and my sisters
(Julie, Anne, and Giselle)
for all the many things they have done with me.

CONTENTS

ACKNOWLEDGMENTS

IT HAS TAKEN a good long while to write this book, and that means there are plenty of people to thank for their efforts along the way. That the book is the culmination of several different studies only expands the number of thank-yous owed.

First, I'm deeply grateful to my wife, Jovi, and my children, Zion and Liel. Without their patience when I was hiding in the bedroom to write and using my dresser as a bookshelf the book couldn't have been written. Without the fun and joy they give me when I crawl out of the bedroom, there wouldn't have been much point to writing it.

While their influence upon me began long ago, I continue to look for support and inspiration from The Congress, my former classmates during my graduate school years at the University of California. They were a brilliant bunch to study with, and they remain a brilliant group of colleagues, even if we are scattered around the country now.

I'm grateful for my current colleagues, especially those in the Department of Religious Studies at Manhattan College, who have given me wide latitude in deciding what kinds of projects to pursue. In addition, the college and its provost, Weldon Jackson, deserve recognition for financially supporting the trip to Pittsburgh that was necessary for chapter two. None of the chapters could have been written without the wonderful library staff at Manhattan College, who cheerfully tracked down books and articles through Interlibrary Loan and generally made my trips to the library pleasant through their gracious assistance and even more gracious friendship. Likewise, I appreciate the secretarial assistance and good cheer of Syrita Newman and MaryEllen Lamonica in the School of Arts, who make all manner of tasks simpler through their help.

Many people sat down for the interviews that form the ethnographic basis of two chapters in the book. Matt Mason, director of the Robotics Institute at Carnegie

Mellon University welcomed me to Pittsburgh as a visiting researcher, gave freely of his time and conversation, and proved a congenial friend. I had many wonderful conversations at the Institute and I appreciate the time that everyone gave to me for interviews, especially that of my friend Dave Touretzky. In addition, the residents of *Second Life* (SL) who spoke with me about their online lives made chapter three possible. I am particularly grateful to Sophrosyne Stenvaag and Giulio Prisco for their conversation, insightful observations and friendship.

Without Vogelman! helping me several years ago to overcome the worst of my bad habits as a writer and thinker, the text would be unreadable. Any credit for adequate writing should be shared with him; any criticism for unbearable writing, I'll shoulder myself.

I've benefitted enormously from peer reviews of my ideas, in particular that which I received from the *Journal of the American Academy of Religion* over an essay there and that which I received for this book from Noreen Herzfeld and an anonymous reader. Their efforts have greatly improved the manuscript, but they certainly cannot be held liable for those ways in which I may have revised imperfectly.

Cynthia Read, my editor at OUP, has been enthusiastic and encouraging from beginning to end. I am profoundly thankful for that. I am likewise grateful for the editorial assistance at OUP, which has enormously improved the manuscript.

Finally, I owe my gratitude to the singer-songwriter Mike Doughty, whose humorous references to robots led me into my present research field many years ago and to my wife's grandmother, Bobby, whose help made it possible for me to read and write, rather than teach, during the winters and summers. Without them, this book might never have been written.

And because they are always the first people I think of when I wake and the last I think of before I sleep, Jovi and the kids should be first and last in these acknowledgments. I'm very much in love with them and am so happy to have such an amazing family.

APOCALYPTIC AI

INTRODUCTION

AFTER I WROTE and published a series of papers on what I termed "Apocalyptic AI"—the presence of apocalyptic theology in popular science books on robotics and artificial intelligence (AI)—I found that much of my research begged a more serious question. I had no doubt that Jewish and Christian apocalyptic categories inform pop science robotics but I wondered whether those pop science books actually mattered at all and, if so, to whom. To answer this question, I stepped outside of my library and began an empirical study of real people working and living real lives.

Apocalyptic AI names a genre of popular science books and essays written by researchers in robotics and AI. These researchers include Hans Moravec and Kevin Warwick in robotics and Marvin Minsky, Ray Kurzweil, and Hugo de Garis in AI. These individuals are professional researchers, some of whom are justly famous for their technical work. In their pop science books, they extrapolate from current research trends to claim that in the first half of the twenty-first century, intelligent machines will populate the earth. By the end of the twenty-first century, machines might well be the only form of intelligent life on the planet.

Apocalyptic AI authors promise that intelligent machines—our "mind children," according to Moravec—will create a paradise for humanity in the short term but, in the long term, human beings will need to upload their minds into machine bodies in order to remain a viable life-form. The world of the future will be a transcendent digital world; mere human beings will not fit in. In order to join our mind children in life everlasting, we will upload our conscious minds into robots and computers, which will provide us with the limitless computational power and effective immortality that Apocalyptic AI advocates believe make robot life better than human life.

I am not interested in evaluating the moral worth of Apocalyptic AI. This book is about the social importance of Apocalyptic AI; it is an anthropological, not a theological work.[1] Furthermore, I am not interested in assessing the truth content of Apocalyptic AI. This book is neither supporting nor debunking the claims of Moravec and Kurzweil. The future is an unwritten story (despite Apocalyptic AI claims to the contrary!) and the fact that I do question some of the assumptions made in Apocalyptic AI does not mean that the authors are wrong in their predictions. As an anthropological study, this book assesses the *significance* and *presence* of Apocalyptic AI in modern culture, not its truthfulness or moral righteousness.[2]

Pop science books, especially those by Carnegie Mellon University's Hans Moravec and AI researcher Ray Kurzweil, take a dualistic approach to the world, one where physical and biological reality and bodily life are computationally inefficient and "bad" while rational, mechanical minds and virtual reality are efficient and "good." Moravec, Kurzweil, and others predict that we will upload our minds into machines and live forever in a virtual paradise. This transcendent future is the subject of Apocalyptic AI and is a marvelous integration of religious and scientific work. In chapter one, I describe the development of Apocalyptic AI and explore its religious roots but, as I have said, this discussion does not suffice to explain whether or not Apocalyptic AI *actually matters*. To understand how Apocalyptic AI influences modern life, I visited the Robotics Institute at Carnegie Mellon University (CMU) as a visiting researcher and held discussions and interviews in the increasingly popular virtual reality world, *Second Life* (SL).[3]

The apocalyptic perspective is not universally approved by members of the robotics and AI communities. Robot manufacturers already anticipate a cultural mixture of human beings and robots, rather than a cultural replacement of the former by the latter. Likewise, most researchers disregard the apocalyptic imagination altogether. The majority of academic researchers concern themselves with making robots and AI software work rather than with grand schemes for saving humankind from ignorance and mortality. Apocalyptic promises do, however, play a role in robotics and AI research: they justify public support and enhance the prestige of research. The prestige garnered by Apocalyptic AI affects not only scientific lay people but also funding agencies, such as the National Science Foundation (NSF), giving both groups added incentive to prioritize robotics and AI research.

I received a warm welcome from Matt Mason, the director of the Robotics Institute at CMU, where I joined Dr. Mason's Manipulation Laboratory research group during the summer of 2007. I was gratified that the other "natives" also welcomed me into their society despite what must have seemed to scientific practitioners a rather odd project. The greater part of this fieldwork became the second chapter of this book. Although many scientists might be suspicious of a religious studies scholar walking around looking for closet theologies, the Institute members engaged me cheerfully and helpfully. No trace of the resentment visible in battles over the so-called science wars marred my interaction at CMU. While physicists may fret over whether their results are "socially constructed" or not—and whether anyone believes the sociologists who say they are—the roboticists I met were comfortable with my intellectual speculation.

I had previously written about the implications of Apocalyptic AI in social struggles for cultural prestige (Geraci 2007a) but I hoped to learn more about what might motivate Moravec and the others. Upon my arrival, I felt that Apocalyptic AI might be a reaction to the moral hazards of accepting money from the military complex but during my residence at the Institute I came to realize that researchers do not seek a way out of the conundrum over military ethics. By and large, they accepted the source of their funding with equanimity, with only occasional exceptions. My thoughts on Apocalyptic AI and military funding appear in appendix two so that they will not disrupt the narrative but will be nevertheless available for those who wish to understand why military ethics does not drive Apocalyptic AI.

Eventually, I gained a clearer understanding of how prestige and public approval of robotics/AI research plays a role in Apocalyptic AI—robotics and AI enjoy government support as a consequence of the fantastic promises made by Apocalyptic AI authors. Promises of intelligent robots and uploaded consciousness could have replicated successfully through science fiction without ever mixing so closely with laboratory science, as they do in Apocalyptic AI pop science books. The value of the apocalyptic imagination lies in its power to create excitement in the lay public and government funding agencies. Pop science in general, and Apocalyptic AI in particular, is a—sometimes conscious, sometimes unconscious—strategy for the acquisition of cultural prestige, especially as such prestige is measured in financial support.

While this research and writing was under way, I was alerted to the online game *Second Life*, where "residents" build houses, buy clothing, go to bars and live music venues, and otherwise act much as they would in real life. I toured *Second Life* as Soren Ferlinghetti (I chose the last name from a list of given possibilities—I appreciated the beatnik reference—and the first from my admiration for Søren Kierkegaard's *The Sickness unto Death*) and I built the Virtual Temple,[4] where I held discussions on topics in religion, most of which were designed to be fieldwork for this book. I invited other people to come and share their ideas about religion and cybertechnologies and was astounded by what some of the residents told me. The Temple gave me a marvelous forum for finding people who wished to discuss a philosophy of *Second Life*. The results of those discussions and the rest of my time spent in the field can be found in chapter three, where I discuss how the promises of Apocalyptic AI play a powerful role in virtual communities.

Although researchers in robotics and AI often disagree with their apocalyptic colleagues, the apocalyptic pop science books of Moravec, Warwick, de Garis, and, especially, Kurzweil have found a welcome home in virtual communities of "transhumanists," "posthumanists," and "extropians." These groups, hereafter consolidated under the term transhumanists, eagerly look forward to the technological salvation promised in Apocalyptic AI, and their visions play a significant role in online gaming. Millions of users have created accounts so that their individual avatars can work, play, and meet other avatars. The residents of *Second Life* often find life online more enjoyable and more conducive to personal expression and self-fulfillment than they do earthly life. Not only is SL heavenly to many of its residents, it is explicitly understood through the categories of Apocalyptic AI. Many SL residents accept apocalyptic visions of transcendent heaven and individual immortality: some believe that their avatars are distinct "persons," without necessary connection to the biological person who created them, and others hope to upload their minds into SL or an equivalent virtual world.

Just as most Americans get their knowledge of robotics and AI through Hollywood, science fiction stories and films helped establish sacred communities of online gamers. Cyberpunk novels from the 1980s manufactured a sacred aura for virtual reality, separating it out from the life of "meat." These stories intertwined with the futuristic promises of Apocalyptic AI authors and have helped shape the public perception of online reality. A significant portion of online gamers would consider spending all of their time in those worlds if it were feasible. What makes online life so attractive vis-à-vis earthly life? Virtual reality is a flight from the mundane, a search for transcendence and meaning, a desire to constantly experience the power of human collectives and of the sacred. It is thus the perfect environment for transhumanist Apocalyptic AI communities.

Apocalyptic AI also drives important new movements in the study of mind, legal and governmental regulation, and theological ethics. Cognitive scientists and philosophers of mind now take account of the ideas advocated by Marvin Minsky, Hans Moravec, and Ray Kurzweil. In particular the idea that our minds are collections of individual agents (our minds are societies) and that, therefore, no true individual "I" exists has considerable cachet in the philosophy of mind despite the incredibly counterintuitive nature of the claim. In addition, the belief that our minds are patterns of information rather than integrally tied to their material substrates (brains) promotes particular ways of thinking about human beings. Whether or not machines actually *do* become conscious, the current conversation on that subject deserves consideration and is deeply entwined with contemporary debates over human consciousness.

In addition to the impact of Apocalyptic AI theorists on the study of the mind, the claims they make about intelligent robots have already been noticed by lawyers and policy experts seeking to prepare our legal and governmental structures for the future. While fantastically intelligent robots may be rather distant in our future, the prospect of their existence is difficult to ignore. At any rate, lawyers and policy makers now engage in debates over them. The prospect of legal rights for robots and of a society with human beings and robots working alongside one another demands considerable attention from today's thinkers.

While intelligent robots offer much grist for the policy mill, they simultaneously loom large in theological and moral debates. Computer scientists and theologians alike have wondered what moral obligations we will owe to robots and, simultaneously, what moral choices they will make. Should we think of robots as persons? Should we include them in our circles of empathy? At the same time, what kind of morality would intelligent robots espouse? Starting with Ray Kurzweil, several computer scientists have proposed that the intelligent robots of the future will have religious sentiments; some scientists argue that robots will even join humanity in our traditional religious practices and beliefs. In addition, the promises made by Apocalyptic AI theorists give theologians pause. In particular, what does it mean for Christian theology that we seek to build intelligent robots? A number of outspoken members of the academic community studying the interactions between religion and science believe that a properly formulated theology, one in which being made in the image of God means that we form loving relationships with others, implies that the goal of robotics should be the creation of new partners in creation. In this regard, Apocalyptic AI has led to a theology of robotic engineering, even though such theologians reject the conclusions of Apocalyptic AI.

Putting these many pieces together helps us understand how modern technoscience operates. While diachronic history is indispensible in understanding the nature of technoscientific progress, we cannot ignore the importance of synchronic historical approaches. Diachronic history is the history of sequential events: this event happened and then that event happened. It ties together the accumulation of knowledge and the shifting of paradigms, but it cannot fully account for the here and the now of any moment in history. Synchronic history, championed by the New Historicists in literary theory (see Veeser 1994), emphasizes the organic connections among texts, social structures, gender, sexuality, class hierarchy, ethnicity, family relations, work relations, etc. Throughout this book, I have omitted most of these, but show the connection between scientific work and a number of contemporary religious, political, entertainment, and literary concerns. A synchronic approach to pop science books in robotics and AI reveals the web entangling robotics and AI and academic, literary, gaming, legal, governmental, and ethical communities based on various strands of one religious ideology: Apocalyptic AI.

Intelligent robots, as portrayed in Apocalyptic AI, matter in contemporary society. They matter to the researchers who benefit from public appreciation. They matter to the communities in virtual reality that might one day include most if not all of humanity. They matter in public policy.[5] Speaking about robots allows us to circulate within these different groups, understanding how both science and religion constitute much of our social cohesion. The integration of religion and science in Apocalyptic AI reflects many of our traditionally religious concerns while at the same time recasting those concerns with a technoscientific aura.

Intelligent machines are boundary objects: plasticity of meaning allows robots to hold pride of place in research, gaming, and legal communities (despite the vastly different ways in which these groups think about and employ robots) while a consensual understanding of robots ensures that we all "know what we are talking about." What passes for a robot at CMU bears only a fuzzy relationship to the hypothetical robot a lawyer might argue could serve as a financial trustee. Yet enough of the robot remains constant over the translation from laboratory to virtual reality to neighborhood communities that we can understand its passage among them. As we follow the robots across cultural boundaries, we will learn a very great deal about modern American life. Apocalyptic AI is a powerful force in modern culture. Through science fiction and popular science, the movement advances technoscientific research agendas, creates the ideology for virtual life, and presses for the acceptance of intelligent machines into human culture.

The integration of religion and technology in Apocalyptic AI should not be ignored. Given how profoundly the movement affects and may continue to affect our society, responsible social analysis demands that we understand Apocalyptic AI in its religious and technoscientific contexts. Fortunately, the tools for such an analysis have slowly become available as scholars have increasingly examined the relationship of science and religion.

For several decades, the study of religion and science has steadily grown, largely with the intent of finding ways for modern people to "be religious" while simultaneously appreciating the contributions of modern science. Frequently, this ethical agenda has led scholars of religion and science to emphasize points of harmony between the two fields and to advocate the reconciliation of religious and scientific truths (see Barbour 1997; Clayton 2000; Gilbert 1997; Townes 1990)[6]. In large part, this exercise was a reaction against the nineteenth-century conflict thesis of Andrew White, who believed that "dogmatic theology," though not religion in its "essence," opposed scientific progress (White [1896] 1923). The reconciliation paradigm grew out of twentieth-century American Protestant thought and was a boon to historical, sociological, and anthropological work in that it established religion and science as a legitimate area of academic inquiry.

Unfortunately, the reconciliation agenda is deeply problematic. In addition to its serious methodological problems (see Cantor and Kenny 2001), it may not be able to bring about what it hopes to achieve. Reconciliation theorists hope that religion and science can come together in a broader metaphysical worldview. In practice, however, the integration of religion and science rarely serves the interests of the liberal Christians who defend such a view. Integration between religion and science is most successful (read, "gains the most adherents") in enterprises that the liberal Christian faithful would likely oppose, such as the Intelligent Design movement among fundamentalist Christians and Apocalyptic AI among pop scientists, online gamers, and transhumanists.

Apocalyptic AI is a powerful reconciliation of religion and science. The sacred categories of Jewish and Christian apocalyptic traditions have thoroughly penetrated the futuristic musings of important researchers in robotics and artificial intelligence. Those categories have serious political effects in robotics research, virtual reality/online gaming, and contemporary disputes over the nature of consciousness and personhood, public policy, and theology (all of which subsequently drive Apocalyptic AI deep into legal and social concerns). Robots, as portrayed in Apocalyptic AI, link these disparate elements of society. To study intelligent robots is to study our culture.

ONE

APOCALYPTIC AI

INTRODUCTION

Excepting rapture theologians of fundamentalist Christianity, popular science authors in robotics and artificial intelligence have become the most influential spokespeople for apocalyptic theology in the Western world. Apocalyptic AI resolves a fundamentally dualist worldview through faith in a transcendent new realm occupied by radically transformed human beings. These religious categories come directly from Jewish and Christian apocalyptic theology; they are the continuation of those theological traditions. Apocalyptic AI advocates promise that in the very near future technological progress will allow us to build supremely intelligent machines and to copy our own minds into machines so that we can live forever in a virtual realm of cyberspace.

The historian Joseph J. Corn implies that the masses of "regular people" are "to blame" for our faith in the possibility of technology to fulfill our salvific dreams. "Ignorance about the rudimentary workings of technology, the lack of what we now call technological literacy, has always contributed to the envisioning of material things as social panaceas" (Corn 1986, 222). Corn might be surprised, then, that the theological promise of AI comes directly from the leaders of our modern technocracy. Although Corn believes that technological ignorance leads to soteriological dreams, a careful look at technological innovators shows that they lead the charge to find salvation in robotics and AI. In fact, if we follow David Noble's account of the rise of technology (1999), we see a steady stream of influential intellectuals who defended the soteriological promise of technology throughout modern history. It is not the scientifically ignorant who champion the religion of technology (though they may well join a movement of it) but the technological leaders who do so.

Allen Newell, one of the pioneers of AI, has given the religion of technology a beautifully mythical cast. "The aim of technology," he says, "when properly applied, is to build a land of Faerie" (Newell 1990, 421). Despite Max Weber's belief that technology fundamentally disenchants the world (Weber 1958), Newell states that it is precisely the enchantment of the world that technology seeks.[1] In the case of artificial intelligence, Newell believes that the incorporation of "intelligent behavior in all the nooks and crannies of our world" (Newell 1990, 422) will succeed at this basic technological obligation.

Artificial intelligence may be the single most important twenty-first-century technology of enchantment.[2] Apocalyptic AI is a movement in popular science books that integrates the religious categories of Jewish and Christian apocalyptic traditions with scientific predictions based upon current technological developments. Ultimately, the promises of Apocalyptic AI are almost identical to those of Jewish and Christian apocalyptic traditions. Should they come true, the world will be, once again, a place of magic.

Apocalypticism refers to 1) a dualistic view of the world, which is 2) aggravated by a sense of alienation that can be resolved only through 3) the establishment of a radically transcendent new world that abolishes the dualism and requires 4) radically purified bodies for its inhabitants. These characteristics of ancient apocalypticisms reappear in Apocalyptic AI. In short, Apocalyptic AI divides the world into categories of good and bad, isomorphic with those of knowledge/ignorance, machine/biology and virtual world/physical world. Apocalyptic AI theorists locate human beings on the bad end of this spectrum due to the human body's limited intellectual powers and inevitable death. Apocalyptic AI promises to resolve the problems of dualism and alienation in a radically transcendent future where we forsake our biological bodies in favor of virtual bodies that will inhabit an omnipresent and morally meaningful cyberspace.

MYSTICAL ENGINEERS

The eschatological and utopian visions of robotic technologies are but one part of a larger technological religion. Before we discuss the theological aspects of pop science books in robotics and AI, however, we should briefly seek to understand how modern science and technology developed out of the universities and monasteries of medieval Christianity. This historical process explains why Christian theology affects the goals of scientific research and technological development in the modern world. "What we experience today," writes David Noble, "is neither new nor odd but, rather, a continuation of a thousand-year-old Western tradition in which the advance of the useful arts was inspired by and grounded upon religious expectation" (Noble 1999, 4). Although nineteenth- and twentieth-century commentators made considerable effort to sever the connections between religion and science, these efforts have almost entirely failed. The vain exclamations of "strong atheists" and Brights (e.g., Dawkins 2006; Harris 2004) aside, technological research has continued to be "suffused with religious belief" (Noble 1999, 5). This is not to say that there is something essential about the connection between science and religion, only that among the many ways in which religion and science have interacted over the millennia, one fact is that—if only by virtue of geographical coincidence—Christian theology has mixed with technoscientific research (in chapter two, I shall briefly discuss how non-Christian theology has intertwined with modern technology). The religious influence upon modern science and technology is neither a good thing nor a bad thing; it is simply a fact of life. I see no reason to believe that science or technology could be completely separated from religion nor have I any reason to believe that such a separation would be of unmitigated benefit to either party.[3]

Scientific thought intermixed with religious ideology throughout the rise of modern science. Francis Bacon (1561–1626), whose advocacy of empiricism makes him one of the founders of modern science, described how technology served Christian aims in his fictional story *New Atlantis*, published in 1627 (Bacon 1951).[4] For Bacon, human progress demands the twin aims of religious and scientific restoration (McKnight 2006). In *New Atlantis*, the people of a remote island have a scientific society (The Society of Solomon's House) which develops technology to increase individual life spans, control the forces of weather, improve upon nature, and finish the divine creation. Their use of technology is explicitly religious, including daily prayers "imploring his [i.e., God's] aid and blessing for the illumination of our [technoscientific] labours, and the turning of them into good and holy uses" (Bacon 1951, 298).[5]

Other key figures in the scientific revolution were equally—if not more—religious. Isaac Newton (1642–1727)—justly famous for his work on calculus, gravity, and optics—wrote more books on prophecy than he did on natural philosophy. Robert Boyle (1627–1691), one of the founders of modern chemistry, sought to demonstrate the existence of God through chemical experimentation. Not only was Boyle a noted philanthropist, he also supported the Company for the Propagation of the Gospel in New England and "became the foremost champion of his day in rebutting the charge that intercourse with science disposed men to atheism . . . and provided in his will for the foundation of a series of annual lectures to prove the truth of the Christian religion" (Moelwyn-Hughes 1964, vii). There were precious few natural philosophers (the word "scientist" was not coined until the nineteenth century) who did not integrate religious and scientific beliefs as they brought about the scientific revolution.

The early modern natural philosophers were near universal in possessing a religious outlook. Since its rise in medieval monasteries, technology has been implicated in 1) the Christian desire to restore humanity to the perfection of Adam prior to his fall and 2) the millenarian struggle between Jesus and the forces of evil that will inaugurate the eternal heavenly kingdom (Noble 1999). Many natural philosophers believed that Adam possessed all scientific knowledge and sufficient powers of observation to understand all of creation. In order to overcome Adam's failure and restore humanity to prelapsarian grace (i.e., the grace before the fall), natural philosophers improved their powers and observations through technology. The rise of Protestantism continued this trend: natural philosophers in seventeenth-century England believed that Adam could "sense all facts directly, including the earth's orbital motion and the circulation of his blood . . . [modern] Experimenters were fallen, so they needed instruments. But armed with these tools they became regenerate, and, according to some, would see what Adam saw" (Schaffer 2002, 503). The devices that modern human beings require (microscopes, telescopes, etc.) in order to understand the world demonstrate humanity's fall but at the same time fulfill the religious obligation to make amends, to overcome sinfulness. At the same time, increased scientific and technological knowledge predicted a coming millennium of peace, a worldly progress that matched postmillenarian Biblical interpretation.[6]

The dominant role played by religion in public life was supposed to dwindle in the twentieth century.[7] In the wake of the Scopes Trial about the teaching of evolution in public schools (1925), Frederick Lewis Allen, in his enormously influential book *Only Yesterday*, saw "the triumph of reason over revelation and science over superstition in modern America" (Larson 1997, 227). And, in fact, this alleged victory of reason and science (now or in the future) has been held crucial for the future of democracy by some secularist advocates, such as the philosopher Richard Rorty (Stout 2008, 535–36).[8]

Despite the claims of secularists, however, religious belief and practice retains its popularity; while secularization is common in "religious economies," it never separates itself from "a countervailing intensification of religion" in other parts of its society (Stark and Bainbridge 1985, 2). Secularism, argue Stark and Bainbridge, stimulates revival in traditional religious practice and—and this is crucial to the remainder of this book—also religious innovation (ibid., 2).[9] Just as all of the world's religions were once on their respective cultural fringes, a new religious movement that revolves around the future of robotics and AI might someday become fully mainstream (its growth is already measurable!).

The growth in scientific knowledge and the rapid deployment of powerful technologies were key to twentieth-century faith in the triumph of secularism. The eminent sociologist Max Weber, for example, argued that science had disenchanted the world (Weber 1958), a trend not susceptible to reversal because once explained scientifically, facts were forevermore overdetermined. For Weber, only the absence of scientific explanations allowed room for enchanted or religious explanations of facts.[10] Secularism has not, however, banished religion to insignificance, nor has it eliminated the religious impulse from technoscientific work. Later thinkers have persistently argued that enchantment remained after the rise of secularism, integral even to the world of technology (Bailey 2005; Noble 1999). As in the past, scientific research will supposedly deliver us from evil and provide an eternal spring of equality and justice. Technological progress has been extraordinary across much of human activity but the most impressive changes in social structure have been wrought by computers, which remain tied to theology and which, in Apocalyptic AI, never stray from the desire to find meaning and purpose in natural science. A high priesthood of divine scientists and engineers will, by building intelligent machines and worlds of virtual reality, lead us forward into the joyous world of life everlasting.[11]

The intersection of religious ideals and digital technology first occurred in countercultural groups that united communalist ideals, New Age spirituality, and technological progressivism. Countercultural groups—especially as led by Stewart Brand and his *Whole Earth Catalog* and spinoffs—expected computers to usher in freedom from the modern world's stultification and alienation (Turner 2006). In the late twentieth-century technocratic circles that emerged out of the countercul-ture of the 1960s and 1970s, modems became the doorways into paradise. Fred Turner calls this "digital utopianism" because the leaders in digital culture believed that the Internet would usher in a new world of harmony among people and the environment. A new peer-to-peer society would promote collective liberation (ibid., 208–9) and a leveling of traditional hierarchies (ibid., 219).

As in Bacon's *New Atlantis*, digital utopianism allows the rise of a new techno-logical priesthood; the abolition of hierarchies through peer-to-peer societies would allow a new social structure grounded in computer meritocracy where designers actually ascend into the heavenly ranks as angels or gods. The creators of com-puter simulations of life have often likened themselves to gods (Helmreich [1998] 2000, 83–84, 193) while simultaneously drawing upon New Age and Buddhist social structures that delegitimate prior hierarchies (ibid., 182–202). This attitude, widespread among the digital utopians, was well publicized by Kevin Kelly, editor of *Wired*. In his "Nerd Theology" essay, Kelly argues that the creators of new com-puter worlds (in computer games, in virtual reality, in artificial life simulations, and more) are the gods of their own theological systems (Kelly 1999, 389), a posi-tion echoed by many designers (Helmreich 1998, 85).[12]

Cyberspace allowed the technocracy to rethink salvation and what it means to be human; properly envisioned, cyberspace created a wonderful new human-machine hybrid. *Wired* magazine equated cyberspace with a new frontier akin to the communes of the 1960s counterculture, which were intended to reverse the routinization of modern life (Turner 2006, 229). Stewart Brand, the founder of the Whole Earth Network and an enormously influential figure in the rise of cyber-culture,[13] saw modern life as stultifying and mechanical, so he fled to the counter-culture. At the same time, Brand advocated the use of cybernetic ideas and high technology that could benefit those living in communes and other countercultural environments. Reunited with technology, the counterculture saw a new way of thinking about human beings and machines. Humanizing machines, rather than dehumanizing persons, could be the ground for a new world.[14]

The desire for cyberspace salvation draws upon the changing religious metaphysics of the modern world. Margaret Wertheim has convincingly argued that modern science has systematically dismantled our Western understandings of sacred space, leaving god, heaven, and the souls of the dead with no particular place to go (Wertheim 1999). She argues that understanding of and mastery over physical space, from astrophysics to genetics, has seen an accompanying loss of spiritual space but, rather than accepting Weber's "disenchantment thesis," she argues that this has led to an empowerment of particular kinds of religious activity. In a literal sense, "we have lost any conception of a spiritual *place*—a part of reality in which spirits or souls might reside" (ibid., 33, emphasis original), and, as a consequence, cyberspace fills a psychological, religious void in modern life (ibid., 30). "Once again we find ourselves with a material realm described by science, and an immaterial realm that operates as a different plane of the real" (ibid., 230).

Cyberspace is sacred space. Cyberspace allows us to build paradise in ways previously unimaginable. Christians have long sought to create heavenly spaces in their cathedrals, with arching roofs and towering spires—but these spaces were all too human and all too earthly. They were limited by the constraints of physics and engineering. Flying buttresses allowed you to put windows into huge stone structures . . . but those windows were too few and too small.[15] Michael Benedikt, an architect and the editor of the influential book *Cyberspace: First Steps*, directly compares cyberspace to the radiant city of the Book of Revelation (Benedikt 1994, 14). Christians anticipate a jeweled and glowing city to be their home in the rebuilt world, and such a city can in some sense be realized in a virtual world.

While digital utopianism (including its architectural branch) owes its precise formulation of a transcendent virtual reality to Apocalyptic AI, its integration of religion and technology is characteristic of much of Western science. Our technoscientific heritage is grounded in the religious life of the Western world, which explains how religious goals and sacred categories are inseparably mixed into its experimental aims. At least in this case, there really is nothing new under the sun and, thus, this is but the newest formulation of an old relationship. Given the extraordinary amount of power at stake in modern technology, however, it has become ever more important that we uncover and understand such relationships.

The enchantment of cyberspace has been a key factor in the rise of a new religious movement: transhumanism. Transhumanism, which I will address more carefully in chapter three, is a philosophical or religious (depending upon who you ask) system that advocates a "better than well" approach to humanity. Transhumanists believe that through judicious choices and technoscientific progress, humankind can transcend its present conditions and obtain healthier, happier and longer, possibly infinite, life spans. While some transhumanists restrict their hopes to the promise of biotechnology, many (in particular the Apocalyptic AI advocates discussed throughout this book) see robotics and artificial intelligence as the keys to a transcendent future. In doing so, they incorporate the apocalyptic categories of ancient Judaism and Christianity into a modern worldview buttressed by the successes of twentieth and twenty-first century technology.

JEWISH AND CHRISTIAN APOCALYPSES

The foundation of apocalypticism is the desire to reconcile a cosmic dualism in which good and evil struggle against one another in the universe. This dualism can only be fixed in a transcendent new world occupied by purified and angelic beings. Apocalypticism cannot flourish, however, without a sense of alienation that accelerates the believer's eschatology (expectation of the world's end). The apocalyptic believer, desperate to end his alienation and resolve the cosmic dualism, anticipates that God will soon rectify human problems by destroying the world and replacing it with a perfect world in which the believer will live in an angelic new body. These basic characteristics can be seen in the major apocalyptic works of ancient Judaism and Christianity, from the Second Temple period of Judaism[16] through the end of the first century CE.

To be precise, apocalypse means "unveiling" or "revelation" in Greek and refers to a (generally eschatological) literary genre from the ancient world in which a prophet receives divine revelation about a transcendent reality to come.[17] Pop scientists have produced no apocalypses in this sense: pop science revelations never come from gods and their authors are not prophets in the traditional sense. The Apocalyptic AI authors draw upon past technological achievements and the presumably overwhelming powers of evolution (now applied to technology rather than biology) to predict the future in terms they consider scientifically certain. Although an apocalypse is technically a literary work, the word can be and is used almost synonymously with the end of the world (the *eschaton*). I will, therefore, occasionally refer to "the AI apocalypse" though this requires that I use the term in conventional, if not technically proper, ways. The AI apocalypse is the series of events predicted by pop science authors in robotics and AI.

The pop science promises of Hans Moravec and others discussed below are religious and apocalyptic despite the most obvious difference between their visions and the ancient Jewish and Christian apocalypses: Apocalyptic AI has no god whose will brings about the new world. The eminent scholar of apocalypticism John Collins, for example, believes that apocalypticism is "the belief that God has revealed the imminent end of the ongoing struggle between good and evil in history" (J. Collins 2000a, vii). It might then appear that Apocalyptic AI cannot, in fact, be apocalyptic: after all, what god enters the realm of popular robotics? This position has been held by Ted Peters of the Center for Theology and Natural Sciences (Peters 2008). Although Collins has emphasized the role of gods in apocalypticism, we do better when we rely upon his other insights to categorize what makes an ideology apocalyptic; Peters believes that a lack of gods makes digital transhumanism non-apocalyptic but offers no particular reason to support that assertion. In fact, no gods are necessary for apocalypticism. Rather, Collins's apocalyptic dualism between good and evil and its resolution in a transcendent future is more productive as a point of discrimination between that which is apocalyptic and that which is not (Geraci 2008a).

Jewish and Christian apocalyptic traditions[18] grew out of the cultural mixture of ancient Israel's prophetic (D. S. Russell 1964; Hanson [1975] 1979) and wisdom (von Rad 1965) traditions, the combat myths of ancient Mesopotamia (R. Clifford 2000), and writings from Greek and Persian cultures (J. Collins 2000b). Collectively, these sources found a home in the social landscape of Second Temple Judaism and early Christianity, where disenfranchised Jews and Christians struggled to reconcile their political and social alienation with divine promises. Both the Jews and the Christians believed that they had an arrangement with God which was not being entirely upheld, as each group suffered particular kinds of discrimination.

Alienation, though not itself sufficient to foster an apocalyptic worldview, is a necessary engine for apocalypticism. Second Temple Judaism and early Christianity were rife with apocalyptic beliefs because the Jews and subsequent Christians suffered from significant political and theological discomfort. Political conflicts were chronicled in the Bible as the Jewish homeland was successively invaded by occupying nations. We see a connection between apocalyptic hopes and political conflicts with Assyria (Isaiah), the Babylonian Captivity and postexilic period (Ezekiel, Isaiah 55–66), Greek rule and the Maccabean Revolt (Daniel, 2 Maccabees, the early elements of the apocryphal 1 Enoch), and Roman rule (the apocryphal 2 Baruch, also known as the Syriac Apocalypse of Baruch, 4 Ezra, which is chapters 3–14 of the apocryphal 2 Esdras,[19] the apocryphal Apocalypse of Abraham, and the later parts of 1 Enoch 37–71).[20]

While early texts such as Isaiah and Ezekiel were not themselves apocalypses, they provided some of that genre's key concepts. Prophetic oracles and hopes for redemption led to full-blown apocalypticism in later generations. Although the Jews were allowed to return to Jerusalem, they experienced only brief bouts of self-rule thereafter. In particular, Greek rule after Alexander proved troublesome for the Jews and it was in this period that the first true apocalypses were written. The subsequent defeat of the Greeks in the Maccabean revolt, which began around 167 BCE, provided the Jews with only a short respite from foreign domination. The Romans conquered the Jews in the year 67 BCE and they remained in power through the rise and early development of Christianity.

These political conflicts were particularly important to Jews because of their covenant with God. Jews believed that if they upheld the covenant (i.e., obeyed God and followed the commandments), they would receive prosperity and control over the land of Israel. Insofar as the Jews continued to obey the commandments, they required an explanation as to why God withheld control of the promised land. Many came to believe that God would soon rectify the inequities of the world and establish a just kingdom. Difficult times led Jews to a new kind of religious vision. "Apocalyptic," notes D.S. Russell, "is a language of crisis" (1978, 6).

Political alienation is not sufficient, by itself, for apocalyptic beliefs, although it may be a necessary ingredient. Stephen Cook, however, argues that apocalypticism is not tied to alienation or deprivation at all; he believes that apocalyptic writings in Ezekiel, Zechariah, and Joel stem from ruling priestly groups (Cook 1995). Likewise, de Boer points out that for Paul,[21] alienation was a consequence, not a cause, of his conversion to Jesus's mission because Paul was a relatively well-off Jew and suffered political attacks only after he converted to the cause of Jesus (de Boer 2000, 348). De Boer's position presumes, however, that Jewish political life was stable and comfortable for Paul. While Paul may not have been subject to political persecution prior to his conversion, large segments of the Jewish community were uncomfortable precisely because political alienation was a constant fact under Roman rule. Horsley suggests that colonialism (in this case imperial domination from Rome) can lead to cultural retreat and, therefore, zealous persecution of sinners, a sequence he attributes as likely in the case of Paul (Horsley 1993, 128–29). By Roman times, prolonged subjugation of Judea meant that Jewish society was "almost continually in circumstances of crisis" (ibid., 4), a position previously held by D. S. Russell (1978). Likewise, as John Collins points out, "even those who wielded power in post-exilic Judah experienced relative deprivation in the broader context of the Persian empire" (2000b, 133) as did those of the Hellenistic period (ibid., 147). It is important, however, to note that a tie between apocalypticism and alienation *does not* indicate that apocalypticism flourished among only conventicles (small religious groups who have lost power struggles).[22] Horsley and Russell rightly demonstrate that the apocalyptic imagination can arise within both powerful and weak groups, both of which can suffer from alienation.[23] Although its degree might vary from era to era, there should be no question that alienation was common in Roman Palestine and is a contributor to apocalyptic ideology.

Just as the Jews were unhappy throughout Greek and Roman rule, so too were Christians in Roman times.[24] In many ways, the followers of Jesus were politically worse off than the Jews. Although the Jews caused some problems for the Romans, the Romans felt that the Jews followed an ancient religion and, thus, allowed its practice. To the Romans, the followers of Jesus appeared to have invented a new religion and they were subsequently persecuted for their refusal to engage in Roman civic religion. The followers of Jesus were eventually thrown out of the

Jewish synagogues and frequently hunted down by Roman authorities, who burned them, crucified them, and threw them to the lions. Thus Christians were utterly homeless, having neither temple nor marketplace in which to find safety.

Ancient Jewish and Christian apocalypses (largely written between 200 BCE and 100 CE) generally agree that radical transcendence will resolve the alienation experienced by their audiences. Apocalyptic communities held to dualistic world-views in which opposing powers oppressed the righteous. In his final intervention in history, God will overthrow the oppressors, create a perfect new world, and resurrect the righteous in purified and glorified new bodies.

Cosmic dualism causes the alienation of apocalyptic believers. When the world is divided up into categories of good/evil and heaven/earth, the believer will be necessarily alienated. Our exclusion from heaven logically necessitates that our surroundings be evil (or, at least, not good), which of course explains how Jews could find themselves out of power despite their commitment to the covenant. The more deeply the believer feels his or her immersion in evil, the more he or she will anticipate the arrival of a solution. Alienation accelerates eschatology; it provides an impetus for the end of the world. The balance of powers in cosmic dualism cannot last because it challenges the authority of God and the goodness of the cosmos. Because apocalyptics are, essentially, optimistic about the goodness of God and the future (Meeks 2000), they expect that the more obvious that evil appears to be the more likely it must be that God is planning to permanently resolve the matter.

Apocalyptic discourse, argues Wayne Meeks, is revelatory, interpretive, and dualistic (Meeks 2000, 462). By revelatory, Meeks refers to the literal definition of apocalypse—that the apocalypse is a revelation from God. Apocalypticism is interpretive in the sense that it reinterprets traditional or older imagery and in that it requires interpretation itself (often by a character within the narrative).[25] For example, God explicitly explains the time frame of the apocalypse to the prophet Baruch (2 Baruch 26–28) and the angel Uriel repeatedly comes to help Ezra understand his vision (e.g., 4 Ezra 5:32). The most critical element in Meeks's study, the dualism inherent to apocalypticism, is what really guides an apocalyptic ideology.[26] "Apocalyptic discourse is dualistic temporally, spatially, and socially. It divides this world from the world to come, earth from heaven, and us from them—dwellers in heaven from dwellers on earth, children of light from children of darkness" (Meeks 2000, 463). The faithful inevitably look forward to the future world, when they will be freed from the constraints of earthly life and offered a chance to live a paradisiacal new life, one that they deserve by dint of their unflagging faith in the eventual triumph of the good and their contribution thereto.

The resolution of cosmic dualism can only happen in a transcendent new world. Apocalypticism is different from utopian eschatology insofar as it leads, not just to a pleasant and peaceful kingdom on Earth, but to a heavenly kingdom (J. Collins

2000b) that eliminates the binary opposition of good/evil (Bull 1999, 80).[27] The ancient apocalypses look forward to such a world; the current world is, as 4 Ezra states, but clay compared to the gold of the next (8:1–3). The transcendent goal of apocalypticism is a remarkable shift in Jewish thought. No longer content to await a messiah who will inaugurate a just and peaceful kingdom on Earth, apocalyptic Jews insist that no earthly kingdom could possibly fulfill the divine plan. Clearly, God must intend to give the Jews a different kind of Jerusalem, one whose splendor could never find equal in the present world.

Because cosmic dualism is resolved in the world to come, that world will be infinitely more meaningful than our present world. In the ancient apocalypses, meaningful activity was defined as prayer and praise of God. In their prophetic travels, apocalyptic visionaries were accepted into heaven, where they witnessed what life would be like in the postapocalyptic kingdom. The apocalyptic heaven looks like a glorious temple, which the visionaries enter after they receive priestly investiture from the angels (Himmelfarb 1993). In heaven, the newly invested prophets witness angels and righteous human beings praying and praising God (2 Enoch 8–9, Apocalypse of Zephaniah 3:3–4, 1 Enoch 39:9–14). In heaven, where cosmic dualism does not apply, praise of God is the highest and most meaningful activity and it therefore occupies the highest levels of heaven. Apocalyptic prophets have no difficulty pointing out how different this is from our own world, where material desires overshadow the spiritual. When the new kingdom is built, it will be just like the heaven shown to the prophets.

Apocalyptic hope for a transcendent world is accelerated by alienation. The hope for a new world was common to ancient Jews and Christians, who expressed it in their writings. "I am about to create new heavens and a new earth," declares God in the Hebrew Bible (Isaiah 65:17). This event is fully realized in 1 Enoch's "Apocalypse of Weeks" (1 Enoch 94:16) around the time of the Maccabees and revisited in John's apocalyptic vision (Revelation 21:1) in the late first century CE. Although such language was originally metaphorical (as in Isaiah or the promise of the resurrection of Israel in Ezekiel 37), 1 Enoch offers a literal expectation of the world's recreation in Jewish apocalypticism (J. Collins 2000b, 141) and this became the standard interpretation of divine promises. John sees a New Jerusalem descending from heaven; in the New Jerusalem, death and sadness will be wiped away (Revelation 21:2–4). God will erase all the Jews' and Christians' political problems. In the New Kingdom, no one needs to worry whether he or she should pay taxes to Caesar!

God is always just about to create a new world in apocalyptic imaginings. The imminent end of the world is predicted among Jews (4 Ezra 4:26, 2 Baruch 85:10) and Christians (Mark 13:30, 1 Thessalonians 4:13–18, Revelation 22:7). For the oppressed, the marginalized, and the ideologically disenfranchised, there would be little solace gained from believing that God will rectify the cosmic dualism and create a perfect world someday in the far distant future. While that might benefit subsequent generations, it would do little for the apocalyptic believer him or herself. Besides the immediate concern for one's own welfare, the immediacy of the apocalypse "underscores the dire nature, the emergency of the current state of affairs" (Schoepflin 2000, 428). Apocalyptic beliefs reflect a concern that this is an important time, a singular time in the history of the world. Faith that God intends to create a perfect world in the very near future gives hope to the downtrodden.[28]

The new world is fully eschatological: it leads nowhere and it never evolves. Flush with the eternal presence of God, it is ultimately meaningful with nothing more to be sought. The faithful will enter the divine temple and conduct perfect praise of God without need of anything else. Whatever else it is that happens in the New Jerusalem, it certainly will not advance history in any conventional sense. Novelty is tied to the binary logic of pre-eschatological life. Novelty is desired precisely because it clarifies the cosmic dualism and advances progress toward the eradication of the dualism. Once the New Kingdom is established, however, there is no need for anything new, no need for historical progression.

God, of course, plans to include the righteous in this wondrous future. Thanks to their resurrection in transformed bodies, the saved will enter the Kingdom of God. Most apocalyptic Jews and Christians believed in a bodily, not a spiritual, resurrection.[29] Indeed, it was the bodily element of resurrection that functioned as the lynchpin of communal self-definition, uniting the disparate elements of Jewish and Christian theologies (Setzer 2004).[30] Bodily resurrection first occurs in Ezekiel 37, where it refers, not to a literal resurrection of the faithful but to a restored nation of Israel: "I am going to open your graves, and bring you up from your graves, O my people; and I will bring you back to the land of Israel" (Ezekiel 37:12; see also Isaiah 25:8 and 26:19). In subsequent writings, resurrection of the body became a key theological doctrine.

Although subsequent apocalyptic Jews and Christians expected bodily resurrection, they did not expect to have precisely the same bodies as those that they possessed in life. Their earthly bodies, tainted as they were by the dualistic world that they inhabited, would not be appropriate in heaven. Instead, resurrected bodies would be new and glorious. God would raise up the dead in purified bodies; made immortal, these glorious new bodies would enable the righteous to join the angels in the Kingdom of God. The bodies of the saved will be incorruptible, imperishable. This tradition begins as early as the apocalyptic portions of Isaiah: "No more shall there be in [the new world] an infant that lives but a few days, or an old person who does not live out a lifetime; for one who dies at a hundred years will be considered a youth" (Isaiah 65:20). Isaiah, however, is not radical enough for the later apocalyptics. They expected the bodily resurrection to do more than just raise bodies from the ground and grant them long life. Apocalyptics believed that bodily resurrection would include a transformation of the body into something superior (2 Baruch 51:3–10, Mark 12:25, Luke 20:35–36, 1 Corinthians 15:42–44), which would partake of the glory of the stars and possess beauty and immortality.

Apocalyptic resurrection beliefs show that the faithful acknowledged the fundamental imperfection of our selves as we inhabit the world. It stands opposite the common Greek notion of escape from the body because it requires a body, but it does not simply accept that our present bodies could occupy the new kingdom. Paul asserts, shortly after the death of Jesus, that "flesh and blood cannot inherit the kingdom" (1 Corinthians 15:50), by which he refers to the impossibility of saving human bodies *as they are in this world*. As the faithful are lifted into the transcendent new world, they must take on new forms. "We will not all die," says Paul, "but we will all be changed" (1 Corinthians 15:51; see also 2 Corinthians 5:1–4). We will all need bodies in the new kingdom, but those bodies must be altogether superior to the ones we have now. God must, therefore, act to transform human bodies into angelic bodies.

In ancient Jewish and Christian apocalyptic traditions, the saved share the glory of celestial bodies (which were believed to be angels). Comparing the resurrected body to the sun, the moon, and the stars, Paul says, "What is sown is perishable, what is raised is imperishable. It is sown in dishonor, it is raised in glory. It is sown in weakness, it is raised in power. It is sown a physical body, it is raised a spiritual body" (1 Corinthians 15:42–44; see also Philippians 3:21). Likewise, the Jewish text 2 Baruch declares that the saved "shall be glorified in changes, and the form of their face shall be turned into the light of their beauty, that they may be able to acquire and receive the world which does not die, which is promised to them" (2 Baruch 51:3–4) and "they shall be made equal to the stars" (2 Baruch 51:9).

The glorious new body will be immortal. Death marks the ultimate degradation of humanity so resurrection in a heavenly body will eliminate mortality. The "perishable body must put on imperishability, and this mortal body must put on immortality" (1 Corinthians 15:53–54). The impure bodies of the world are mortal. God promises a new body, one that belongs in the New Jerusalem. Reconfigured bodies will combine humanity with the divine glory of the celestial realm. These bodies will be eternal, perfect, and immortal . . . just like the world to which they go.

Apocalyptic ideology has surpassed the traditional boundaries of Jewish and Christian theology and has become instrumental in American popular culture. Modern apocalyptic fervor includes prophecy belief among Christians (Boyer 2000, 293–339) but also pop culture apocalypticism in which human intellect, rather than divine providence, is expected to bring about apocalyptic salvation (Schoepflin 2000, 427). Perhaps as a result of the alleged "generational sensibility" of those who grew up in the shadow of the atomic bomb during the Cold War (O'Leary 2000, 393), authors, musicians, moviemakers, and even scientists imagine the world in apocalyptic terms (O'Leary 2000). Just as it does in other areas of pop culture, the apocalyptic imagination governs pop robotics and AI, as articulated by Hans Moravec, Ray Kurzweil,[31] and others.

Apocalyptic AI influences robotics worldwide but it is a particularly American phenomenon. For two centuries, Americans have sought distinctly American ways of reinterpreting Christian thought and practice in new forms of Christianity and new religious movements (Albanese 1999, 217). New religious movements in nineteenth-century America were strongly eschatological. Though few actual dates were espoused after the Great Disappointment of October 23, 1844,[32] participants in later religious movements expected an imminent end to the world and the construction of what they considered appropriate social structures. New religious groups (e.g., the Mormons, the Christian Scientists, and the Seventh Day Adventists) held restorationist views of Christianity and eschatological hopes for the future because of the self-understood newness and open possibility of American life (ibid., 247). Though the perils of progress were so amply demonstrated in the middle of the twentieth century, twenty-first-century American culture remains deeply tied to the salvific promises of its past. Just as the Branch Davidians inherited nineteenth-century American eschatology, so too, in its own way, has Apocalyptic AI.

Apocalyptic AI borrows from the nineteenth-century expectation of a "this worldly" millennium of saints but simultaneously expands upon it through the integration of a radically "other worldly" approach to the end of the world. Many nineteenth-century American religious practices—such as the Mormons' effort to rebuild Zion in the desert of Utah—encouraged the belief that an age of peace would emerge in the new world, America. Moravec and his followers believe that a new age is coming out of worldly progress but it will shortly give rise to a transcendent new world, a virtual kingdom of Mind. The promise of a new world, so meaningful in the rise of the American nation, has been part and parcel of American technological culture and, ultimately, pop science in robotics and artificial intelligence.

POP SCIENCE REVIEW: A WHO'S WHO OF APOCALYPTIC AI

Hans Moravec and Ray Kurzweil are the two most significant figures in Apocalyptic AI, but they also have additional support. Luminaries such as Marvin Minsky and Allen Newell have applauded their ideas, as have other researchers, including Kevin Warwick and Hugo de Garis. Like Moravec and Kurzweil, Warwick and de Garis have written entire books that offer evidence in support of the AI apocalypse and advocate it on morally normative grounds.

Before his retirement, Moravec was principal research scientist at the famed Carnegie Mellon University Robotics Institute, where he founded the Mobile

Robotics Laboratory. His work in mobile robotics was seminal; he is a "living legend" (Gutkind 2006, 93). One of his former colleagues considers Moravec the single most important figure in mobile robotics, which is the field of getting robots to navigate through physical environments (Choset 2007). In addition to his technical work, Moravec is well-known for popular writings, including the books *Mind Children: The Future of Robot and Human Intelligence* (1988) and *Robot: Mere Machine to Transcendent Mind* (1999). Moravec effectively began the Apocalyptic AI movement in 1978, with his publication of "Today's Computers, Intelligent Machines and Our Future" in *Analog*, a science fiction magazine. In that essay, Moravec predicts human-level machine intelligence by 1988 and describes an operating room in which human minds are transferred to computers. This transferal will provide faster computation time (i.e., greater intelligence) and virtual immortality. Eventually, human beings will form a community mind in cyberspace and bring other animal life-forms into it. "We now have a picture of a super-consciousness, the synthesis of terrestrial life, and perhaps jovian and martian life as well, constantly improving and extending itself, spreading outwards from the solar system, converting non-life into mind" (Moravec 1978). Moravec's 1978 essay forms the basis of his later popular books and thereby the subsequent books by other Apocalyptic AI authors.

Ray Kurzweil is an influential researcher in AI and a key innovator in music synthesizers, AI speech recognition and reading devices for the blind. He is a past winner of the $500,000 Lemelson-MIT Prize (2001) and the National Medal of Technology (1999) and is a member of the National Inventors Hall of Fame. Like Moravec, he has complemented his innovative research with pop science writing. He began his pop science career with *The Age of Intelligent Machines*, in which he argues that in the future computers will be more intelligent than human beings (Kurzweil 1990, 21), but he does not advocate apocalyptic ideas. Kurzweil subsequently wrote *The Age of Spiritual Machines* (1999), an elaboration and extension of Moravec's ideas, and *The Singularity Is Near* (2005), a powerful argument for the evolution of technology toward transcendent machine intelligence. Both *The Age of Spiritual Machines* and *The Singularity Is Near* make extensive use of apocalyptic imagination. Kurzweil also began a website, www.KurzweilAI.net, which publishes his own essays as well as those by leading futurists and transhumanists, and which has become a popular forum for Apocalyptic AI proponents, as well as an occasional detractor.

Marvin Minsky has supported Apocalyptic AI for years. A longstanding professor at the Massachusetts Institute of Technology (MIT), his shadow has loomed large over the development of both robotics and AI. Although Minsky has not written an apocalyptic book per se, he did coauthor a science fiction book with Harry Harrison in which a machine becomes more intelligent than human beings by having a human being's sense of self-identity downloaded into it (Harrison and

Minsky 1992, 245) and in which a human being has a computer implanted into his brain, making him more machine than human being (ibid., 422). As a frequent cheerleader of Moravec, Minsky has supported both the potential for highly intelligent robots[33] and the uploading of human brains into machines. In particular, the essay "Will Robots Inherit the Earth?" (1994), which he published in the pop science magazine *Scientific American*, clearly aligns him with Moravec (whom he cites) and Kurzweil. When the Extropy Institute, a transhumanist group, was still operational, Minsky was a member of its board of directors.

Warwick and de Garis are latecomers to the Apocalyptic AI scene and are less well known than their forebears. Both, however, are tireless advocates of their beliefs, speaking, for example, in the documentary *Building Gods* (Gumbs 2006). Warwick even joined the virtual reality world *Second Life* to give a presentation on cyborg technologies to transhumanists (Warwick 2007). Warwick, a roboticist at the University of Reading in the U.K., argues that machines will soon take over Earth and in order to prevent catastrophic enslavement of humankind we must become cyborgs. Warwick does not accede to Moravec's dream of immortal minds (Warwick [1997] 2004, 180) but is otherwise in line with the general thrust of Apocalyptic AI; he simply replaces uploaded minds with massively powerful brain implants. We must enhance our mental faculties with computer implants so as to compete with the robots. De Garis, an Australian-born researcher who has lived in Cambridge, Belgium, and Japan, is an adjunct associate professor of physics at Utah State University and an instructor of computer science and math at Wuhan University in China. His primary research has been in neural-net machine intelligence, which he calls "brain building." In *The Artilect War* (2005), de Garis claims that human beings will soon fight a war over whether or not to build superintelligent machines. He believes that the "cosmists" (those who want the machines) will win after all or nearly all human beings kill one another, and that intelligent robots will thereafter conquer the universe.

One additional figure is worth mentioning in the context of pop AI. David Levy, an AI expert from Scotland, has written a pop science book on robots that should be considered utopian, and perhaps eschatological, but not really apocalyptic. Levy led the team that won the 1997 Loebner Prize for artificial intelligence, which is given annually to the program judged most humanlike in a conversation (no program has yet fooled the judges into thinking it actually *is* a human being), and was the chairman of the Rules and Arbitration Committee for the Garry Kasparov vs. Deep Junior chess match in 2003 (which was a draw). Levy, a chess expert, also won several well-publicized bets with AI luminaries such as John McCarthy and Donald Michie regarding the time frame in which a computer would beat him at the game. Levy's book, *Robots Unlimited* (2006), paints a rosy picture about our future in which robots become our friends and lovers[34] but do not reach the transcendent heights advocated by the apocalyptics.

Nevertheless, Levy has acknowledged an "underlying sympathy" for Moravec's and Kurzweil's position (Levy 2009).

Collectively, Moravec, Kurzweil, Minsky, Warwick, and de Garis have a loud voice in technological circles. Their beliefs are sufficiently powerful to have elicited the criticism of influential fellow technocrats, like the virtual reality pioneer Jaron Lanier (2000) and the former chief scientist at Sun Microsystems Bill Joy (2000). Several of these authors (the most notable exception being the rather reclusive Moravec[35]) speak in a wide array of forums and willingly sit on the boards of directors for transhumanist groups. They regularly evangelize and, indeed, oftentimes their technical research takes a backseat to their futuristic predictions.

The rest of this chapter explores the apocalyptic scenario that these authors predict. Apocalyptic AI is a pop science movement that resolves a dualistic conflict between the mundane physical and the transcendental virtual in a cyberspace future inhabited by disembodied superminds. Apocalyptic AI advocates divide the world into a cosmic opposition of good/bad, knowledge/ignorance, machine/biology, mind/body, and virtual/physical. Resolving this opposition is particularly important to advocates of Apocalyptic AI who feel fundamentally alienated by embodied existence. Their bodies prevent their minds from reaching the heights they desire, so they look forward to a future when they can depart the physical and biological world altogether, downloading their minds into computers and living forever in cyberspace.

DISAPPOINTMENT AND THE SINGULARITY SOLUTION

Apocalyptic AI, like its predecessor movements in Jewish and Christian history, starts with a dualistic view of the world. The entire world can be separated into two morally distinct categories, with little fuzziness in the boundary. Although for Jews and Christians dualism entails a difference between that which is good and that which is evil, the analogous formulation in Apocalyptic AI is the conflict between that which is good and that which is bad. The forces of good and bad can be lined up in opposition to one another. On one side stand mind, machine, and virtual reality. On the other side stand body, biology, and the physical world. Apocalyptic AI offers resolution to this dualist stance in the abolition of the finitude of biological reality in a transcendent new world of pure mind. Exponential growth in technological progress will produce a "singularity," in which progress occurs inconceivably fast, leading to a meaningful future that abolishes cosmic dualism and resolves the experience of alienation.

The cosmic dualism of Apocalyptic AI divides the world into complementary dichotomies of good/bad, knowledge/ignorance, virtual/physical, and machine/biology. The good/bad value system runs through the other dichotomies, providing a worldview and direction for action in the world. Although many of Apocalyptic

AI's bad things might also be considered evil (and one roboticist whom I consulted readily agreed to do so) it would be excessive allegiance to my apocalyptic analogy to insist upon calling them so. While the morality of evil may not motivate Moravec or Kurzweil, escaping the confines of what is "not good" certainly does. The goal of Apocalyptic AI is to disentangle the world from its inherently "bad" qualities by merging machines and biology in superintelligent computers.

Apocalyptic AI's cosmic dualism combines with a sense of frustration at the boundaries implicit in the dualism; such frustration leads to alienation, which emphasizes the eschatological faith in the singularity (described below). The principle form of alienation in Apocalyptic AI is distaste for human bodily finitude. Apocalyptic AI advocates are, however, also potentially politically alienated, as demonstrated by their desire to establish cultural authority to protect their research funding from perceived cultural threats (Geraci 2007a).

Revelation of the political nature of modern science has led to alienation in some scientific circles. Studies indicating the prevalence of politics in scientific research (Greenberg [1967] 1999) and progress (Kuhn [1962] 1996) revolutionized the way that sociologists and philosophers approached science. Science's seemingly unassailable air of epistemological purity dissolved in a cacophony of critical stances, from the sociological (Barnes, Bloor, and Henry 1996) to the feminist (Harding 1988; Haraway 1997). One universally accepted standard among commentators, if not scientists themselves, is that science is certainly not separated from the rest of society, able to arrive at empirical conclusions in a purely "objective" manner.

The critical approach to sociological interpretations of science led to the "science wars," in which scientific advocates argued for the independence and epistemological certitude of scientific research against the apparent relativism of Science and Technology Studies (also called Science, Technology, and Society [STS], a field that broadly captures the many humanistic and social scientific approaches to understanding science within modern culture). This blew up dramatically with the publication of Alan Sokal's "Transgressing the Boundaries: Toward a Transformative Hermeneutics of Quantum Gravity" (Sokal 1996a). The patently absurd essay, which extensively quotes major STS figures (deliberately out of context) was published by *Social Text*, a leading journal of cultural theory. At the same time as its publication, Sokal revealed the essay as a hoax in the journal *Lingua Franca* (Sokal 1996b). His hoax essay, including such nonsense as "the infinite-dimensional invariance group erodes the distinction between observer and observed; the π of Euclid and the G of Newton, formerly thought to be constant and universal, are now perceived in their ineluctable historicity; and the putative observer becomes fatally de-centered, disconnected from any epistemic link to a space-time point that can no longer be defined by geometry alone" (Sokal 1996a, 222), was published by the editors of *Social Text* without a single peer review, much less one by a qualified scientist. Sokal took this successful hoax as proof that the humanistic study of science is nothing but folderol, as did his many admirers.[36]

The Science Wars have been very important to twenty-first-century scholarship and have raised a certain amount of fear that "relativistic" accounts of science—that is, accounts that describe its progress with respect to its social relations—could lead to widespread public disapproval of science and an accompanying loss of research funds. The politics of research funding plays a role in Apocalyptic AI, as shall be demonstrated in the next chapter. For now, however, I shall return to the bodily alienation that Apocalyptic AI shares with apocalyptic Judaism and Christianity.

In a criticism to the essay "Apocalyptic AI: Religion and the Promise of Artificial Intelligence" (Geraci 2008a), Ted Peters denies that Moravec and Kurzweil experience alienation. Peters says it "is difficult to see how millionaire industrial leaders or authors who publish with Harvard University Press belong to the class of alienated victims of social breakdown" (Peters 2008). This criticism depends upon two key issues: one is that all alienation is that of social breakdown and the other is that alienation requires that one suffer economic privation. Neither, as was discussed above, is true.

Apocalyptic AI advocates have a profound distaste for bodily existence, which sickens, dies, and limits the kind and quantity of intellectual effort a scientist produces.[37] "There are things worse than death" is an old cliché: in the case of Apocalyptic AI, those "things" are loss of information and the end of rational thinking. Fortunately, the AI apocalypse will end the "wanton loss of knowledge and function that is the worst aspect of personal death" (Moravec 1988, 121).

Even were we to somehow live forever (as some biotechnology enthusiasts have, in fact, promised we will), our bodies would continue to erect barriers between us and transcendental learning—living forever will not, by itself, solve the alienation experienced by our minds. Computation takes a wide array of different forms; the most obvious are through biological nervous systems and computers. Of the two, computers are far more efficient. Our nervous systems use chemical neurotransmitters to signal to one another, a process that is far slower than the incredible speeds at which silicon transistors can communicate. Human beings—all protein-based life-forms—will never think as fast or as well as machines will in the future (Moravec 1988, 55–56; Moravec 1999, 55; Minsky 1994; Kurzweil 1999, 4; Kurzweil 2005, 8–9; Warwick [1997] 2004, 178; de Garis 2005, 103). Beyond the necessary limitations of speed, our brains pale in comparison to the memory capacity and accuracy of computers. Human recollection suffers from a wide variety of difficulties that are impossible for a computer; as long as the computer is functional and has sufficient storage, it will accurately remember a colossal amount of information and rapidly retrieve individual facts from within.

Barring mechanical breakdown, computers can recall with perfect accuracy and amazing speed. While you sit and struggle to think of a word "on the tip of your tongue," a computer will have found the desired word along with sixteen synonyms it has compiled. While you wonder about the capital of Idaho, your computer could tell you those of all fifty states plus the national capitals for every country in the world (assuming, of course, that it has ever "learned" these things).

A computer can also process information far more rapidly than a human being. Mathematics, logic, map directions, and correct spelling are all much faster for the computer than the person. Though people still have the advantage in pattern recognition, natural language recognition, and other tasks too complicated for today's computers, this advantage will diminish and possibly disappear in coming generations of computers. Chemical synapses simply cannot transmit information as rapidly as silicon transistors. Fortunately say Apocalyptic AI theorists, the solution to our limited lifespan will simultaneously solve our computational problems.

Disappointment about the frailness of human life and the limitations of human learning are not new. Solutions to the former, if not the latter, usually come in traditionally religious packaging. Most Apocalyptic AI advocates, however, see the widely held belief in souls and spirits as a feeble psychological ploy. William Sims Bainbridge, coeditor of two substantial National Science Foundation (NSF) volumes on twenty-first-century technology, argues that improved cognitive sciences will squeeze out the last of our religious superstitions (Bainbridge 2006, 207–8). Marvin Minsky says that beliefs in souls are *"all insinuations that we're helpless to improve ourselves"* (Minsky 1985, 41, emphasis original).[38] In his sci-fi book *The Turing Option*, Minsky claims that souls do not exist (Harrison and Minsky 1992, 163) and implies that belief in gods is an invalid superstition (ibid., 386). Although traditional religions allegedly fail in their efforts to "fix" human life, faith in technological salvation will not. The enthusiasm shown by the Apocalyptic AI advocates when they articulate how robotics and AI will save us from our problems is a perfect analogue to the passionate excitement that Wayne Meeks has described in apocalyptic Judaism and Christianity.

The Apocalyptic AI advocates are enthusiastic indeed; they are, in fact, absolutely positive that technological progress will fix the miserable facts of human life that leave our minds alien to their world. In popular robotics and AI, Darwinian evolution guarantees the inevitability of our salvation. Evolution has brought about human intelligence, and evolution will now inevitably lead to intelligent robots. As Kurzweil says, "the next stage of evolution . . . is technology," particularly intelligent machines (Kurzweil 1999, 35; see also Kurzweil 2005, 374). Moravec believes that near-term intelligent robots are inevitable (Moravec 1999, 13) and that the robots will replace humankind as Earth's dominant species because Darwinian evolution is "weeding out ineffective ways of thought" (Moravec 1999, 165).[39] This process will lead to an unstoppable Mind Fire, a spread of cyberspace computation throughout the universe (ibid., 167).[40]

Moravec and his allies argue that the natural laws of the universe necessitate the Mind Fire. Kurzweil argues that the emergence of life necessitates the emergence of technology (Kurzweil 1999, 17) and that subsequently the speed of technological computation—computer speeds—will inevitably increase at an exponential rate (ibid., 18), leading to an "inexorable emergence," which was the title of his prologue to *The Age of Spiritual Machines*. Hugo de Garis believes that the "evolution" of "godlike" machines is a cosmic inevitability (de Garis 2005, 173) and may well be inherent in the laws of physics (ibid., 175). The future is set, the rise of supremely intelligent machines is inevitable: "we have started a time bomb ticking . . . and we will be unable to switch it off" (Warwick [1997] 2004, 302).

In order to justify the seamless transition from biological evolution (which operates according to laws of natural selection, sexual selection, geographical isolation, random genetic drift, etc.) to technological progress (which proceeds according to no known laws, apart from those conjectured by Moravec and Kurzweil), Apocalyptic AI borrows on the technological successes of "Moore's Law." In 1965, Gordon Moore of Intel noticed that the number of transistors on an integrated circuit doubled roughly every twelve months, which means that the speed of computers doubles in that period. It may be that computer speed doubles more like every eighteen months than every twelve (by 1975, Moore argued for a twenty-four-month period) but the point remains that computation speed has increased exponentially for decades and will likely continue to do so at least until 2020, when the transistors will be so small that quantum interference will prevent them from shrinking further.

Kurzweil argues that Moore's Law is a natural law that expresses a universal Law of Accelerating Returns. Exponential growth in computing, Kurzweil argues, began prior to the invention of the integrated circuit, which "suggests that exponential growth won't stop with the end of Moore's Law" in 2020 (Kurzweil 1999, 25). Kurzweil believes that a Law of Accelerating Returns applies to all processes in which order and chaos struggle. He believes that as order increases in a system, the returns from that system will improve exponentially. "The Law of Accelerating Returns," he says, "is not a temporary methodology. It is a basic attribute of time and chaos" (ibid., 33; see also Kurzweil 2005, 7–21). If the Law of Accelerating Returns is a true natural law then Kurzweil might be right to believe that an equivalent of Moore's Law will take over after Moore's Law expires. Of course, not everyone agrees with Kurzweil that there is anything natural about accelerating returns.[41]

Kurzweil did not always make such strong claims about the inevitability of the AI apocalypse. In *The Age of Intelligent Machines*, he predicted that a computer would pass the Turing Test[42] "sometime between 2020 and 2070. . . . Of course, there is no assurance that *my* prediction will be any more accurate that Turing's" prediction of the year 2000 (1990, 416, emphasis original). By the time of *The Age of Spiritual Machines* a decade later, however, Kurzweil was quite convinced by his newly devised Law of Accelerating Returns (hereafter LAR). "The nature of time is that it inherently moves in an exponential fashion—either geometrically gaining speed, or, as in the history of our Universe, geometrically slowing down" (Kurzweil 1999, 10). Kurzweil means that the time between "salient events" increases or decreases exponentially; this is because things happen faster if there is more order in the system. In the beginning, just as the universe's expansion in the Big Bang had begun, it was very orderly and things happened swiftly; now that the universe has spread out, things happen quite slowly.

Kurzweil uses the evolution of life as one of his examples for the LAR (Kurzweil 1999, 73–75). Prokaryotic life arose on Earth 3.4 billion years ago, followed by eukaryotic (multicellular) life 700 million years ago. After the rise of eukaryotic life, it took only another 100 to 150 million years to develop vertebrates and most modern plant and animal body types. Humanoids arose 15 million years ago, relatively swiftly followed by *Homo sapiens* 500,000 years ago and thereafter by *Homo sapiens sapiens* 40,000 years ago.[43] Kurzweil masterfully covers a wide array of technological data in *The Singularity is Near*, making a powerful case for the Law of Accelerating Returns by extrapolating it from different innovations.

Just as the emergence of life took billions of years before speeding up rather swiftly, Kurzweil believes that technology has undergone an exponential evolution. In the nineteenth century, for example, human beings utilized widespread and vastly longer canals, improved steam ships, paved roads, and used steam-powered railroads, telegraphs, photography, bicycles, sewing machines, telephones, typewriters, phonographs, motion pictures, automobiles, and light bulbs, among other innovations. Truly, the nineteenth century was an extraordinary time, where new inventions appeared far faster than they had in the past. Moving to the twentieth century, however, we begin to feel that nineteenth-century people were dullards, taking forever to create new technologies. In the twentieth century, we seem to see major new improvements every day, especially in the computing industry. According to Kurzweil, the LAR "forbids" us from calming or stopping technological innovation (Kurzweil 1999, 130).[44]

This process of accelerating innovation will lead to a "singularity" in which progress accelerates so rapidly that shocking and impossible to truly conceive progress will occur "over night." The singularity was first named by the mathematician and science fiction author Vernor Vinge in a 1993 presentation at the annual conference of the Association for the Advancement of Artificial Intelligence (AAAI) that was subsequently published in the *Whole Earth Review*. According to Vinge, "the acceleration of technological progress has been the central feature of this century" and will lead to intelligent computers between 2005 and 2030 (Vinge 2003[45]). Intelligent computers will be able to improve themselves far, far more rapidly than human beings can improve them, which means that progress will run away out of human control. Vinge had an enormous influence on Kurzweil, who subsequently touted the power of the singularity to radically change our lives and the world.[46] The singularity solution reflects Schoepflin's (2000) apocalyptic immediacy; both the need for a new world and the faith in the importance of our own world emerge in expectations of a singularity. Likewise, it is the equivalent of what Meeks (2000) referred to as historical dualism, the divide between the present and future worlds.

All Apocalyptic AI advocates agree that the exponential rise in computing power will lead to intelligent robots in the first half of the twenty-first century. Those who believe we will build intelligent machines have generally accepted Moravec's dating scheme (Vinge 2003), though Minsky has insisted that we already have sufficient computing power to duplicate human intelligence, if only the software problems were solved (Hall 2007, 252). Moravec initially predicted that we would build robots with humanlike performance by 2030 but, in *Robot* (1999), revised this date to 2040. Kurzweil believes the feat could be achieved in a supercomputer by 2010 and in a $1,000 personal computer by 2025. In 2060, he says, a $1,000 computer will be as intelligent as all human beings put together and by 2099, one penny's worth of computation will be one billion times greater than that of all human beings combined. "Of course," he continues, "I may be off by *a year or two*" (Kurzweil 1999, 105, emphasis added). Using the Law of Accelerating Returns as justification has helped Kurzweil greatly enhance his level of certitude since the publication of *The Age of Intelligent Machines.*

Apocalyptic AI advocates leave no question that robots will dominate the future and that such a world will be, in a very important sense, good for humanity and for the entire cosmos. "Will robots inherit the earth? Yes, but they will be our children. We owe our minds to the deaths and lives of all the creatures that were ever engaged in the struggle called Evolution. Our job is to see that all this work shall not end up in meaningless waste" (Minsky 1994). As Minsky indicates, meaningfulness is integral to the AI apocalypse; without it, the entire resolution of dualism would be impossible.

The moral dualism of Apocalyptic AI becomes transparent in discussions of the singularity because it is in these that a value system expresses itself. Kurzweil, for example, believes that, in the coming singularity, evolution is bringing about an event of "greater import" than anything in the history of the world (Kurzweil 1999, 5). The activities of superintelligent robots will be as far "above" our own as ours are above those of bacteria (Moravec 1992a, 20) as the future brings "meaningful" computation everywhere, including to "boring old Earth" (Moravec 1999, 167). "We will turn into robots," says Moravec, "it is inevitable and desirable" (quoted in Chaudhry 2000). It is not just that the AI apocalypse is inevitable but that it is *good.*[47] This is why de Garis advocates it despite his fear that all human beings will be wiped out in warfare over the development of intelligent machines. Even one artificial intellect is more valuable than all people put together (de Garis 2005, 174).

The AI apocalypse will demolish the difference between the physical and the intellectual, leading to a world where moral value can be found in the ubiquity of rational computation. Apocalyptic AI dissolves cosmic dualism in a world where the line differentiating the machine from the living explodes in a singularity that will sneak up on us like a thief in the night. Slow computation, limited recall, insufficient ability to share one's insights, and inevitable death presently restrict the mind from realizing its full potential, but a radical change in life itself will unlock the powers of mind and unleash them upon a universe completely unlike the one we presently occupy.

TECHNO-SALVATION: A HEAVENLY LIFE TO COME

Apocalyptic AI promises a transcendent heavenly future in a traditional two-stage apocalyptic scenario.[48] Just as many of the ancient apocalypses anticipated that a period of peace and justice would reign on the earth prior to God's final dissolution of the world and establishment of an eternal realm of goodness, Apocalyptic AI anticipates that advances in robotics and AI will create a paradise on Earth before transcendent Mind escapes earthly matter in an expanding cyberspace of immortality, intellect, moral goodness, and meaningful computation. This second stage, the Age of Mind, will inevitably succeed the first stage of the apocalypse, the Age of Robots.

Throughout the modern era, scientists, philosophers, and theologians have linked technological progress to a biblical millennium of peace. Faith in the scientific millennium is analogous to (and has been frequently identified with) Christian postmillenarian thought. Contrary to the premillenarians (who believe that Jesus will come to Earth in order to inaugurate the kingdom), postmillenarians believe that progress in human culture will bring about the millennium of peace, after which Jesus will arrive to end the world and establish the new kingdom. From the thirteenth century on, technology has also been presumed necessary for the war against the Antichrist (Noble 1999). Faith that scientific progress would "fix" the earth and ready humankind for the millennium continued into the exploration of the Americas and the creation of a new political order there (Nye 2003).

The earthly paradise proposed by Moravec and his followers is nothing new for the religion of technology; it is simply the preapocalyptic culmination of earthly history. In order to return Earth to its origins in Eden, Apocalyptic AI promises a series of improvements upon human life that will, eventually, negate many, if not all, human problems. First, robots will do all of our work for us, creating economic equality and ensuring that no one need fight over basic necessities. Second, human beings will upload our minds into robotic bodies in order that we will no longer become ill, die, or suffer mental decline. Our new robot bodies will enable us to overcome the limitations of human thought: we will learn quickly, remember everything and teach one another at very nearly the speed of light.

The Age of Robots will lift the burden of human subsistence from our shoulders and improve the quality of human life. Robot corporations will move manufacturing into outer space, eliminating pollution and freeing human beings for a life of leisure. Universal ownership of the robot corporations will ensure that all human beings have a source of income (Moravec 1999, 134).[49] The resemblance to Francis Bacon's seventeenth-century work *New Atlantis* is uncanny: we will control the weather (Moravec 1999, 155), manufacturing of all goods will be free (de Garis 2005, 67–68), and all human needs will be fulfilled (Kurzweil 1999, 2). The robots capable of delivering us from evil will arise by the middle of the twenty-first century. Moravec believes that as robots do more and more of the work that human beings are accustomed to doing, we will have leisure time to begin a "comfortable tribalism" (Moravec 1999, 136–37). We will retreat from the stress of urban life and return to the supposedly noble past to which we are better evolved. Nationhood and warfare will become obsolete in the "garden of earthly delights," which is "reserved for the meek" (ibid., 143).

No matter how wonderful such a garden may appear, it does not eradicate sickness, age, or death; resolving the problem of death can happen only if we depart our biological bodies.[50] "Everyone wants wisdom and wealth. Nevertheless, our health often gives out before we achieve them. To lengthen our lives, and improve our minds, in the future we will need to change our bodies and brains. . . . In the end, we will find ways to replace every part of the body and brain—and thus repair all the defects and flaws that make our lives so brief" (Minsky 1994). Nearly all of the Apocalyptic AI advocates agree that human beings will eventually learn to "upload" a human mind into a robot body (Moravec 1988, 108–10; Moravec 1999, 142–43; Minsky 1994; Kurzweil 1999, 126; Kurzweil 2005, 198–202; de Garis 2005, 77–78), a position first advocated by Moravec in *Analog* (Moravec 1978).[51] The robot bodies vary by author, of course, though they universally offer immortality, massive intellectual powers, and near-magical abilities. Kurzweil believes that nanotechnology will allow human beings to build new bodies that have all the benefits of the old (warmth, softness, self-repair, cuddliness) while providing entirely new abilities, such as resistance to temperature and pressure changes, strength, speed, increased mental faculties, immunity to disease, and limitless life span (Kurzweil 1999, 136). Moravec touts the wonders of "robot bushes," which are entirely unlike human bodies. The robot bushes are composed of branchlike structures resembling, obviously, a tree's root and branch system. Each branch breaks off into ever smaller appendages until the bush tapers off in a trillion nanoscale digits capable of manipulating the world in an unprecedented fashion.[52] For the robot bushes, "the laws of physics will seem to melt in the face of intention and will. As with no magician that ever was, impossible things will simply *happen* around a robot bush" (Moravec 1988, 107–8, emphasis original).[53]

Robot bodies would allow human minds to take advantage of the superior computational powers of silicon. In many ways, it would be wonderfully convenient if we could learn and adapt as fast as computers. If I want my computer to read spreadsheets, I can download the latest version of OpenOffice from the Internet and within a few minutes of downloading plus a few minutes of installation, it is ready to go. Everyone in 1999 wished, upon watching Keanu Reeves learn kung fu in a matter of seconds (in *The Matrix*), that he or she could have some—if not all—knowledge implanted directly into his or her brain just as though it were a computer (forget for the moment the impossibility of learning a physical skill without adjustments to the body's muscular, skeletal, and endocrine systems and the chemical synapses of the neural system). Need to fly a helicopter? Just make a quick phone call and you'll be prepared in seconds.[54] Want to speak Italian on your upcoming vacation? Unfortunately in the real world you will need to devote an awful lot of time to learning it and, unless you are a child, you will lack desirable fluency no matter how hard you study. And if you want to learn how quantum dynamics explains aspects of our material universe you must prepare for a years-long odyssey that still does not guarantee that you will truly understand. There is much to be learned and we will always be limited in our ability to remember and manipulate it.

While there might be much to laud in the way human learning requires that we overcome obstacles and struggle through adversity, in Apocalyptic AI the biological world receives persistent criticism for the ways in which it limits the powers of mind. This criticism hinges upon a fundamental dislike of the body, which is presumed to be, in a very important sense, separate from the mind even if minds do not presently exist outside of brains.

The legacy separating mind and body draws greatly from the work of Rene Descartes (1596–1650). Descartes believed that the mind (*res cogitans*) was nonphysical but connected to a physical body (*res extensa*). The mind operated on the body through the pineal gland in the brain. His theory had very important ramifications. First, it mechanized the body and brain, turning them into machines. Second, upon the discrediting of the pineal gland theory, it left little room for such entities as "minds," "souls," or "spirits" to have real worldly presence.[55] Without a *res cogitans*, all we have left is a *res extensa*, a physical substance that responds precisely to mechanical input-output laws. The brain, by this logic, is no different from the rest of the body: it is a machine for computing data and responding to given circumstances.

If the brain is nothing but a machine, then how can mind be separated from it in the Apocalyptic AI account? Mind, say the advocates of Apocalyptic AI, is a pattern of information housed in the brain and nothing more. Further, there is nothing special about the brain that makes it a particularly appropriate house for that pattern. Therefore, the brain can be replaced. All we have to do is identify the pattern and copy it exactly into a computer. The pattern is the important part, says Moravec, if it "is preserved, I am preserved. The rest is mere jelly" (Moravec 1988, 117; see also Kurzweil 1999, 54, and Warwick [1997] 2004, 90, 104).

Despite the enormous technical hurdles for mind uploading (assuming that such a thing is even possible), Apocalyptic AI authors believe it will be available soon. Kurzweil believes that his Law of Accelerating Returns absolutely guarantees that noninvasive scanning technologies, such as Magnetic Resonance Imaging (MRI) will soon allow scientists to scan and record the estimated 100 trillion neural connections in a human brain (Kurzweil 1999, 123). That we are nowhere close to understanding the brain or even looking at it carefully is no discouragement to the apocalyptic imagination. The LAR will, says Kurzweil, quickly dispel such problems.

Once we learn how to upload our minds into computers, we will be but a short step from our eventual salvation in the transcendent world of cyberspace. Robot bodies will give us wondrous powers but even these will pale before the limitless possibility of virtual reality. In the Age of Mind, physical reality will lose relevance as it is alchemically transmuted into cyberspace. The movement of robots throughout space will be a "physical affair. . . . But it will leave a subtler world, with less action and even more thought, in its ever-growing wake" (Moravec 1999, 163). Moravec calls this the "Mind Fire," which will be a "friendly" world (Moravec 1988, 146) and will allow us to transform the cosmos, including our destiny—in the Mind Fire, we will have control over our evolutionary future (ibid., 158–59; see also Kurzweil 1999, 260 and Kurzweil 2005, 487).

Human beings seem to require bodies but we will, according to Moravec and Kurzweil, overcome this physical need through improved technology. Sensory deprivation does very bad things to people, causing hallucinations and a variety of mental ills even over short periods, but if we provide the sensory stimulus that a body would have provided, presumably we can keep our minds functional. "We don't always need real bodies. If we happen to be in a virtual environment, then a virtual body will do just fine" (Kurzweil 1999, 142). All meaningful activity—our senses of selfhood and liveliness included—will depart the physical realm and enter virtual reality. We will be, according to Kurzweil, software, not hardware (ibid., 129). Within virtual reality, we can walk/swim/slither/fly/teleport around in whatever kinds of bodies we like, experiencing heaven as we once experienced Earth. By 2099, however, we will no longer have defined bodies, instead representing ourselves however we please (ibid., 241–42).

Eventually, we will find ways to eliminate our need for bodily sensations in virtual reality. Because we will compete with AIs,[56] we will have to forego any computations that limit ourselves. Moravec believes that "a human mind would lumber about in a massively inappropriate body simulation, analogous to someone in a deep diving suit plodding along among a troupe of acrobatic dolphins. . . . Maintaining such fictions increases the cost of doing business"; thus many people "may feel a great economic incentive to streamline their interface to the cyberspace" (Moravec 1992a, 19–20). Why should we think of money as gold coins in a chest if we can find ways of dealing with it as nothing but 0s and 1s? Why should we conceive of information as a book when it could be nothing more than 0s and 1s?[57] Thus, while the Age of Mind might at first appear to be rather like the old world, only better, it will end up radically different from our physical reality.

In the Age of Mind, physical matter will become irrelevant, transformed by the Mind Fire. Apocalypticism, as noted above, demands an escape from our present reality, a movement into a transcendent realm. Intelligence will be purified (Crevier 1993, 307) in a world of transcendent information (ibid., 48) that will overcome the physical world. The "inhabited portions of the universe will be rapidly transformed into a cyberspace, where overt physical activity is imperceptible, but the world inside the computation is astronomically rich" (Moravec 1999, 164). The initial tendency to build robotic bodies "will be overtaken by a faster wave of subtle cyberspace conversion, the whole becoming finally a bubble of Mind expanding at near lightspeed [sic]" (ibid., 165).

The transmutation to Mind will provide the universe with meaning. "Physical activity will gradually transform itself into a web of increasingly pure thought, where every smallest interaction represents a meaningful computation" (Moravec 1999, 164). This move will resolve the basic dualism of Apocalyptic AI. As we enter the Age of Mind, the physical world gives way to the primacy of cyberspace, knowledge banishes ignorance, and the entire cosmos is filled with meaning.[58] In "a well-developed cyberspace every bit will be part of a relevant computation or will be storing a useful datum" (Moravec 1992a, 15; see also Moravec 1999, 166). Once "boring old Earth" has been "swallowed by cyberspace," it will "host astronomically more meaningful activity" (Moravec 1999, 167).[59] Or, as Kurzweil puts it, "the Singularity will ultimately infuse the universe with spirit" (Kurzweil 2005, 389) and "will make life more than bearable; it will make life truly meaningful" (ibid., 372).

As the Age of Mind takes hold, it will collapse our traditional notion of time, ending history in its conventional sense. Within cyberspace, "entire world histories . . . will be resurrected" (Moravec 1999, 167). When all of history can be simulated with perfect accuracy and "fast forwarded" to reveal the future of each historical simulation, time has utterly lost its traditional meaning—all times are copresent in the virtual kingdom come. The collapse of time enables other, more traditional religious promises, such as the resurrection of the dead, which is promised by Moravec (1988, 122–4; 1999, 167–8), Kurzweil (Kushner 2009; Ptolemy 2009) and other commentators such as Giulio Prisco (2007a, 2007b, 2007c), to whom we shall return in chapter three. If computers can simulate with perfect accuracy, then why mourn the loss of your grandfather, child, or spouse? As we approach the Age of Mind, the human survivors will restore their lost loved ones to (virtual) life.

Most of the time, Apocalyptic AI authors limit themselves to describing the religious *benefits* of their research; Hugo de Garis, however, also claims that the products of his research deserve religious *worship*. He argues that the artilects will be gods (2005, 12) and worthy of worship (ibid., 104). In fact, if Kurzweil is wrong about the Law of Accelerating Returns and we can intentionally bring technological progress to a halt before creating artilects, such an act would be "deicide" (ibid., 20). De Garis offers faith in the artilect mission as a "powerful new religion" (ibid., 105) capable of competing with the "superstition" of older religious traditions (ibid., 91).

The religious value of robotics and AI has been seen and positively expressed by Kurzweil and the other leaders in the Apocalyptic AI movement, who do not seem to share de Garis's willingness to sacrifice all of humankind. In *The Singularity is Near*, Kurzweil claims that "we need a new religion" to enhance morality and encourage the spread of knowledge (2005, 374–5) and Giulio Prisco believes that a religious "front end" will enable transhumanism to compete with traditional religions and thus create a religion free from the bigotry that be believes has characterized the history of religious practice (2007b). Although Kurzweil denies the need for a "charismatic leader" for this new religion, he certainly fits the bill for such a position, having not only done an enormous amount of work to lead Apocalyptic AI into mainstream pop culture conversations (Geraci 2010) but also having gained a loyal following among transhumanists.

Pop science robotics and AI draw on the traditional apocalyptic categories of ancient Judaism and Christianity, promising a transcendent world occupied by purified beings. Mind, freed from its bodily fetter, will soar into a virtual realm of perfect bliss, experiencing happiness (Kurzweil 1999, 236), the end of all need (Moravec 1999, 137; Kurzweil 1999, 249), better sex (Kurzweil 1999 148, 206; Levy 2007), the end of nationalism and war (Moravec 1999, 77),[60] immortality (Moravec 1988, 4, 112; Kurzweil 1999, 128–29; de Garis 2005, 67), and the infinite expansion of intelligence (Moravec 1999, 167; Kurzweil 1999, 260; de Garis 2005, 189). In the Mind Fire, predict Apocalyptic AI advocates, heaven will absorb Earth and the rest of the cosmos, spreading infinitely in all directions and providing a home to resurrected, reconstituted, and immortal minds.

CONCLUSION

Apocalyptic AI is a technological faith that directly borrows its sacred worldview from apocalyptic Judaism and Christianity. Like these, it refers to 1) a dualistic view of the world, which is 2) aggravated by a sense of alienation that can be resolved only through 3) the establishment of a radically transcendent new world that abolishes the dualism and requires 4) radically purified bodies for its inhabitants. The apocalyptic worldview has deeply penetrated the technological worldview of modern life, as expressed in popular robotics and AI and (as will be apparent in subsequent chapters) science fiction depictions of intelligent machines.

Ancient apocalyptics believed that God would soon bring about the end of the world and provide them with the unlimited bliss they desired. Lacking a God, Apocalyptic AI advocates turn to evolution[61] as transcendent guarantor but insist that their vision of the future is as inevitable as the one that once belonged to ancient Jews and Christians. The Jews and Christians looked forward to the resolution of their political dilemmas through the establishment of a new kingdom that they would inhabit in new bodies. Apocalyptic AI advocates see the spread of intelligent computation in cyberspace as the solution to the limits of the human body. They intend to upload human consciousness into machine bodies and permanently occupy virtual reality.

Apocalyptic AI constructs the world in aligned categories of knowledge/ignorance, machine/biology, virtual/physical, which it evaluates in the equivalent dichotomy of good/bad. Though ancient apocalyptics tended to see the world in terms of good and evil that relied upon God, Apocalyptic AI advocates place the basis of their moral system in a portrait of human life that idolizes rational intellect and scientific knowledge, occasionally without regard for other aspects of human life. Moravec, Kurzweil, and their allies interpret all of history through the Apocalyptic AI worldview, as even developments in physics, biology, and noncomputer technologies all seemingly predict the rise of intelligent robots. Laws of physics, evolution, even progress in telegraphs, railroads and other technologies are all taken as evidence that intelligent robots are destined to take over the cosmos.

It is important to keep in mind that the religious nature of pop science robotics and AI does not immediately invalidate the claims made by its expositors. Moravec and Kurzweil are brilliant and accomplished individuals who may, in fact, have accurately identified the general course of our future. To recognize the religiosity inherent in their enterprise is just that; it is not a denial of their claims.

When the robots arrive, they will allegedly accelerate technological progress and enable human beings to join them in mechanical bodies by scanning and uploading mind patterns (which are presumed separable from their physical instantiations—brains). Eventually, we will forego physical bodies altogether, becoming, in Kurzweil's words, software rather than hardware. We will jump from computer to computer, living in cyberspace with whatever virtual bodies we choose. Salvation.

The promise of Apocalyptic AI has taken root in our culture, having definite effects outside the world of popular science appreciation. Apocalyptic AI is a social strategy for the acquisition of research funding (chapter two), an ideology for online life (chapter three), and the inspiration for philosophical, legal, and theological reflection (chapter four). The AI apocalypse cannot be ignored, no matter how little we wish to credit pop science as profound or influential. At its best, pop science is both of these things. With Moravec and Kurzweil as its intellectual champions, Apocalyptic AI has entered contemporary life.

As a poetic end to this chapter and as a transition into the chapters that follow (all of which deal with real-world applications of Apocalyptic AI), I would like to quote Allen Newell, a Turing Award winner[62] and one of the founders of artificial intelligence, as he expresses the mystical aims of technology more eloquently, perhaps, than any other Apocalyptic AI advocate.

> I wish to assert that computer science and technology are the stuff out of which the future fairy land can be built. My faith is that the trials can be endured successfully, even by us children who fear that we are not so wise as we need to be. I might remind you, by the way, that the hero never has to make it all on his own. Prometheus is not the central character of any fairy tale but of a tragic myth. In fairy tales, magic friends sustain our hero and help him overcome the giants and witches that beset him (Newell 1990, 423).

LABORATORY APOCALYPSE

INTRODUCTION

Dreams of robotic salvation will not help a robot navigate a room or help a blind person read a book, so Hans Moravec's and Ray Kurzweil's striking development from technical researchers to apocalyptic theologians requires explanation. In chapter one, I discussed how a desire to reconcile a metaphysical dualism and escape the limitations of our bodies played a role in the development of Apocalyptic AI but that kind of wish fulfillment[1] could have happened anywhere—it did not need to appear in a robotics laboratory and yet it has prospered there in power and social acceptability. Apocalyptic AI has become so integral to our understanding of robotics and AI that the *IEEE Spectrum*[2] devoted an edition to essays on the singularity.[3] To clarify why Apocalyptic AI arose requires that we think about how it fits into its own technoscientific milieu. While the religious inspiration for Apocalyptic AI traces from science fiction, the desire for social prestige (and its accompanying advantages) drives Apocalyptic AI, which promotes the public authority of robotics and AI researchers.

I visited the Robotics Institute of Carnegie Mellon University (CMU), where Moravec worked from 1980 to 2003, to understand what Apocalyptic AI means to the researchers there and what led Moravec to his influential role in the movement's beginnings. Early in my stay, I introduced myself to the faculty at a lunch/research presentation. Upon hearing I was a professor of religious studies, everyone looked bewildered but most smiled in bemusement when I explained I was at Carnegie Mellon to learn why Moravec began writing what was, to me, apocalyptic theology. "If you can figure that out," said Chuck Thorpe, former director of the Robotics Institute (RI) and current dean of the CMU campus in Qatar, "we'll all buy your book." He was smiling along with his colleagues. Quite clearly, many of the faculty were fond of Moravec but simultaneously mystified by his religious claims.

The mundane reality of robotics research bears little resemblance to the apocalyptic imagination of Moravec or his followers. Roboticists build fire-fighting robots, robots that play pool, ping-pong, air hockey, and soccer, Mars-exploring robots, rescue robots, robots that communicate with other robots to build things or search rooms, robots that wander factories, and more. No one is building a super-intelligent robot that will either a) take over all human work or b) take over the world.

Finding out why Moravec wrote *Mind Children* (1988) was something like a detective story. One member of the RI suggested to me that Moravec wrote his pop science books purely for fun and that there was nothing else to it. This opinion was echoed by a few other colleagues. It is difficult to believe, however, that a labor-intensive writing like *Mind Children* could be solely a game for its author. After all, every book has an intended audience and an intended message. Pop science, however close it may come to science fiction, is not science fiction. Not even Marvin Minsky's sci-fi book *The Turing Option* (Harrison and Minsky, 1992) looks like it was written "just for fun," so I do not believe that *Mind Children* was. Though I imagine it was a pleasant break from Minsky's other responsibilities, *The Turing Option* further popularizes Minsky's scientific ideas about computers, human minds, and even the relative importance of AI research. As much as any "purely" pop science book, *The Turing Option* is an evangelical text. Pop science, by its very nature, seeks to educate more than entertain (though a good pop science book will do the latter as well). Education is a goal-oriented process; it drives toward something. In what direction, then, do *Mind Children* and *Robot* point?

Although factory robots seem rather distant from the promises of Apocalyptic AI, Moravec sees the two as complementary. My detective work was made more challenging because the star witness was impossible to pin down. Unfortunately, Moravec was too busy with his current company, Seegrid, to sit down and chat about his books during the time that I visited the Institute.[4] He did, however, tell me that his work at Seegrid leaves him "too busy making the plan happen to want to spend time talking about it" (Moravec 2007). In an interview given at Seegrid's launch, he clearly stated that Seegrid's vision-navigation products are a step toward his long-term predictions (Walter 2005).

When I arrived in Pittsburgh, I expected to find that the ethics of military funding would be important to my inquiry. After all, many projects are funded by the military and few researchers make a point of talking about it (Menzel and D'Aluisio 2000, 27; Gutkind 2006, 221). More recently, however, debate has begun, especially with regard to robots that might kill autonomously (Abate 2008). As I walked around the RI and spoke with grad students and faculty, however, I started doubting my intuition. Indeed, there are members of the community who feel ambivalent about accepting military funding and even one or two who absolutely refuse to apply for it but, for the most part, military funding does not pose the problem that I expected.

Concerns about the military were relatively rare but interest in science fiction was commonplace. Although few researchers proposed that robotics or AI research might arise directly from science fiction or that there was a definite relationship between sci-fi and Apocalyptic AI, the genre came up in nearly every conversation I had (sometimes at my instigation but far more often not). The writers Isaac Asimov, Philip K. Dick, and Neal Stephenson and several TV shows and movies were all brought up by grad students, faculty, and researchers. Science fiction has a persistent presence in the lives of the RI faculty and students, so it takes little imagination to appreciate how it might affect the ideology of Apocalyptic AI.

The blurring between science fiction and science fact is of considerable interest given that it shows the kinds of inspirations that scientists experience and also the way in which the future appears amenable to human intervention; more importantly, however, in Apocalyptic AI we see the sociocultural power of pop science. Pop science in general—and Apocalyptic AI in particular—is an effort to create and expand technoscientific power. Apocalyptic AI advances the social agenda of roboticists and AI researchers by dramatically illustrating the importance of present and future research while thereby justifying public expenditures upon them. Funding is part of the larger picture of prestige and authority for robotics and AI; greater cultural prestige should, theoretically, lead to increased research funds. The pop science books of Moravec and Kurzweil strengthen the field by defending the importance of advanced research through an effective merger of religion and science.

AN ASIDE ON THE STUDY OF SCIENCE AND TECHNOLOGY

Progress in science and technology requires that scientists assemble theories, experiments, institutions, funding, publications, conference presentations, and interpersonal relationships into a cohesive network. Scientists do not have a mystical connection to deep, inner truths about the universe; rather, consensus emerges that a scientist has done good work by conducting carefully constructed and repeatable experiments, through publication in high-quality journals, and through a scientist's own personal reputation (Latour and Woolgar [1979] 1986; Latour 1987; Collins and Pinch [1993] 1998). A radical claim made by a Nobel Prize winner, for example, will receive greater initial credibility than if it were made by an unknown scientist thanks to his or her prior work, the various institutions and individuals who support him or her and the expectation that such a person would make only the sort of claim that can be defended.[5]

One of the major problems for science studies has been the debate between realism and constructivism: either scientists gain knowledge through direct perception of the things "out there" in nature or else they "construct" their knowl-edge through social practices of publication, presentation, and argument—"trials of strength," as put by Bruno Latour in his classic *Science in Action* (1987). Although major figures in science studies hold ontologically realist positions of one sort or another, they tend to be epistemologically relativist. That is, few members of sci-ence and technology studies would deny the presence of "real" things out there, which come into contact with "real" human beings. However, the identification of those "real" things does not come through unproblematic, immediate access to the "real" but, rather, comes through a constant series of social mediations (observa-tions, experiments, publications, presentations, social networks, etc.).

The debate over realism is further complicated by the fundamental split in social scientific research between an ontology of nature and an ontology of society (Latour 1993; Latour 1999). We either believe that scientists study nature "in itself" with society offering little or no impact upon scientific results or we believe that scientific progress results solely from social processes of belief formation and group politics. This latter position, first defended by the Edinburgh School, also called both the Sociology of Scientific Knowledge (SSK) and the Strong Program in the Sociology of Science (e.g., Bloor [1976] 1991; Barnes, Bloor, and Henry 1996), clearly shows the influence of society upon science. Though this influence can no longer be doubted, many authors have reviled the "relativism" of it. According to the SSK, a given empirical phenomenon will be classified, manipulated, and understood according to social principles: the social world in which the scientist acts. A given empirical event is "real" because it leads to analysis but the nature of the analysis is structured entirely within society (Bloor 1999b).

Latour and his colleagues in Actor-Network Theory (ANT) have challenged the SSK theorists, seeking to restore a measure of realism they feel disappears in the SSK approach. Latour, for example, argues that Bloor and the SSK community have divorced reality into two kinds of causality: first, the empirical, which leads the scientist to the second, the social, which is where scientific knowledge is de-cided. Whether this severance of causality makes comprehension easier or more difficult depends upon whom you ask.[6] Latour's chief complaint is that SSK has eliminated the material world from scientific explanations. Michel Callon, one of Latour's primary ANT colleagues, famously argued that in order to understand scientific progress, you had to address both natural and social actors. In his study of the scallops of Saint-Brieuc Bay in France, human actors such as the fishermen, the scientific community, and the researchers themselves were studied alongside the scallops, a natural actor given equal attention; Callon even speaks of "negoti-ating" with tidal currents in the bay (Callon [1986] 1999).

To follow the ontology of Latour, Callon, and their ANT colleagues means to line up all the people, institutions, ideas, places, and objects that contribute to scientific outcomes. What ANT theorists propose is that we should look at all of these simultaneously, and at their internal relatedness, in order to understand how science operates. We cannot, for example, talk about how Pasteur discovers the cause of anthrax without aligning his biological laboratory in Paris, the anthrax bacillus, the rural farms, the cattle, Pasteur, his ideological framework, the hygienists who supported his work, etc. (Latour 1988). Star and Griesemer's history of Berkeley's Museum of Vertebrate Zoology is among the best adaptations of Actor Network Theory (Star and Griesemer 1993). Like Latour and Callon, they label nonhumans (e.g., dermestid beetles) as "allies" alongside people, institutions, and places. In addition, however, they expand the intersections of the network, permitting more than one "obligatory passage point."[7] Likewise, the history and philosophy of technology requires thick description, a multitude of voices and actors; to streamline a technology into simple parts without a full accounting of all the relationships of which they are themselves parts is thin to the point of immaterial (Latour 2007).

What we have learned from science and technology studies is that we cannot reduce successful scientific paradigms to an ontology of nature and unsuccessful ones to an ontology of society. That is, we used to say that scientific errors were caused by social mistakes but scientific successes were caused by eliminating all social factors in order to uncover the object "in itself." Scholars of science have shown that social factors play a role in *all* scientific positions, be they "true" or "false." Scientific prestige, the distribution of publications, the awarding or removal of research funding, attention by popular media, and more all affect the way in which truth is established in science. In addition, even a community's way of functioning directly influences how it practices technology (Bijker 2007).

Those sociologists and anthropologists and, to a lesser extent, historians who have studied science have done tremendous work exploring the inner workings of scientific research but have all too often ignored the fact that religion, being an important part of social life, should play a significant role in their analyses. The more attention it pays to Religious Studies, the more effective Science and Technology Studies (STS) will become and, indeed, vice versa (the study of religion and science has almost entirely ignored the contributions of STS, which could provide data and methodological sophistication to the broader study of religion and science).

Of course, even fans of science studies may have difficulty swallowing the proposition that religion is an influential part of that social process in science. In general, the alignment of mediations in STS assigns human actors to varying scientific groups, for example, but rarely looks very hard at their connections to religious groups. More commonly, STS ignores religious environments. All too often, a scientist might be tied to some formalized religious institution without regard for the broader religious world in which that individual lives. As STS scholars rarely train in the study of religion, this absence is not surprising but nor is it entirely excusable. Societies are constituted by more than institutions. Religious ideas have (*pace* Marx!) real world affects upon social life even when social actors do not ascribe to particular religious institutions. Through education, pop culture, media, and even an architecture of religious ideas, a way in which they are built into the landscape, religious ideas infuse the thinking of all persons, including those who have rejected institutional religions and even the explicit promises and beliefs of those religions. What the conscious mind rejects in one format, it reformulates subconsciously and adapts to new conscious thoughts, as I showed with regard to apocalypticism in religion and technology in chapter one.

The religious environments in which scientists research in robotics and artificial intelligence do make a difference to their work. In Japan, where Shinto and Buddhism have far longer and far more significant traditions than does Christianity, we see entirely different technological emphases than in the United States. In Japan, the sanctification of nature and positive evaluation of bodily human life emphasize embodied robots (including a fascination with humanoid robots) rather than the effectively disembodied[8] artificial intellects glorified in Apocalyptic AI (Geraci 2006). *Showing that science is a part of society is not to say that there is something "wrong" with science. We are, after all, creatures of society; so it should come as no surprise that society has something to do with our scientific endeavors.* The mixture of technological goals and religious ideologies simply reiterates the powerful ways in which technoscientific culture remains, first and foremost, human culture.

Apocalypticism appears in both religious literature and pop science, but does that mean it plays a role in science itself? Another way of asking this would be to wonder whether pop science is science at all. Perhaps pop science is, in fact, closet religion while science is something entirely different, safely ensconced within the walls of laboratories and the internal computations of its robots. Certainly, many people have sought to build and maintain a barricade between religion and science and the belief that scientific facts might be influenced by religion frightens some scientists. This separation between the two, however, is rarely absolute (Derrida 1998). Latour has begun illustrating methodological similarities between religion and science, though he maintains a distinction between the two (Latour 2002). Pop science is not research science, but neither is it something wholly alien to the scientific enterprise. Indeed, as a strategy for bridging the gap between scientists and the lay community and as a roadmap for future research, it is very much a scientific endeavor. Pop science is, therefore, critical to technoscientific power.

CARNEGIE MELLON UNIVERSITY'S ROBOTICS INSTITUTE

Although Moravec and Kurzweil wax eloquent about the ramifications of robotics and AI research, their apocalyptic imagination bears little if any significance for the assembly and programming of real robots. Their positions are an extreme interpretation of current technological trends while everyday research requires a much more detailed approach to immediate problems. In solving any particular scientific problem, the ordinary researcher is far removed from the transcendental positions advocated in Apocalyptic AI. The gulf between apocalyptic visions and detail-oriented research is precisely why many (if not most) researchers place little stock in Apocalyptic AI. Researchers are passionate about the small details they study and these details dissolve in the broad brushstrokes of visionaries (Choset 2007). In order to trace the religious imagination within robotics and AI, I visited the intellectual home of both: Carnegie Mellon University. Herbert Simon and Allen Newell, who were among the earliest pioneers of the birth of AI in the 1950s, both worked at CMU. They helped establish the Department of Computer Science, which has been since elevated to the School of Computer Science. The School of Computer Science regularly appears at the top of computer science rankings and has had an influence upon the study and construction of computers, artificial intelligence, and robotics that extends throughout the world. The Robotics Institute gives Moravec leverage in his apocalyptic claims, providing the authority of an eminent research institution, but—as we will see by the end of this chapter—the aim of Apocalyptic AI is actually to acquire social significance and subsequently return more prestige and power to robotics research than was initially invested thereby.

Founded in 1979, the CMU Robotics Institute, a division within the School of Computer Science, is a power player in the robotics world. With hundreds of researchers (faculty, staff scientists, students, postdocs), the Institute delivers an astounding number of papers at academic conferences and plays a role in the development of nearly every aspect of robotics and AI. No other program in the world rivals the RI for its scope and only a few can boast of similar quality researchers.

The Robotics Institute occupies parts of Newell-Simon Hall, Smith Hall, Wean Hall, and the Gates Center for Computer Science on campus, in addition to the Robot City Roundhouse and other locations in Pittsburgh. Robot City is home to Red Whittaker's field robotics group and was the site for a DARPA (Defense Advanced Research Projects Agency) qualifier for the 2007 Urban Challenge during my stay at CMU (DARPA officials came to observe Boss, the robot Chevrolet Tahoe, as it drove itself around a course, avoiding obstacles, stopping at stop signs, ceding right of way when necessary, and doing a three-point turn).[9] On campus, graduate students share offices or have cubicles that contain textbooks, computers, and, of course, robots, such as a Roomba robot vacuum cleaner with a camera mounted to the top. Faculty offices are crammed with books, computers (often several per person), robots, and papers. Laboratories include machining tools, electrical tools, robots, computers, books, chalkboards, whiteboards, and, of course, faculty, grad students, postdocs, and occasionally even undergrads.

The life of the roboticist is rarely as exciting as one might hope from reading *The Age of Spiritual Machines*. Strolling through the halls and poking into offices or labs, I was likely to see nothing more than people staring at, and possibly typing on, computers. Anyone working on a robot was most likely tinkering with it in the hopes of overcoming some engineering difficulty, not rejoicing in his or her robot as it triumphantly accomplished heretofore impossible tasks or acquired self-awareness. Referring to the difficult task of fitting the servo controller, the motor controller, and the Linux-based computer he needs into a foot-long robot chassis, Dave Touretzky said, "I never thought that after I got a PhD in computer science I would be running to Radio Shack every other day to pick up low-profile connectors" (Touretzky 2007b).[10] Robotics research is difficult work. A good robot, whether simple or complex, will likely be a marvelous mix of programming and engineering. Getting all the right parts together, making them work in partnership, and coding autonomous behavior all require a lot of work. Success never comes easily, though at CMU it comes more often than it does elsewhere.[11]

Conveniently, CMU—already important to the development of robotics and AI—is also home to Apocalyptic AI. Hans Moravec, the founder of Apocalyptic AI, was a principal research scientist at the CMU Robotics Institute before leaving to become chief scientist at Seegrid. While few of his colleagues could be labeled as "allies" in the apocalyptic movement, many appreciated his influence within the field and, indeed, *Mind Children* was sufficiently valued as an intellectual exploration that it helped Moravec in promotion considerations (Mason 2007).

The religious nature of Apocalyptic AI does not exclude it from the world of science; it does not even mean that *Mind Children* is "bad science"—whatever that would be. Two of the roboticists that I interviewed, Howie Choset and Matt Mason, saw Moravec's apocalyptic writings as an outgrowth of his research and, in Mason's words, "not that different" from it (Mason 2007). We should not, therefore, be quick to assume that, simply because it is theological, Apocalyptic AI is necessarily different from robotics research or that it is, in some fundamental sense, opposed to it. The integration of robotics and theology in Apocalyptic AI, while mystifying to some researchers, counts as intellectually important or interesting to others (though likely they would hesitate before proclaiming *Mind Children* religious, as I have done[12]).

Few roboticists at CMU concern themselves at all with Moravec's apocalyptic promises. Although widespread agreement exists that human beings are, in a meaningful sense, "just" machines, this does not automatically lead to the conclusion that machines will one day surpass human intelligence and we will upload our minds into computers so as to live forever. "I'm glad," one graduate student told me after reading my research proposal, "that you note how most roboticists don't think about these things. Because we don't. I've never had a discussion about it with anybody" (Hollinger 2007). When I asked one faculty member, "does anyone here think he's going to download his mind into a computer and live forever?" he replied, "I don't know because we never talk about it" (Atkeson 2007).

No graduate student at CMU told me that he or she had read Moravec's apocalyptic writings, and the faculty were only somewhat more likely to have read them. Older faculty told me they had read *Mind Children* when it came out but few had seen *Robot*. None of the graduate students or younger faculty that I met had read either book and several were unaware of the books' existence. For the most part, everyone is just too busy to follow philosophical discussions of robotic research unless it somehow bears upon his or her work. *Mind Children* and its successors, says Lee Weiss, were not written for the robotics community (Weiss 2007). Of course, the growing significance of Apocalyptic AI, in both public and research communities (e.g., the *IEEE Spectrum*'s singularity edition) might change this in the near future.

When we did discuss Apocalyptic AI, most faculty were dismissive of the movement, either because they thought Moravec's time frame for intelligent machines too short or because they didn't believe we could upload our minds into computers or because they felt that Apocalyptic AI had missed what is important about robotics and AI. In his response to an open letter presented by the Artificial General Intelligence Research Institute (AGIRI), which advocates responsible development of post-singularity artificial intelligence research, Dave Touretzky wrote that we are, at the least, centuries away from creating a machine with general intelligence (the ability to perform a wide array of human tasks). Propounding upon the singularity, he wrote, is "wishful thinking, and perhaps a bit of grandstanding" (Touretzky 2007c). Other faculty suggested that building robots so that they can take over the world is an unreasonable and/or foolish enterprise—robots are built to work for human beings.

Many Institute researchers were unaware of Moravec's pop science books because they are engaged in very "local" kinds of research. They are not willfully ignorant of Apocalyptic AI or the broader implications for robotics and research as portrayed within that field. Indeed, many faculty and students were happy to take time away from their already busy schedules to chat with me. Rather, their research requires that they study technical details and that they devote their time to solving particular kinds of intellectual and mechanical problems. Howie Choset, for example, spoke eloquently of the details involved in robotics research and of the passion that researchers feel for their work. Most of the creativity in robotics and AI happens at a precise level. Only rarely does a researcher such as Moravec expand his creative insights to the bigger picture.

To some extent, *Mind Children* was a product of this creative passion exploded beyond the usual boundaries of robotics. Choset believes that Moravec was just having fun, while Matt Mason, the director of the Institute, echoed Choset, saying that Moravec was writing what he found exciting, what he had found exciting since his childhood (Mason 2007). Without question, Moravec loves visionary thinking and surely enjoyed writing his apocalyptic books. There is good reason to believe, however, that *Mind Children* and *Robot* were more than simply the idle playtime of an enthusiastic researcher.

Pop science has a target audience and the relationship between author and audience must be considered when we seek out an author's motivations, be they conscious or not. Thus, *Mind Children* was certainly more than a game, if by the latter we mean play with no serious ramifications.[13] The stereotypical audience for science fiction books, for example, is young males (though it is unclear that this stereotype adequately describes the actual demographics). The audience for pop science is decidedly older and more educated. It is almost inconceivable that any book written as pop science could just as easily have been science fiction. While the two genres may overlap in important ways (including, of course, in their audiences, which often age from one genre into the other), they are not the same.

The author-audience relationship explains Moravec's desire to write pop science rather than science fiction. The sheer thrill of writing apocalyptic pop science cannot be disentangled from the excitement of science fiction, but pop science, however fantastic, is decidedly *not* science fiction. Before we can understand how pop science diverges from science fiction (through its author-audience relationship), we must first understand how closely the two are related.

SCIENCE FICTION SACRED

If Moravec found Apocalyptic AI fun and exciting, even as a child, we must ask what brought about such a passion. I genuinely believe that Moravec enjoyed writing *Mind Children* and enjoyed engaging in his futuristic ideas but such engagement often has a precursor and almost always has a purpose. For Moravec and his Apocalyptic AI allies, the most likely precursor is science fiction.[14] Though often marginalized as a "trash" genre, science fiction has deeply influenced technological culture, including the rise of Apocalyptic AI. Science-fiction authors reinterpret religious categories in their literature and film and pass these new ideas on to researchers in robotics and AI. Science fiction provides an authoritative voice for the religious environment; it transmits religious ideas even to those people otherwise reluctant to accept them and condones them in the minds of those people who are already religiously faithful.

The public generally regards science fiction as a genre for little boys (Benedikt 1994, 6) but this image is dissipating. Science fiction is allegedly the sort of literature that one "grows out of" as one gets older, discovers girls, and plays more sports. Of course, public perceptions are often bigoted and wildly inaccurate. Social pressure led some authors, however, to seek popularity through "mainstream" novels. Philip K. Dick, one of the treasured authors of sci-fi, tried repeatedly to publish mainstream fiction (Sutin [1989] 1991, 86–88) but succeeded only with *Confessions of a Crap Artist* (1975). Science fiction is a marginalized genre, even if the typical sci-fi fan is unfairly caricatured by "Trekkie" stereotypes.[15] After decades of ignoring sci-fi, academics have since accepted the genre into the literary canon. The influence of authors like Dick has continued to spread and literary critics have made science fiction a respectable area of academic study.

Despite the common denigration of science fiction, it is an extremely important genre for understanding contemporary life, especially with regards to technology. Science fiction tells us about science, society, ourselves, even religion. "If," as Lawrence Sutin asks, "Heraclitus is right—and 'the nature of things is in the habit of concealing itself'—then where better to look for great art than in a trash genre" (Sutin [1989] 1991, 1)? According to Sheila Schwartz, science fiction is the "most accurately reflective literary genre of our time" (Schwartz 1971, 1043). Science fiction has become an important medium for understanding modern life; while it often purports to be about the future, in fact it merely uses the future as a setting to explore contemporary concerns (Huntington 1991; Spark 1991; Sterling 2007).

We rarely see explicitly religious characters in science fiction but religion nevertheless plays a serious role within the genre. Religious language and themes persist in science fiction (Brantlinger 1980, 31; Miller 1985, 145). For example, science fiction borrows regularly from the Bible, including language and traditions of messiahs, angelic beings, Edenic paradises, and cosmic wars between good and evil. Theology even serves the methodological interests of science fiction, which borrows heavily upon apocalyptic ideology in order to bring about a new cognitive world for the reader (Ketterer 1974). The most powerful religious symbol in science fiction is, naturally, the intelligent machine. In science fiction, artificial humans "represent a combination god, externalized soul, and Divine Human" (V. Nelson 2001, 269). Our attribution of near omnipotence to machines demonstrates their divine potential.

Power alone is insufficient, however, to define divinity; science fiction blurs the line between technology (particularly AI technology) and the divine by according robots and computer AIs with the characteristics of the Holy, as they are described by Rudolph Otto. In his masterpiece *The Idea of the Holy* ([1917] 1958), Otto argued that the religious experience has two components: the *mysterium tremendum* and the *fascinans*. The *mysterium tremendum* refers to God's "wholly other" nature. God is totally different from human beings and full of divine power; this scares us. At the same time, the *fascinans* also characterizes God. God is fascinating because only through God can we acquire salvation. Naturally, Otto's description of the sacred is particular to his own brand of liberal Lutheranism and does not necessarily apply to all religious traditions. Nevertheless, his description is eerily similar to the role of intelligent machines in science fiction (Geraci 2007b).

In science fiction, we tend to both fear and adore our intelligent machines. Hollywood blockbusters, such as the *Terminator* and *Matrix* sagas, demonstrate our fear of and fascination with robots. Arnold Schwarzenegger stalks

John Connor through a shopping mall in the beginning of *Terminator 2: Judgment Day* (1991) but instead of killing Connor, it saves him from the T-1000 that has also come back in time. In *Terminator 3: Rise of the Machines* (2003), the T-800 (still played by Schwarzenegger) that goes back in time to save Connor again is the same one that kills him in the future (it was reprogrammed by Connor's wife after it killed him and then sent back to rescue the young Connor and his future wife). A similar dynamic appears in *The Matrix* trilogy. Though he has spent his newfound career as "The One" battling intelligent machines in the series, Neo needs them to form a symbiosis powerful enough to defeat Agent Smith at the end of the trilogy. In these movies and more, we cannot live without the robots[16] but we fear their ability to disenfranchise and to strip us of all of our uniqueness and, indeed, of even our lives.

Intelligent machines have an overwhelming kind of power. Just as the Holy, according to Otto, strikes fear in us through its magisterial power, science fiction robots always possess something just outside of our control. Modern Americans maintain a subconscious faith in the divinity of machines (V. Nelson 2001, 251), such as when supremely intelligent computers control all of human affairs in the final story of Asimov's famed *I, Robot* collection. The Machines are gods, able to create a paradise on earth, restoring the lost Garden of Eden (Thomsen 1982, 29). In order to create this heaven on earth, however, the Machines must eliminate certain people from positions of power. Their manipulation, of course, cannot help but remind us of the Holy. Susan Calvin (the "robopsychologist" and protagonist of many of the stories) and Stephen Byerley (the World-Coordinator) realize that the Machines now control human destiny. While Byerley calls this "horrible," Calvin calls it "wonderful" (Asimov [1950] 1977, 192). No doubt both are correct. The Machines' domination of human life means the reduction of humankind to mere instrumentality but also means the possibility of human happiness. Simultaneous damnation and salvation—which leads to fear and fascination intertwined.

In the West, we have what Asimov considered a deplorable tendency toward the Frankenstein complex: we are sure that the robots will turn on us and ruin our lives. This has led to excellent book sales and a movie contract for Daniel Wilson (PhD from the CMU Robotics Institute) who wrote the humorous but educational book *How to Survive a Robot Uprising* (2005). But it also means that whenever roboticists are interviewed, they have to field questions about evil robots taking over the world (Rosheim 2006, 61). Honda was sufficiently concerned about Western responses to robots that they sent a representative to the Vatican seeking reassurance that it would not oppose Honda's humanoid robotics program (Yamaguchi 2002, 101).

Despite our fear of a robot uprising, however, we have an insatiable hunger for robot technologies and stories. Millions of iRobot Roombas testify to our desire for robots: Roombas cannot clean floors as well as ordinary floor vacuums but buyers still want them. The idea that robots might make our lives leisurely is a powerful brand of earthly salvation. In science fiction, the primary locus for interpreting robotic technology, no amount of terror over a robot uprising can wipe away the fascination and allure of the robots. In science fiction, *the allure of intelligent robots cannot be separated from the fear they engender—the robots are akin to the Holy* (Geraci 2007b). In real life, no amount of concern over economic disenfranchisement or robotic enslavement has curbed the growth of the robotics industry.

Science fiction reflects a broad array of cultural issues and it becomes both carrier and interpreter of those issues for its audience. Science fiction readers often become scientists themselves. The very people who build and use computers are often the ones who first learned about them in science fiction novels when they were children. The science fiction worldview can, therefore, make powerful contributions to the nature of technological progress and it has played a role in transhumanism, the belief that humankind will surpass its current limitations, as in Apocalyptic AI (Alexander 2003, passim; Tirosh-Samuelson 2007).

Science fiction has even played a role in elite technology education. Early cyberpunk stories from the 1980s, for example, helped shape the way researchers thought about their problems. In an Amazon.com book review, Olin Shivers of Georgia Tech University described the importance of Vernor Vinge's *True Names* to his graduate studies in artificial intelligence. According to Shivers,

> When I was starting out as a PhD student in Artificial Intelligence at Carnegie Mellon, it was made known to us first-year students that an unofficial but necessary part of our education was to locate and read a copy of an obscure science-fiction novella called *True Names*. Since you couldn't find it in bookstores, older grad students and professors would directly mail order sets of ten and set up informal lending libraries— you would go, for example, to Hans Moravec's office, and sign one out from a little cardboard box over in the corner of his office. This was 1983—the Internet was a toy reserved for American academics, "virtual reality" was not a popular topic, and the term "cyberpunk" had not been coined. One by one, we all tracked down copies, and all had the tops of our heads blown off by Vinge's incredible book (Shivers 1999).

True Names is a story about computer hackers who can enter a virtual reality cyberspace and manipulate it through the quasi-magical powers of computer programming. One of the hackers, Mr. Slippery, joins forces with another to locate and defeat an enemy (the Mailman) who is systematically taking control of the "Other Plane," Vinge's cyberspace. In the end, Mr. Slippery's partner permanently uploads her consciousness into the matrix so that she can forever safeguard it against similar attacks.

As far as I can tell, no CMU faculty still "require" that graduate students read *True Names* or any other science fiction story. Nevertheless, it is significant that a time existed when, at least loosely, this was the case. The AI department at CMU is among the world's very best and has trained many professional and academic computer scientists. Students can be an impressionable community, so faculty advocacy of particular science fiction stories (as opposed to other kinds of stories or even other science fiction stories) could have a profound effect upon the way graduate students go about their future careers.

At the same time that *True Names* was required reading for CMU grad students in AI, sci-fi deeply influenced research in that other East Coast technological haven: the Massachusetts Institute of Technology (MIT). "Science fiction is *the* literature at MIT," according to Stewart Brand, who spent time at the MIT Media Lab in the mid-1980s (Brand 1987, 224, emphasis original). Decades later, MIT's Cynthia Breazeal, a pioneer in the construction of social robots, cited Asimov, Dick, Stephenson, Brian Aldiss, the movie *Star Wars*, and the android Data from the television show *Star Trek: The Next Generation* as influences on her work (Breazeal 2002). There can be no doubt about the continuing influence of science fiction on researchers. Just as an explicitly religious environment can change the way people do scientific work (as in Judeo-Christian apocalypticism in the U.S. and Shinto and Buddhism in Japan, above), the science fiction environment—which often borders on, or even crosses over the border of religion—can affect how scientists practice. As Brand recognizes, science fiction and science fact often "are so blurred together they are practically one intellectual activity" (Brand 1987, 225).

Marvin Minsky deserves much credit for science fiction's continuing relevance at MIT. It was he, after all, who disparaged all twentieth-century philosophers as "just shallow and wrong" compared to science fiction authors, especially Isaac Asimov and Frederik Pohl (quoted in Brand 1987, 224). Minsky has enthusiastically involved himself in the science fiction community: he wrote the afterword for *True Names* and cowrote *The Turing Option* with Harry Harrison.[17] In *The Turing Option*, he defends the intellectual merit of science fiction and glorifies its audience as "in the top percentile" of readers (Harrison and Minsky 1992, 79). Minsky has even advocated a visiting professorship in science fiction to bring writers to the Media Lab, an idea seconded by Brand (Brand 1987, 259).[18] Although the Media Lab has yet to establish such a post, Minsky's influence on the Lab and on the students and faculty of the Lab is without question; he is, after all one of the grand old fathers of artificial intelligence. If Minsky says "jump," surely more than one member of the Lab buys a copy of Asimov's *I, Robot*.[19]

Vinge's *True Names* ([1981] 2001) is not the only science fiction book to deeply affect robotics and AI. In addition to Asimov's famous stories about robotics, which may be why many researchers enter the field in the first place, cyberpunk gave the imaginative impetus for much current research. Shivers, for example, cites the novels of William Gibson and Neal Stephenson as better prognosticators and better illustrations of technological implications than the nonfiction of Negroponte, Gate, or Dertouzos (Shivers 1999). At MIT, according to Brand, "every computer science student knows and refers to John Brunner's *Shockwave Rider*, Vernor Vinge's *True Names* ... William Gibson's *Neuromancer*" (Brand 1987, 224). Had Brand visited MIT just a few years later, no doubt Stephenson's *Snow Crash* (1992) would have been on the list.

Gibson's *Neuromancer* was critical to the formation of virtual reality research. Although pioneering work had already been done in the entertainment industry by Morton Heilig, inventor of the unsuccessful but extraordinary Sensorama (Rheingold 1991, 49–67) and in scientific areas of medical research, molecular biology, architecture, and planetary data imaging (ibid., 34–46), the virtual community coalesced under Gibson's book. *Neuromancer* "triggered a conceptual revolution among the scattered workers who had been doing virtual reality research for years" (A. Stone 1991, 98). Focused under the new conceptual umbrella of "cyberspace," a vast array of researchers imagined themselves "together"[20] and thus was a new way of practicing science born.

The Association for the Advancement of Artificial Intelligence (AAAI) claims that "for those interested in AI, science fiction offers a window to the future, a mirror for the present, and even interesting career opportunities" (AAAI 2007). The AAAI is *the* official voice of AI research in the United States and it explicitly defends the truth value of science fiction—and not only with regards to interpreting present culture but as a way of predicting the future! If the AAAI accepts and argues for the significance of science fiction, it should not surprise us that Shivers, Brand, and others describe that significance within various academic programs.

Jason Pontin, former editor of the dot-com magazine *Red Herring* and current editor in chief of MIT's *Technology Review*, reports that science fiction directly influences technological research. Life imitates art: researchers try to build the fascinating things described in science fiction (Pontin 2007). For example, it was a William Gibson short story published in OMNI magazine that led the VRML (Virtual Reality Modeling Language) architect Mark Pesce into his career of virtual reality development after he flunked out of MIT (Wertheim 1999, 254). Pontin claims that scientists such as Marvin Minsky, Seymour Cray, Tim Berners-Lee, and Jaron Lanier were all influenced by science fiction (Pontin 2007; see also Rheingold 1991, 140). Berners-Lee, the creator of the World Wide Web, is a perfect example of how science fiction can affect a research program. Berners-Lee read science fiction as a youth and was particularly impressed with Arthur C. Clarke's "Dial F for Frankenstein" (Wright 1997). In Clarke's story, many telephone switching stations are linked together and become conscious (to humanity's detriment). Berners-Lee's most noted accomplishment, of course, has been the linking of computers: he was responsible for designing the hypertext markup language (HTML) used in creating Web sites and pairing it to protocols for communication between computers, thus making the Web possible. Fortunately, the Web—unlike Clarke's switching stations—has yet to take over the world.

Just as elsewhere in digital technology, science fiction has had a major impact upon robotics. Isaac Asimov's stories remain inspirational reading for roboticists and a number of researchers trace their current robotics projects to science fiction. Brian Aldiss's book *Supertoys Last All Summer Long*, for example, influenced David Hanson's Zeno, a robot boy designed for interactive learning and human emotion (Slagle 2007). Joseph Engelberger,[21] who promoted the first industrial robot (designed by George Devol in 1954), was an Isaac Asimov fan (Hornyak 2006, 79), and in Japan, nearly every researcher credits the significance of *Tetsuwan Atomu* (Mighty Atom, known in the United States as Astro Boy) for encouraging his or her love of robotics (ibid., 54). Those who grow up with science fiction are likely to find inspiration in it in their career choices and in their research agendas, just as the AAAI suggests.

Carnegie Mellon professors may not require science fiction reading but their graduate students remain fans of the genre. Geoff Hollinger suspects that at least 50 percent, if not closer to 80 percent, of the RI graduate students and faculty have read Isaac Asimov's *I, Robot*. Members of the RI are continually amazed by Asimov's prescient stories, which often revolve around technical predicaments that have become commonplace in robotics research (Hollinger 2007). Other students echoed Hollinger's interest in science fiction; most mentioned Asimov but they also referred to the cyberpunk authors, such as Gibson and Stephenson. In my online survey of robotics enthusiasts, 80 percent of respondents interested in robotics either occasionally or regularly read science fiction while another 13.7 percent used to read it.[22] In a seminar I held with grad students and faculty at the Robotics Institute, there was general accord that, while pop science did little to influence roboticists directly, many Apocalyptic AI concepts reached the robotics community through science fiction (Geraci 2007c).

Science fiction may do more than carry sacred themes; it may operate as an ersatz religion for some scientists. In *The Artilect War*, Hugo de Garis explicitly ties his enjoyment of science fiction to his need for religious fulfillment (2005, 92).[23] He feels that his scientific outlook prevents him from adopting any traditional religious beliefs (a position that is considerably less than universal among scientists) but continues to feel a longing for meaning and value. He gains such things from science fiction, which thus crosses the boundary between science and religion.

Hans Moravec's key theological aim—the establishment of a transcendent new reality occupied by purified Mind—does have precursors in science fiction. The first appearance of mind uploading occurs in Sir Arthur C. Clarke's *The City and the Stars*, first published in 1953. In that book, Clarke describes a world where people's personalities are stored in a computer memory and then downloaded into bodies cloned for them at predetermined times (Clarke 2001, 18–19). Frederick Pohl, glamorized by Marvin Minsky as one of the twentieth century's greatest philosophers, describes human minds uploaded into robots in his story "The Tunnel under the World," first published in 1955 and subsequently republished (Pohl 1975). In the story, the protagonist repeatedly wakes to the same day (June 15) and eventually realizes that his entire world is a marketing arena. The rulers of the city test out various advertising mechanisms for commercial and political enterprises upon the minds of people who died in a cataclysmic explosion. The marketers instantiated each individual's mind in a miniature body living in a miniature version of the town that the operators shut down each night to wipe the day's memory from each resident.

Although mind uploading does not carry a positive aura in "The Tunnel under the World," it is largely beneficial in Clarke's *The City and the Stars* and within a few decades became widely appreciated.[24] In Roger Zelazny's *Lord of Light* (1967), for example, individuals technologically "transmigrate" through biologically grown bodies, carrying their identities with them just as in Clarke's story. Though the characters in *Lord of Light* and *The City and the Stars* are not robots, the same underlying logic of mind identity and uploading enables the transfer of identities.[25] Indeed, identity and mind were separate from the material bodies in Clarke's work (just as they now are for Moravec and Kurzweil), where he describes a being called Vanamonde that is made of pure mind, free of the "tyranny of matter" (Clarke 2001, 263). Likewise, in *2001: A Space Odyssey*, Clarke posits alien life-forms that have evolved from biological forms, through mechanical forms, and eventually into "frozen lattices of light," who—like Vanamonde—escape the "tyranny of matter" (Clarke 1968, 185). The book's protagonist, David Bowman, interacts with alien technology and transcends the human condition, becoming the "Star-Child" that returns to Earth as a god, "master of the world" (ibid., 221).

The concept of mind uploading, the preservation of an individual's personality and the instantiation of it in a biological or digital body, gained scientific credibility in Moravec's writings. Moravec, first as a graduate student at one of the nation's premier computer science universities (Stanford) and later as an eminent researcher at another of the nation's premier computer science universities (CMU) provided respectability to what had been "just" an aspect of visionary science fiction. The sci-fi concept of mind uploading was combined with the hidden apocalyptic ideology of Jewish and Christian traditions for the first time in Moravec's writings and from there became a staple of both science fiction and popular science robotics and AI.

Science fiction carries a camouflaged sacred into technological research. I do not suggest that science fiction endorses religion and that its readers accept that endorsement and happily carry it into technological careers. Indeed, many sci-fi authors reject institutional religion, such as when Clarke refers to it as a "disease" (2001, 142). Rather, science fiction borrows from the Christian tradition because it is the output of a Christian environment. Insofar as it inspires and influences those who become scientists, it has real world affects on the progress of technology. Science fiction is part of technological culture and it prominently inhabits the worldview of researchers in robotics and AI. Therefore, a feedback loop forms, strengthening certain aspects of our relationship to technology. Early modern experiences with technology led to both enthusiasm and dread (think of the Luddites!), and when these appear in science fiction they return to our culture even stronger. Thus, by the late twentieth century, science fiction regularly portrayed intelligent machines in the same powerful language employed by Rudolph Otto to describe the Christian god.

The adoption of religious categories by Apocalyptic AI reflects the broader integration of the sacred into our cultural apperception of technology. Science fiction illustrates how Marvin Minsky or Hans Moravec or anyone else could begin integrating religion and technology in his or her worldview. The love of science fiction, of *what if?*, inspires Apocalyptic AI and makes it fun, but the real power of Apocalyptic AI is in its cultural politics.

THE POLITICS OF APOCALYPTICISM

If a dualist worldview provides the religious zeal of Apocalyptic AI and science fiction gives it a visionary road map, it is the popular politics of funding and prestige that gives Apocalyptic AI its evangelical incentive, its raison d'être. Apocalyptic AI, like much of popular science, seeks cultural authority for its heroes in the form of tangible assets like research funding and intangible assets like prestige.[26] Popular science books serve several purposes. One is to educate the general public on scientific matters but it would be naive beyond measure to suggest that this is the sole aim of such books. Apocalyptic AI works establish their authors as critical thinkers in our culture; they present them as authorities. At the same time, insofar as authors become cultural authorities, scientific research is glorified within the realm of human work, which increases public support of technological research. Pop science writing creates political and cultural power, which explains the origins of Apocalyptic AI and its significance for scientific research in robotics and artificial intelligence.

The relationship between funding and techno-religious promises appears elsewhere in twentieth- and twenty-first–century science. Brian Alexander notes that "bravado"—claims about the miraculous potential of biotechnology—provided impetus for massive cash funding in corporate IPOs in the late 1990s and early 2000s (2003, passim). Such rhetoric also helped get funding into government labs (ibid., 96) and led to major corporate involvement in biotech, as when the British pharmaceutical giant SmithKline (now GlaxoSmithKline) endorsed the pharmaceutical company Human Genome Sciences and put millions of dollars at the new company's disposal (ibid., 101). The religious faith in a biotech millennium provided the fledgling biotech industry momentum and justified the enormous influx of cash into the community.

Despite the measurable increase in robotics and AI funding, those in the field continue to press for increased public and government participation. Bill Thomasmeyer, president of the National Center of Defense Robotics (NCDR) and executive vice president of The Technology Collaborative, claims that robotics is essential to American political and economic goals (Atwood 2007). Thomasmeyer emphasizes his point by raising the specter of our borders and security needs (evidently referring to illegal immigration and terrorism, respectively). Any drop off in the rate of engineering and science graduates trained in robotics research will be a "real threat to our country" (ibid.). Robotics industry groups (including the National Defense Industry Association [NDIA], the Robotics Industry Association [RIA], the Association for Unmanned Vehicle Systems International [AUVSI], and the NCDR) worked together to help congressmen Mike Doyle (D-PA) and Zach Wamp (R-TN) launch a congressional caucus on robotics, which is now co-chaired by Doyle and Phil Gingrey (R-GA). Robotics groups see continued and increased congressional support as crucial to their operations and so are committed to publicizing robotics and encouraging congressional representatives' investment therein.

Pop science advocacy pushes for greater public excitement over robotics research. For example, the magazine *Robot* is the foremost popularizer of robotics and though the magazine is read by professional researchers (I saw more than one copy of the latest edition while visiting the CMU Robotics Institute), it primarily speaks to the scientific lay public. *Robot* does not include academic essays but instead has short updates on cutting-edge research, information on educational robotics and local communities, helpful tips on programming or building robots, and reviews of commercially available robots. It is clearly a popular magazine, a magazine of the people. In it, Thomasmeyer urges people to write to their representatives requesting that they join the Congressional Bi-partisan Robotics Caucus, an effort seconded by the magazine's editor in chief, who interviewed Thomasmeyer. *Robot* is thus part of the broader movement among roboticists and robot manufacturers to raise public awareness of and appreciation for robotics research.

Pop science books, especially those in the Apocalyptic AI movement, conform to the field's need to enhance the visibility and social significance of research. Magazines like *Robot* generally preach to the choir; after all, any subscriber to the magazine is almost destined to support a congressional caucus on robotics. Pop science books, although they have built-in audiences, also expose new people to their fields. You are not expected to know anything about robotics before you pick up *Mind Children*; indeed, you may not even care much about robots when you start. The book will teach you a little about robots and their history while showing you why you should care. In order to accomplish this, one of the chief aims of Apocalyptic AI has been to elevate the social status of the author. You should care what he has to say because he is an important person, a master of the technology that will dominate our future and save us from confusion, ignorance, and death.

Historically, the ability to create an artificial person is attributed as an honorific and as evidence for an individual's worth. Legends of manufacturing a person demonstrate the spiritual, intellectual, or technological prowess of the creator (for a longer description of the history of automata and artificial humanoids, see appendix one). In Judaism, for example, the ability to create a Golem[27] is proof of an individual's spiritual prowess (Goldsmith 1981, 36–37; Idel 1990; Sherwin 2004, 14). Rabbi Elijah of Chelm (d. 1583) and Rabbi Judah Loew ben Bezalel (c. 1520–1609), for example, were the primary heroes of modern Jewish Golem legends. Rabbi Chelm was otherwise known as the *gaon* (genius) of Vilna and was the first rabbi to receive the title Baal Shem ("Master of the Divine Name") and Rabbi Loew was called "the great rabbi." Earlier figures—the Biblical patriarch Abraham, Ben Sira (the author of the deuterocanonical book Sirach), and others—occasionally attached to the Golem history also received widespread admiration. Golem manufacture is simply not attributed, in Jewish literature, to anyone of less than paramount spiritual authority.

Similarly, Greek legends show how the ancients credited certain brilliant heroes with the power to create artificial life. In the famous myth of Pygmalion, the statue Galatea comes to life, in part out of Aphrodite's recognition that Pygmalion loves the statue but also out of respect for Pygmalion's artistic merit (which made his love possible). One human being, according to Greek legend, was able to build "living" automata: the engineer Daedalus, who was reputed to have designed moving statues. The only other Greek myths in which artificial beings are created attribute this to the clever (though physically lame) god Hephaestus. Daedalus, then, has the creative and technological wizardry of a god.

In medieval Europe, masters of theology, philosophy, and arcane lore benefited from legends of their automata. Pope Sylvester II (c. 945–1003 CE) and Saint Albertus Magnus (c. 1200–1282 CE), for example, were believed to have talking heads that could answer questions put to them by their masters. Sylvester and Magnus were prodigious scholars and leading members of the church (the former was a pope, the latter is a saint). Contemporaries attributed technical wizardry (and perhaps a hint of sorcery) to Magnus and Sylvester out of respect for their eminence. Legendary automata, like Golems, represent the two Christians' power in politics, philosophy, and theology.

As an honorific, anthropogonic attributions had powerful practical influence in business, providing individuals with economic benefits. Paracelsus (1493–1541 CE), a medical doctor, claimed he could create a homunculus, a living person made through alchemical means. Just as Daedalus compared to Hephaestus in ancient

Greek mythology, Paracelsus likened himself (and other alchemists) to the demi-urge, or lesser god of creation in Platonic and Hermetic lore (Newman 2004, 199), and declared the creation of a homunculus more honorable than the creation of gold (ibid., 165). The power to make a homunculus clearly reflects upon Paracelsus's ability to heal the infirm; he who can create life from nonlife must have the power to maintain life in the already living. In early modern Europe, the clock maker Pierre Jaquet-Droz (1721–1790 CE) and his sons built amazing automata— life-sized piano players and scribes—in order to sell more clocks (if they can build a piano player, how great must their clocks be!). The power to create a humanoid and endow it with life is one of the chief ways in which Westerners have claimed spiritual, social, and even technological prowess. Apocalyptic AI is a part of this tradition.

The financial and social benefits of evangelizing Apocalyptic AI reflect the on-going ways in which the fabrication of artificial life has reflected the power and prestige of the fabricator. Pop robotics and AI are rife with pronouncements de-claring the enormous significance of technical research. Roboticists are leading us in the final phase of evolution (Moravec 1988, 2), through "one of those rare times in history when humanity transforms from one type of human society to another" (Hillis 2001, 29–30). Indeed, the "emergence in the early twenty-first century of a new form of intelligence on Earth that can compete with, and ultimately signifi-cantly exceed, human intelligence will be a development of greater import than any of the events that have shaped human history" (Kurzweil 1999, 5) and whether to build intelligent machines will be the most significant political issue of the twenty-first century (de Garis 2005, 11). Such claims, if true, elevate roboticists and AI researchers—especially those prophets of the apocalyptic future—to the high-est spiritual and political echelons possible. If they can bring about such events, surely these technological wizards are among the very elite of society.

Self-promotion and a certain amount of grandstanding for robotics and AI run hand in hand through Apocalyptic AI. "Gushing"—breathless enthusiasm—sells books, ideas, and inventions and it is a common strategy in technological circles (Brand 1987, 15). It also elevates a speaker's social standing. Hugo de Garis, for example, seems to get more important to the history of the world with every passing word of his text, which is a considerable feat given that the second sen-tence of his book is "I'm the head of a research group which designs and builds 'artificial brains,' a field that I have largely pioneered" (de Garis 2005, 1).[28] De Garis believes that he "can see more clearly than most" the potential of twenty-first-century technologies (ibid., 2) and that he is the only one who foresees the real problems of artificial intelligence (ibid., 17); he expects to be known as either the "father of the artificial brain" or the "father of gigadeath[29]" (ibid., 18–19); he is the equivalent of the Manhattan Project's Leo Szilard[30] (ibid., 24); he is an "intellec-tual" (ibid., 27); he is too sophisticated for his native country, Australia (ibid., 28)

and his adopted country, Japan (ibid., 29–30); he is multicultural and more stimu-
lating than "monocultured" people (ibid., 29); he is an international media darling
(ibid., 30, 52); he is the subject of several film documentaries (ibid., 54); he is the
father of an entire academic research field, evolvable hardware (ibid., 38); he is
more sophisticated and morally responsible than the average engineer or scientist
(ibid., 48–49); he is in the Guinness Book of World Records and hobnobs with
billionaires at the World Economic Forum in Davos, Switzerland (ibid., 50); he
innovates where others have not (ibid., 35, 40); he is a "visionary" (ibid., 126); and,
if not for the dot-com crash, he and his "miraculous" invention would have secured
his justly deserved place in the history of computing (ibid., 43–44). No reader
could possibly fail to notice de Garis's overwhelming confidence in his own importance, nor would he or she likely miss the fact that de Garis considers himself
smarter than the readers.[31]

Hugo de Garis is not the only self-assured member of the Apocalyptic AI community; Hans Moravec is probably the only one who does not place himself repeatedly in the public spotlight. In *The Turing Option*, Marvin Minsky, who throws out
nearly the entire twentieth-century Western philosophical heritage (Brand 1987,
224), also disparages Marcel Proust's exploration of memory, touting instead the
potential of an AI researcher to study it (Harrison and Minsky 1992, 116). Kevin
Warwick describes himself as a "white knight" ([1997] 2004, 210), labels himself
the world's first cyborg, and implies that—because of his "cyborg implants"—he is
the forerunner of our evolutionary future (2003). One faculty member at the Robotics Institute told me he felt that the whole point of Apocalyptic AI is to convince
the reader of how smart the author is. "Ray Kurzweil is the smartest person in the
world and he wants you to know it," he stated. Kurzweil's first popular science
book, *The Age of Intelligent Machines*, is a sophisticated volume of essays by Kurzweil
and other leading figures in AI and philosophy. The Association of American Publishers (AAP) named it the Most Outstanding Computer Science Book of 1990 and
it was well received in academic circles. It did not, however, earn him the kind of
public praise and media attention that he garnered from *The Age of Spiritual
Machines*, which made him a poster boy for the future. This latter book, in which
he advocates the transhumanist future of Apocalyptic AI, features several references to his prowess at predicting the technological future (1999, 74–75, 170–73,
217) and highlights his various technological innovations (84–85, 174–78). Despite
this rhetoric, however, in person Kurzweil is quite modest and sociable. Self-
aggrandizement is a tool; it promotes the reader's appreciation for the author and
it gives the author an aura of genius rather than the appearance of being a crank.
In the end, convincing the reader of the author's intelligence promotes public
appreciation, which is most tangible in funding politics.

Pop science educates the public so as to raise public interest in scientific
research projects. A cursory examination of other pop science books outside of

Apocalyptic AI demonstrates that the genre is very often political in motivation. Steven Weinberg's *Dreams of a Final Theory* (1992), for example, points toward the political and financial issues in pop science writing. In the late 1980s and early 1990s, Weinberg served as an expert for the congressional hearings on the Superconducting Super Collider (SSC),[32] then under construction in Texas. Building the SSC, Weinberg argued, would help physicists uncover basic facts about the construction of the universe. The colliders presently available could not produce the kinds of reactions that Weinberg believed would confirm or deny state-of-the-art theories in physics, so he passionately argued for the completion of the SSC.

The purpose of *Dreams of a Final Theory* was not to educate the public but to excite it and to advocate for scientific spending. The book's physics lessons are, loosely speaking, comprehensible to a lay audience, which means they will do little as a primer in particle physics (which requires too much math to make for light reading). The history and instruction were designed to offer a rationale for all the money required to complete the SSC. With congressional budgets shrinking, every government-funded project in the United States required advocates. An enormously expensive scientific laboratory with negligible tangible payoff required more than a little support, especially as its cost ballooned from 4 billion to 12 billion dollars. *Dreams of a Final Theory* was Weinberg's effort to convince the lay public to support the SSC. With enough public support, the project would certainly outlast its congressional critics.[33] In the end, *Dreams of a Final Theory* was unsuccessful; the SSC was cancelled and will almost certainly never be built in the United States.

Even before the twenty-first-century explosion of interest in robotics and AI, follow-up books by Moravec, Kurzweil, de Garis, and Warwick prove that Moravec's 1988 work was better appreciated than Weinberg's *Dreams*. Moravec published *Robot* in 1999 with little of substance (aside from the time frame and the language) changed from his 1988 offering and the other authors have all achieved a certain degree of popularity or notoriety based upon their work in the field. Whether or not Weinberg would care to write it, I am hard pressed to imagine a public audience for a sequel to *Dreams*. Moravec mostly updates his earlier arguments in slightly different (and often clearer) language but, not only did he receive a new publication contract, he has sold many copies of *Robot* despite the influx of competitors to the market. Interest in the SSC has evaporated while interest in Apocalyptic AI has increased in both scientific and lay communities.

The role of religion in pop science helps explain the contrasting success levels of Weinberg and Apocalyptic AI. Although *Dreams of a Final Theory* is a well-written and intelligent book, it is no longer anything more than a popularization of physics—an act of Congress cancelled Weinberg's evangelical agenda. Apocalyptic AI advocates have been more successful than Weinberg in part because they use religious categories to heighten the allure of their subject matter.[34] Weinberg regularly casts aspersion upon religion in *Dreams of a Final Theory*; he argues that physics reveals the universe as meaningless and reflects his own personal atheism. There is little emotional appeal in such claims. In contrast, Apocalyptic AI provides meaning and casts a religious shadow across the future, one in which the hopes and dreams of Western civilization are reconfigured but nevertheless accomplished in robotics and AI. Naturally, Apocalyptic AI will not likely appeal to the traditionally religious faithful, but it finds a ready audience among the religiously disaffected who might find a "powerful new religion" (de Garis 2005, 105) and a new kind of god to worship (ibid., 104) in the movement's promises.

Without sacred language or categories, *Dreams* totally fails to inspire real social movements. Apocalyptic AI, on the other hand, has an eager audience. Not only have science fiction fans welcomed the books as promising glimpses into the future but transhumanists have taken the books as "gospel truth." Transhumanists and virtual reality gamers (described in chapter three) demonstrate the power of Apocalyptic AI. The religious framework of Apocalyptic AI makes it a functional ideology for social construction. The absence of such a framework—indeed, a vituperous indictment of religion altogether—prevents *Dreams* from succeeding in several important ways. It is a fine popularization of physics but a poor text for acquiring converts.

I am not suggesting that Apocalyptic AI is a deliberately Machiavellian response to Weinberg's failure to protect SSC funding.[35] I highly doubt that Moravec, Kurzweil, or anyone else thought to himself, "oh, well Steve's efforts don't look too good so I guess I better try something else . . . religion might work!"[36] *Mind Children* antedates *Dreams of a Final Theory*, so that suggestion would be foolish. What we can see, however, is that two different strategies for gaining public approval coincided in Moravec's *Mind Children* and Weinberg's *Dreams* and that only one of these strategies still possesses any charismatic affect. No one cares about the SSC anymore (excluding, perhaps, the local physics community) whereas Apocalyptic AI matters for transhumanists, online gamers, journalists, and even governments. Considering Kurzweil's appearance in the pages of *Rolling Stone* (Kushner 2009) and the acceptance of a documentary about him to the 2009 Tribeca Film Festival (Ptolemy 2009), evidently Apocalyptic AI matters in popular culture as well.

Weinberg sought to raise the prestige of physicists by denigrating religion, whereas Apocalyptic AI raises the prestige of roboticists and AI researchers by hybridizing science and religion. The use of role-hybridization as a strategy for the acquisition of scientific prestige was first noticed in the 1960s by Joseph .Ben-David, the 1985 winner of the John Desmond Bernal Prize[37] for his work in the sociology of science. Ben-David argued that young scientists seeking jobs or prestige in over-crowded fields often hybridized the roles of more prestigious positions with less prestigious positions to forge an entirely new scientific path (Ben-David 1991). The hybridization of religion and science combines the separate authorities of science and religion in a powerful unit that grants cultural prestige to Apocalyptic AI advocates (Geraci 2007a).

Apocalyptic AI draws on the strengths of both religion and science; its religious promises grant us solace and hope while its scientific claims ground that hope in the successes of modern technology. Apocalyptic AI promises freedom from alienation, financial security, long-lasting health, immortality, and even the resurrection of the dead. At the same time, the use of the Law of Accelerating Returns (by Kurzweil), Moore's Law of integrated circuits, and Darwinian evolution allegedly offers a scientific guarantee for the unstoppable course of progress that will satisfy all of these wants.

According to Ben-David, role-hybridization benefits young scholars most but Apocalyptic AI has been frequently championed by senior researchers. For lesser known figures such as de Garis and Warwick, Apocalyptic AI role-hybridization may offer a path to scientific significance, but why would seminal academics and professionals—such as Moravec, Minsky, or Kurzweil—step outside their usual scientific worlds? Why would they risk their academic credibility by hybridizing religion and science? It is because they stand to gain cultural authority, not scientific. Pop science books give them a voice among the lay community of non-scientists. The books prove the significance of robotics and AI research by showing the profound effects these fields will have upon our immediate future. Thus, as with Weinberg's popularization of modern physics, pop robotics is about real world power. By advancing the importance of research in robotics and AI, these authors encourage respect and admiration and, thereby, financial support. All of these elements establish genuine power for robotics and AI.

Science and technology scholars recognize the political importance of laboratory work but have not yet seen how pop science also creates power. Bruno Latour long ago recognized that "it is in laboratories that most new sources of power are generated" (1983, 160) and that scientific articles apply "pressure on readers, convincing them to change what they believe, what they want to do, or what they want to be" (1988, 94).[38] Taking scientific politics into the realm of the lay public, Donna Haraway has argued that "scientific projects are civic projects; they remake citizens" (1997, 175). Haraway has gone further than Latour in recognizing the political power of technoscientific work but she has stopped short of offering a serious evaluation of how pop science applies social leverage and enhances technoscientific prestige.

Authority requires a complex combination of factors, but the most powerful authorities in our culture always depend upon the power of the sacred. Religious backing authorizes an individual's right to speak. Bruce Lincoln, a noted historian of religions, has done much to explore the significance of authority in the modern world. While he first believed that the right mixture of speaker, audience, staging, and message would suffice to establish the credibility of a leader (Lincoln 1995) he subsequently came to appreciate that the sacred grounds ultimate authority (Lincoln 2003). Martin Luther King Jr.'s "I have a dream" speech, for example, borrows from the sacred twice over: it occurred at the Lincoln Memorial, grounds sacred in American civil religion (see Bellah and Hammond 1980) and repeatedly references a god who encourages, even demands, racial equality. Without the sanctity of the Lincoln Memorial, much would have been lost. Without the guarantee of God's justice, even more would have been. King grounded his hope for a just society in the divine desire for one. In like fashion, the religious background of Apocalyptic AI gives it an authority that Weinberg's *Dreams* lacks.

The desire to acquire cultural prestige entails a corresponding desire for research funding. Just as Weinberg's *Dreams* aimed at popular support for research funding, Apocalyptic AI books subtly suggest that public support for robotics and AI would be wise. In the 1980s, AI claims about the near-term power of intelligent machines were directly tied to government and military funding (Dreyfus and Dreyfus 1986, 11–13). A similar strategy helped Nicholas Negroponte and MIT's Media Lab obtain funding (Brand 1987, 11). Researchers can sometimes get funding more easily when they promise solutions to serious human problems than when they "lose the forest for the trees" by focusing upon technical details. Pop science claims that the scientist will offer great service and thus heightens the prestige of the individual and his field. The reader can then wholeheartedly support research (including and especially through government funding).

Apocalyptic AI is, indeed, a request for money. Moravec says that his first apocalyptic essay, "Today's Computers, Intelligent Machines and Our Future" (1978), "called for someone to invest billions of dollars in computer hardware" (Moravec 1999, vii). Moravec also hints that more funding is needed in *Robot*, where he discusses his research and indicates that too little of its relevance has been recognized. "The perceived potential of robotics is limited, and the engineering investment it receives consequently modest" (Moravec 1999, 91). Here we see a direct connection between the educational aim of the book and its financial aim. Given that a few years later Moravec left academia to work full time in developing the industrial technologies being described lends credence to the belief that *Robot* was, among other things, a way of raising interest among corporate investors.

Obviously, such an investment would benefit Moravec and other researchers in robotics and AI enormously. Hugo de Garis is even more obvious in his requests, making multiple references to his need for grant funding, the benefits that government funding would accrue for the grant-awarding nation, and the inevitability that "powerful men of industry and politics" will be Cosmists and support his vision because they, their companies, and their countries have so much to gain from it (de Garis 2005, 47–48, 112). Kurzweil also indicates that computer technologies will have enormous market success (Kurzweil 1999, 195) and that investing in them will reap large benefits as early as 1999 (ibid., 201).[39] In 2009, Kurzweil opened Singularity University, a for-profit university with programs for graduate students and also for executives and public policy experts, the curriculum of which is based upon Kurzweil's writings on the singularity. The first cohort of graduate students worked on projects that aim toward helping people with an understanding that technological growth is exponential and heading toward Kurzweil's vision of the singularity. Each group of students prepared technological solutions to one of humanity's "grand challenges" (in the environment, transportation, poverty, etc.) and then explained their work not just to the faculty and their fellow students but also to a group of potential investors (R. Metz 2009). Apocalyptic AI clearly works toward the acquisition of funding.

Pop science is not the only arena for apocalyptic promises; quite often they appear in grant applications and research project descriptions. Jutta Weber of the Staatsbibliothek zu Berlin, for example, argues that "fairy tale" promises appear in applications for research grants to the European Union and the German Department for Education and Research (Weber 2007).[40] Standards for belief in such promises are hard to find even within the scientific community, which has no rigorous way to establish their credibility or lack thereof (Nordmann 2007). Weber was told that in Germany the scientific community generally pays little attention to researchers who make fantastic technological predictions. She found, however, that in reality many researchers (including those who found futuristic predictions disreputable) use them in grant applications, which are most successful when they promise groundbreaking work of immense social significance (J. Weber 2007, 89–90).[41] Although the transcendent salvation of Apocalyptic AI should likely be out of place in a grant application, these latter have been increasingly filled with promises of a near-term "return to Eden." The blind shall see and the lame shall walk (indeed, the research here is very promising) and our society's ills shall be conquered.

Popular science publications raise a scientist's visibility and thereby improve the odds of public funding. "With the increasing importance of third-party funding comes increasing pressure for 'visibility,' for a presentation of one's research that draws public as well as media attention. A stronger presence of science and research ideas in public discourse is needed, accomplished through communication of one's own research on a popular science level, which at the same time should restore the eroded trust of humans in science and technology" (J. Weber 2007, 92). Pop science—for Weinberg, Moravec, and others—is part of a general strategy to improve the public's appreciation for science and scientists. At the same time, this push for cultural prestige, which takes place in pop science books, aims to increase scientific resources. Scientists' need for public understanding cannot be separated from scientists' desire for prestige and their need for research funding. Although pop science books only occasionally include a direct plea for money and while apocalyptic ideas have only a tenuous position among the research community, in the popular arena and in funding politics these go hand in hand.[42]

It is hard to believe that writing *Mind Children* would influence the pocketbooks at government agencies such as DARPA, where funding decisions should be more pragmatic than to reflect upon the cosmic future of humankind, and yet even roboticists who do not write popular science recognize the value such books have in just these kinds of financial decisions. At a seminar hosted by the Philosophy of Robotics Group at CMU (Geraci 2007c), participants promoted the idea that Apocalyptic AI is a plea for financial backing.[43] One student, Daniel Leeds, immediately answered that the authors were drumming up money. When another student disputed his position, arguing that Apocalyptic AI would be unlikely to benefit researchers applying for grant money, others defended Daniel's position. Another grad student, Katie Rivard, pointed out that apocalyptic promises make your project look "shiny" (and, of course, shininess is good) while Sebastian Scherer pointed out that politicians use such rhetoric regularly and from them it can trickle down to funding groups.[44] In a separate discussion, the director of the Institute agreed that Moravec's work is good for the field (Mason 2007). Of course, grant applications can be as arbitrary and mystical as anything in religion, with success coming for reasons of merit or of social connections or good timing or without any clear explanation at all. Given the arbitrariness of such procedures, it certainly does not hurt to promise eternal happiness as a consequence of your research.

A conference sponsored by the National Science Foundation (NSF) and the Department of Commerce (DoC) in 2001 (and subsequently published as *Converging Technologies for Improving Human Performance* in 2003) reveals the presence of Apocalyptic AI in American government funding agencies' advance planning. The editors, Mihail Roco and William Sims Bainbridge, organized the volume in order that society could prepare for key technological improvements and aid in the improvement of human performance. They argue that enhancing human performance should be a national priority at all levels of education and across a wide expanse of social institutions (Roco and Bainbridge 2003, xii-xiii). As a consultant for the project and contributor to the final volume, Warren Robinett (famous for his invention of the first graphical action-adventure computer game, Atari's *Adventure*, and for his work with educational software) recapitulates the Apocalyptic AI faith that, if we can simply learn enough about brains we will succeed in uploading our minds into computers and transcending physical reality (ibid., 169–70). *This is the published "visionary" position from an NSF/DoC-funded project designed to shape the way we prioritize (and hence fund) future projects.* Although neither the NSF nor the DoC has made Apocalyptic AI an official priority, when *Converging Technologies* acknowledges Apocalyptic AI promises, it does so within the domain of these key funding agencies.

Following the completion of their NSF/DoC work, Roco and Bainbridge continued to receive NSF support in exploring their ideas, which were published in a second edited volume (Roco and Bainbridge 2006). While the first conference addressed the question of whether nanotechnology, biotechnology, information technology, and advances in cognitive science (NBIC) would affect the future, the subsequent work addresses when and how these will do so. Obviously influenced by Apocalyptic AI, Roco and Bainbridge argue that the NBIC technologies are progressing at an exponential rate and will solve the problems of human need if appropriately applied (ibid., 2). Bainbridge further implies that the promises of Apocalyptic AI—immortality and freedom from fear, confusion, and sin—will be accomplished, though not immediately (Bainbridge 2006, 206).

From their perch within American funding agencies, Roco and Bainbridge successfully bridge the gap between transhumanism and American politics and give voice to their ideological allies. Their *Managing Nano-Bio-Info-Cogno Innovations* is rife with techno-utopianism in which nearly every author advocates "convergence" (the prioritization of converging NBIC technologies for human enhancement) as both a moral and technical goal. "Indeed, the use of converging technologies to improve human performance is the explicit goal of the NBIC conferences, whose participants are often influential leaders in government, industry, and academia" (Hughes 2006, 286). Contributor James Hughes, who explicitly advocates transhumanism,[45] asserts that the adoption of new technologies (along with ethical safeguards) could lead to "unimaginably improved lives and a safe, healthier, more prosperous world" (ibid., 304). Bainbridge is also a transhumanist, speaking at transhumanist conferences and joining their associations, such as the Order of Cosmic Engineers (OCE, see chapter three). He eloquently expresses the need for a new religion that will carry humankind safely through the perils of modern life and would see such a religion grounded in transhumanist promises (Bainbridge 2009). The "convergenist" approach he takes in his NSF-sponsored work is clearly evangelical; he attempts to bring about the AI apocalypse through public advocacy and governmental funding.

Roco and Bainbridge's influence appears tangible in American policy, as when the U.S. Congress took note of Apocalyptic AI in directing American research priorities. The 21st Century Nanotechnology Research and Development Act, signed into law December 3, 2003 (U.S. Senate 2003), encourages ethical and legal analysis of nanotechnologies and artificial intelligence that promise improvements to human intellects (cyborgs) and machines of greater than human intelligence. Such research is supposed to ensure equal access to AI technologies among all Americans (ibid., Section II-10-C). In considering the National Nanotechnology Initiative (NNI), the U.S. Congress invited Kurzweil, chief spokesman for Apocalyptic AI, to speak on its behalf. In supporting nanotechnology, Kurzweil announced, "I would define the human species as that species that inherently seeks to extend our own horizons. We didn't stay on the ground, we didn't stay on the planet, we're not staying with the limitations of biology" (quoted in Hughes 2006, 298–99). The 21st Century Nanotechnology Research and Development Act, which authorizes the

NNI and other work, allows for long-term nanotech research that, among other priorities, should emphasize the provision of Apocalyptic AI promises to all members of our society. This cannot help but have direct impact upon the nature of nanotech funding decisions, nor can the fact that Roco, who believes that nanotech will increase the human lifespan and enhance human capability, heads the NSF's nanotech programs. The amount of funding dedicated to nanotech after the 2003 act (double its 2001 level) demonstrates the priority being placed on nanotechnology designed to attain new levels of human technological mastery.[46]

The influence of Apocalyptic AI in politics and in research funding is visible in Kurzweil's testimony before Congress and the prevalence of convergenist ideas in the NSF-sponsored conferences and books but Apocalyptic AI authors can also gain converts among the lay public. Weinberg seems to have deliberately used *Dreams of a Final Theory* as a propaganda effort for the SSC but Apocalyptic AI garners the same (or probably greater) effect without such obvious deliberation. "Will funding automatically follow intellectual excitement? I don't know but I think it's a positive correlation," said the Robotics Institute director Matt Mason (Mason 2007). Popular books, he thinks, are definitely good for the field as a whole (ibid.). Pop science influences government and broader social opinion, encouraging research priorities in fields that might otherwise take a back seat to more mundane social concerns (infrastructure and social services, for example). If not for the amazing promises of Apocalyptic AI, all related technologies (robotics and AI, but also nanotech and biotech) would receive far less support than they do.

Apocalyptic AI exudes excitement but it also lures the reader into participation through its religious categories. In *Dreams*, Weinberg explicitly rejects religion, which he calls "wishful thinking" (1992, 255). He likewise argues that there is an "inconsistency in temperament" between belief in religion and belief in many scientific postulates (ibid., 248).[47] Apocalyptic AI authors do not attempt to drive a wedge between their readers and religious belief. Instead, Apocalyptic AI, as shown in chapter one, absorbs religious categories and uses those categories to bolster the authors' claims. Moravec talks about a "garden of earthly delights" (Moravec 1999, 143); de Garis calls Cosmism a religion (de Garis 2005, 99) and calls artilects the objects of religious worship (ibid., 104); and Kurzweil promises advanced spirituality when our minds have been uploaded into machines (Kurzweil 1999, 151–53), believes that a new religion is necessary (Kurzweil 2005, 374–5), and is comfortable with saying that the universe will be suffused with "spirit" and that evolution moves toward realizing a particular "concept of God," though without ever quite attaining the ideal (Kurzweil 2005, 389). Like Kurzweil, the sociologist of religion William Sims Bainbridge argues that a new religion ust emerge to bring about the evolution of our species (Bainbridge 2009). Such language works because it carries all the cultural authority possessed by traditional religion.

While there are no gods necessary to Apocalyptic AI, and many if not most advocates express agnosticism or atheism, the movement's philosophical position nevertheless does not rule out divine beings.[48] Traditional religions receive little to no attention in Apocalyptic AI; they are ignored rather than confronted. Rather than offending their audience with a defense of atheism, the Apocalyptic AI authors simply ignore the subject of earthly religions altogether. Moravec does, however, offer an explanation for our belief in god. He argues that, just as superbly intelligent computers of the future might simulate other worlds or our past, we could already be living in a computer simulation (1992b). Whoever created the simulation would be the god or gods of our religious beliefs. Already, many computer programmers, virtual world designers, and technology advocates believe that the creation of digital worlds marks the apotheosis of humankind (Kelly 1999, 391; Helmreich 1998, 85; Bartle [2003] 2004, 247). It would, of course, be impossible to tell the difference between a physical world and a sufficiently detailed virtual world, so we cannot rule out Moravec's hypothesis, which he asserts to be "almost certainly" the case (Moravec 1992b, 21).[49] In addition, other Apocalyptic AI advocates have argued that gods might emerge out of digital technology. Kurzweil believes the universe might "wake up" as a sort of divine being (Kurzweil 2005, 375) and members of the Order of Cosmic Engineers conjecture that human beings might one day ascend to godlike status (OCE 2008).

Moravec is, as his colleagues told me, clearly having a good time when he entertains the idea of a god of the simulation; the infectious nature of his fun could well further the political goals of Apocalyptic AI. If the authors enjoy themselves, then their audience will enjoy itself. So their fun leads to public fun, which subsequently leads to funding (and possibly a few new students). Dour predictions about the future rarely engage the public but thrilling scenarios of robot bushes and "resurrected" virtual friends can. Public excitement is a good thing, because it helps scientific projects gain social stature and research support.

Apocalyptic AI is generally a bit more subtle in its request for money than Weinberg was in *Dreams of a Final Theory*, but it supplies its audience with plenty of reasons to support research. Apocalyptic AI demonstrates the value of robotics and AI for society; it promises relief from many of life's burdens and, in the end, it offers salvation. If the researchers can uphold even half of that bargain, robotics will be one of humankind's greatest achievements. Even the most casual reader will come away from *Robot* or *The Singularity Is Near* with an understanding of how life might benefit from progress in robotics and AI. If robots can produce cheap, efficient energy, reduce traffic accidents, eliminate earthly pollution, prevent military deaths, care for the elderly, and produce food at almost no cost, then who would resist the moral value of robotics research and who would begrudge our saviors a few extra dollars? Thus while scientific papers produce one kind of power, a power that creates systems of belief and provokes institutional and financial support, pop science books produce another kind of power. The authority installed by Apocalyptic AI develops outside of laboratories but benefits those laboratories by creating public and governmental acknowledgement of the significance of research.

While Apocalyptic AI may do little to benefit its authors individually, it has a corporate effect upon robotics and AI, making research funding justifiable for government and industry groups. Progress in robotics and AI will benefit so many people in so many different sectors of our community that it, in the Apocalyptic AI argument, deserves whole-hearted public support. Of course, should robotics only disenfranchise millions of workers without providing alternate means for their subsistence, it will create more problems than it solves. Apocalyptic AI, naturally, promises that progress will surpass such problems. In this respect, it gives reason to forgive robots that take away jobs from the poor or, eventually, the middle class. Eventually, we will all enjoy a return to Eden.

Apocalyptic AI is both an ideology and a pop science genre, with the latter arising out of the former as a strategy to raise the public profile of robotics and AI in general and the Apocalyptic AI authors in particular. Roboticists, like the Golem makers of medieval Judaism, become spiritual, moral, and intellectual heroes. The researchers then ascend to the rarified air breathed by only the highest benefactors of the human race, inoculated against criticism and prepared to receive the praise and sacrifices of the public and its institutions.

CONCLUSION

The gulf between Apocalyptic AI and the everyday practice of robotics and AI tempts us to believe that no connection exists between the two. Apocalyptic AI has, however, a strong presence in the public profile of robotics and AI, always engaging Latour's trials of strength in the public sphere. Apocalypticism is about commitment to actions and attitudes (J. Collins 1984, 215); nowhere is this more evident in the pop science call to support research. Apocalyptic AI asks its lay faithful for ideological and financial reinforcement; it presents researchers in the field as spiritual and intellectual leaders who deserve our admiration and unflagging support.

Asking questions about religion and religious practices reveals important aspects of how robotics and AI fit into modern culture. In order to understand how religion has adapted to modern life, we must look at laboratories alongside temples, pop science alongside Bibles. Religious beliefs and practices can have very definite implications for scientific research. In the United States apocalyptic theology has been integrated to robotics and AI in pop science while in Japan, Shinto and Buddhist principles help promote the social integration of robots into human society and a powerful desire to build humanoid robots (Geraci 2006). No social study of robotics and AI, therefore, will be complete without a grounding in the ways religion and technology intertwine therein.

Many of the religious aspects of Euro-American robotics and AI find their way into science through science fiction. Science fiction contains religious themes and these capture the imagination of young people who will eventually have technical careers. The holiness of machines combines with the thoughtfulness and philosophical acceptability of science fiction to have a significant effect upon robotics and AI. Science fiction authors have been powerfully influential in digital technology circles so it should come as no surprise that Marvin Minsky wants a visiting position available to them at MIT. Science fiction acts as a conduit for some of Apocalyptic AI's most sacred commitments; it both imports religious culture into robotics and AI and exports it (transformed) into wider culture.

The religious ideology of Apocalyptic AI gains much of its internal drive from science fiction but its external motivation (i.e., its reason for pressing beyond the boundaries of the scientific community into the broader public) is political. Although it would seem that omnipresent military funding plays a role in Apocalyptic AI, reservations about military spending are relatively rare. Apocalyptic AI advocates do not need to make religious promises as extenuating circumstances that justify their close ties to the military. They make such promises because those promises strengthen their public prestige and help validate public funding. Apocalyptic AI is a political strategy that raises the profile of robotics and AI; it offers cultural prestige to the authors and justifies the money spent on robotics and AI research. Science derives power from successful pop science and Apocalyptic AI must be counted among the most effective of such political efforts. Apocalyptic AI, seen alongside traditions of Golems, homunculi, and automata clearly works to establish scientific authority. The success of this program can be measured in American government policies and in the advisory process to them, which depend upon the actions of advocates of the AI apocalypse.

THREE

TRANSCENDING REALITY

INTRODUCTION

Virtual gamers commonly view their online lives in categories and terms borrowed from Apocalyptic AI. Transhumanist communities actively spread Apocalyptic AI in online gaming, but much of the ideology also appears inextricably linked to our cultural view of virtual reality (VR) worlds. In particular, many residents of the online world *Second Life* see it as the precursor to the digital paradise of Apocalyptic AI.

The line between the real world and the virtual world has blurred. Perhaps once upon a time we could easily demarcate between fact and fiction, life and games, but online games now challenge the barriers that might have once been solid. The virtual world, though intangible, is now quite real and gaining importance in mainstream techno-culture. The median age of online gamers (depending upon the game) ranges from mid-twenties to early thirties; these games are not just for kids! For many, *World of Warcraft*[1] has become "the new golf" as younger colleagues get together online to battle the forces of evil rather than meeting on the greens (Hof 2006). People play with parents, uncles, aunts, cousins, spouses, and friends. They create virtual families and, not infrequently, virtual relationships bleed into the earthly world, leading to dating and marriage. Even earthly politicians, from Mark Warner of West Virginia to the two-time presidential candidate John Edwards, have entered *Second Life* to give interviews and build campaign centers (Pickler 2007). According to the technology and research advising company The Gartner Group, 80 percent of active Internet users will participate in virtual worlds by 2012 (Gartner Group 2007). They may be games, but *Second Life*, *World of Warcraft*, and the rest of the massively multiplayer online games (MMOGs[2]) are serious business.

Computer games have fast become one of the world's major media and a major locus for story telling. As money and talent (both intellectual and artistic) pour into the games, they will take more and more significance away from other pop culture media, such as print and film. A 2007 article in *Wired* suggests that the game *Mass Effect*[3] (played on the Microsoft Xbox 360 game console) has the same cultural cachet as that of George Lucas's renowned *Star Wars* franchise (Lee 2007). A heady claim, indeed! The rapid growth of players and their increasing devotion to virtual life will make MMOGs a crucial element in cultural life.

Millions of players have bought massively multiplayer online role-playing games (MMORPGs) such as *Ultima Online, EverQuest,* and *World of Warcraft,* which usually involves purchasing the CD-ROM and then paying a monthly subscription fee.[4] *Ultima Online, EverQuest,* and *World of Warcraft* are all set in fantasy worlds where players choose to be warriors, wizards, priests, etc., and go on quests to find treasure, slay monsters, and rescue those in need. Other MMORPGs exist, including some which are science fiction, superhero, or mystery based, rather than fantasy based. In all of these games, questing lures players into a larger story framework, one whose conclusion is collectively experienced by all of its participants. The cowritten/participatory nature of MMORPGs is, in fact, one of their principle characteristics and a primary part of their allure (King and Borland 2003, 162; T. L. Taylor 2006, 159).[5]

The popular stereotype of a computer gamer is of a solitary soul staring deeply into his or her computer, cut off from the world, but this representation is far from accurate. The Internet allows gamers to connect with one another; it builds communities. Even at the earliest levels of Internet communication, the Defense Department's ARPAnet—which allowed limited data transfer over telephone lines via modems—e-mail and message boards created ongoing "societies" (Waldrop 1987, 33). Although online gamers are perceived as out of touch and solitary, the focus of the games they play is, in fact, deeply social. In their history of computer gaming, King and Borland trace the profound sociality of computer gaming from its earliest influences in role-playing games (especially *Dungeons & Dragons*) through contemporary "shoot-'em-up" games and online role-playing games (King and Borland 2003). Jakobsson and Taylor have given an ethnographic and sociological account of the social ties present within virtual reality in the game *EverQuest,* which they liken to the mafia in the way "family" ties take precedence over other matters (Jakobsson and Taylor 2003). Online games provide an environment far better suited to the creation and maintenance of societies than mere e-mail. As a result, they integrate features of social life that earlier electronic communities lacked. The social significance of online life is growing for individual users as they immerse themselves ever deeper in virtual reality.

Some games focus more upon the building of communities than do others. Among these, Linden Lab's *Second Life* is by far the most popular. *Second Life* (SL) underwent explosive growth in 2006 and 2007 after Linden Lab started allowing free accounts (a controversial decision for many older users). With 20,000 total users early in 2005, *Second Life* had nearly 7 million users by June 2007 (of whom nearly 2 million had logged on in the previous month). Not all accounts are used (many people create accounts, grow bored, and never return) and some individuals pay for more than one account, but *Second Life* is the clear leader among "social" games[6] and, as of October 2008, had over 50,000 concurrent users at any given time. *Second Life* is not a game of battle, nor a game of quests, puzzles, or strategies. It is a community game. Although there is money to be made through building objects (homes, furniture, vehicles, guns, clothing, etc.), *Second Life* is principally a place for gathering together. Some people do gather to hold battles but most show up to dance, gamble (prior to mid-2007, at which point it was made illegal), shop, listen to music, etc., but these are not the "purpose" of the game; instead, they are locations for social contact.

As *Second Life* has expanded, arguments over its economic and social worth have arisen. Making money in *Second Life* is not easy, especially considering how cheaply everything comes and how sparsely the population of potential buyers is spread out. Randy Pausch, a former CMU professor of human-computer interaction, says that big businesses have come to *Second Life* not to make money, but to get cheap publicity for their earthly products (Pausch 2007; see also Rose 2007; Rosmarin 2007). Every time a major company opens an SL business, earthly news outlets trumpet the move, which means that Coca-Cola or Honda or whoever is launching an island in SL stands to sell real products, not virtual ones. Certainly, the SL islands that house earthly businesses are generally empty and bring in no income (Rose 2007). On the other hand, IBM representatives claim that *Second Life* will make money for them and other businesses eventually while the VR pioneer Jaron Lanier says that in the future "we will all get rich buying and selling virtual goods" and the people making virtual reality work are "in [his] opinion . . . saving civilization" (C. Metz 2007).[7]

Lanier is not alone in his breathless gushing over the potential of online games. Edward Castronova, well-known for his studies of online life, believes that an "exodus of . . . people from the real world, from our normal daily life of living rooms, cubicles, and shopping malls, will create a change in social climate that makes global warming look like a tempest in a teacup" (2007, xiv–xv). It may be that Castronova thinks little of the dangers of climate change but we cannot doubt that he rates virtual reality as the most important thing in our political and social radars. And like Lanier, Castronova believes that virtual reality will save civilization. Social participation will require participation in virtual worlds (ibid., 82) and as more and more people play online games and grow accustomed to the fun of living there, they will demand that earthly governments turn away from economic ends toward the manufacturing of a happy society (ibid., 70).

The significance of *Second Life* does not, as many of its critics allege, hinge upon the world's economic viability. Like Pausch, some commentators have attacked SL as mere hype (though certainly technically innovative hype) without long-term prospects. They believe that SL is bound to go the way of other VR communities such as LambdaMOO and Habitat for the Commodore 64—historical anachronisms with little contemporary relevance. This view, however, is utterly problematic in its regard for SL and in its regard for SL's predecessors. The mere fact that these critics consider the various worlds to be in some sense continuous proves the significance of SL. If this *kind* of world has occupied the last twenty years of technological culture we ought to presume that it responds to some kind of real community need.[8] That is, even if SL itself ends up in economic ruin, a successor will carry on the tradition of online communities in which people gather for "purely" social interaction. This chapter applies to SL's successors as much as it does to SL itself.

Second Life is not a game of acquisition or advancement, although both of which are easily had therein; it is a game where only the user's creative energies (be they social, commercial, religious, or other) determine the user's interaction with the community. *Second Life* residents do frequently revel in commercial acquisitions (as when they show off new outfits to one another) but the acquisition is not actually integral to continued enjoyment of the world. In other online games, such as *World of Warcraft*, users must overcome challenges, gain new levels, and acquire new and more powerful objects if they wish to proceed in the game. In *Second Life*, converting a few U.S. dollars into Linden dollars and spending some time searching and teleporting around will suffice to buy you anything you might like to own. The purpose of the world, obviously, is not acquisition. As Phillip Rosedale, Linden Lab's founder, says, "you can get everything you want on the first day. What's interesting is what you do the next" (Newitz 2006).

CYBERSPACE SACRED

Online life has become increasingly interesting, increasingly meaningful, increasingly sacred. The techno-enchantment of Apocalyptic AI results, ironically, from the rise of modern materialism. According to Margaret Wertheim, as modern science increasingly viewed the world physically, banishing the realm of the spiritual from ontological necessity, it left a void in the Western worldview; cyberspace—the digital world—takes on a sacred aura precisely because people need to locate spiritual realities somewhere (Wertheim 1999). In a literal sense, she writes, "we have lost any conception of a spiritual *space*—a part of reality in which spirits or souls might reside" (ibid., 33, emphasis original). Investing cyberspace with sacred significance answers this existential concern. Apocalyptic AI provides the ideological and intellectual worldview that crystallizes this new sacred aura.

Game programmers and designers wrote the apocalyptic agenda into virtual reality. Many designers automatically assign sacred labels upon activity in virtual reality games and feel those games promote an idealized life and human transcendence (Aupers and Houtman 2005). Indeed, many of the game programmers see game design as a specifically theological enterprise, as when the famed Richard Bartle[9] declares that "deities create virtual worlds; designers are those deities" (Bartle [2003] 2004, 247) and asks whether "those lacking a god's motivation [should] assume a god's powers" (ibid., 293). In a similar vein, a number of programmers see the design and construction of virtual reality worlds as the apotheosis of their players, who take on the role of gods (Helmreich [1998] 2000, 85–86).

The computer world was deeply affected by the utopian dreams of 1960s counterculture, particularly as mediated by Stewart Brand, publisher of the *Whole Earth Catalog* and its subsequent spin-off projects (Turner 2006). "Digital utopians" sought freedom from alienation through computer technologies and the advent of the Internet heightened such dreams. The digital utopia of late twentieth-century techno-enthusiasm borrows directly from religious themes and expectations. John Perry Barlow, who became an influential spokesperson at the intersection of the digerati and the counterculture, believed that cyberspaces "offered what LSD, Christian mysticism, cybernetics, and countercultural 'energy' theory had all promised" (Turner 2006, 173; see also A. Stone 1991, 90). The desire to escape alienation, suffering, and impotence has promoted the "relocation of the sacred to the digital realm" (Aupers and Houtman 2005).

Even before online games became powerful, programmers infused computer worlds with a sense of the sacred and attributed to themselves a divine status. Stefan Helmreich, in his extensive fieldwork among Artificial Life (ALife)[10] scientists, describes the ways in which Artificial Life "has come to perform functions that normatively Christian Western secular culture associates with religion" (Helmreich [1998] 2000, 182). Mystical visions led several of the key figures in ALife to see their worlds as potentially salvific, offering the cosmos a better form of life (ibid., 191, 201–2), and themselves as the worlds' gods (ibid., 83–84, 193). Alongside basic Christian themes, which Helmreich believes have been adapted from wider culture, the 1990s ALife community made frequent use of Eastern mysticism, decoupled from its historical contingency, as a way of understanding the role of the individual self in the wider world (ibid., 185–87).

Virtual reality pioneers frequently raise a religious standard for technology. Bonny de Vargo has enthusiastically described the experience of being godlike in cyberspace and Brian Moriarty has echoed this, asking "why should we settle for avatars, when we can be angels?" (Aupers and Houtman 2005).[11] Likewise, Mark Pesce, the co-creator of VRML (Virtual Reality Modeling Language), called the virtual world Osmose a "virtual kundalini, an expression of philosophy without any words, a state of holy being which reminds that, indeed, we are all angels" (Davis 1996) and Nicole Stengers, a virtual reality artist, declares that on "the other side of our data gloves we become creatures of colored light in motion, pulsing with golden particles. . . . We will all become angels, and for eternity" (Stengers 1991, 52). Stengers believes that cyberspace is the realm of heirophany—the breaking forth of the sacred (ibid., 54–55). Cyberspace advocates have infused the realm with a magical aura and expect the divinization of humankind in cyberspace. The religious agenda of cyberspace belongs in equal parts to the programmers, who were avid readers of fantasy and cyberpunk (King and Borland 2005, 95), and the gamers, whose shared reading list brought them into contact with the paradisiacal dreams of the digital utopians.

Fundamentally, *Second Life* residents revel in virtual reality because they find it superior to their current reality. For some users, the online world is *"the only decent place available"* (Castronova 2005, 65, emphasis original), though many residents of SL explicitly reject Castronova's belief that they like SL because they dislike their conventional lives. The reasons for and degree to which SL is "more decent" than real life will depend upon the user but given the high number of residents (more than 50 percent according to my survey) who would at least consider uploading their personalities to SL it is crystal clear that many find online worlds to be very decent indeed.

The magic of virtual worlds emerged in 1980s science fiction literature through the seminal work of Vernor Vinge, William Gibson, and others. Vinge's *True Names* ([1981] 2001) introduced us to the Other Plane where computer hackers traveled to gather together or visit the linked computer systems of governments, banks, and corporations. Gibson's *Neuromancer* (1984) added a flashy name for virtual reality (cyberspace) and a brilliant story of artificial intelligence, anti-hero chic, and personal redemption in which cyberspace became the focal point for power and value (both economic and aesthetic). *Neuromancer*, the only book to ever win the Hugo, the Nebula, and the Philip K. Dick awards, glorifies cyberspace and derides the "meatspace" where everyone but the hackers resides.

Life in cyberspace is a popular part of virtual reality literature. Just as Vinge ended *True Names* with an individual uploading herself into the Other Plane, other books by popular authors have advocated transcendent immortality. Charles Stross, who described the singularity and life with hyperintelligent robots in *Accelerando* (2005), has defended the belief that virtual reality will eventually occupy most or all of our lives in *Halting State* (2007). Upon entering a virtual reality game, one of his characters thinks "someday we're all going to get brain implants and experience this directly. Someday *everyone* is going to live their lives out in places like this, vacant bodies tended by machines of loving grace while their minds go on before us into strange spaces where the meat cannot follow" (Stross 2007, 104, emphasis original). Stross is among the darling sci-fi authors of the twenty-first century and carries considerable prestige. His work shows how tightly intertwined Apocalyptic AI and science fiction are, but also how closely connected these fields are to *Second Life*. Stross has been to SL as an invited speaker and has agreed to return for an explicit conversation, hosted by Giulio Prisco, on transhumanism (Prisco 2007e).

Though Vinge and Gibson were the trendsetters in cyberspace literature, much of the talk that surrounds *Second Life* derives from a later work, Neal Stephenson's masterpiece *Snow Crash* (1992). *Snow Crash*, which *Time* magazine listed among its top 100 English-language novels (post-1923), is a complicated story of archaeology, cryptography, religion, politics, and computer science in which the protagonist has helped develop the "metaverse," a virtual reality world in which individuals act through their avatars. Though he is one of the designers of the Metaverse, Hiro Protagonist is impoverished and isolated due to his poor business acumen and equally poor relationship skills. Though his adventures likely resolve at least half of these problems, it is not so much the emotional affect of the book but its compelling portrait of the future's virtual world that carries so much weight in today's society. In Stephenson's book, the Metaverse is a fully immersive environment, one that looks and feels like reality thanks to direct neural input from computers.

Stephenson sets the Metaverse apart from its predecessors by illustrating it as a world much like the real world, only far more brilliant—it is this feature that makes the world so captivating as a portrait of things to come. Whereas Gibson was content to imagine cyberspace as a matrix of geometric shapes that represented particular corporate or business computer systems, Stephenson revolves the entire Metaverse around the crowded and surpassingly hip Street that resembles "Las Vegas freed from constraints of physics and finance" (Stephenson 1992, 26). The Street is a mass of businesses, clubs, and neon lighting—it is the shining world of the richest, most impressive members of humanity. The significance of Stephenson's work shows in the language that SL residents employ and in their own efforts to think about the significance of SL with respect to *Snow Crash* (e.g., DaSilva 2008b, DeCuir 2008). Today's users of *Second Life* adore *Snow Crash*, in large measure, because it presents a realistic view of the world (that is, a cyberspace that would be comfortable and appealing to Western nations) while enhancing that world with a sheen of wonder absent from everyday life.

Apocalyptic AI has thoroughly infiltrated the way SL residents think of their new world, particularly through the science fiction promises of 1980s cyberpunk. Cyberpunk is a style of science fiction that melds high technology and a modern pop underground, usually in a dystopian future (Sterling 1986). The hacker residents of this world, described most famously in *True Names*, *Neuromancer*, and *Snow Crash*, prefer it to the real world. Although fantasy has also played a significant part in the rise of digital worlds,[12] cyberpunk infuses them with the promise of salvation. Thanks to science fiction, cyberspace has become the place where the hacker can escape "the prison of his own flesh" (Gibson 1984, 6), a religious vision that does not occupy fantasy literature or its role-playing offshoots. Cyberpunk has become an invisible part of our social world and online users have adopted its worldview. Most important, users—despite the end of the cyberpunk literary movement—desire to spend increasing amounts of time in cyberspace, if not the rest of their lives. *Second Life* occupies more and more of its residents' time and emotional commitment and many users believe that such virtual immersion will be complete or near complete in the future (nearly 20 percent of my survey respondents would spend all of their time in SL if possible and a majority of the rest would like to increase their time commitment to the world). When such belief intertwines with the possibility of emigrating one's consciousness permanently into cyberspace, it becomes the template for the virtual realm of Apocalyptic AI.

Second Life demonstrates the cultural power of Apocalyptic AI because its residents see it (or its successor) as a potential realm for the realization of Moravec's virtual future. The sacred allure of SL is so profound that the world naturally breeds Apocalyptic AI ideas. Transhumanist communities have happily set up shop in *Second Life*, offering information and holding seminars and conferences, but even where transhumanism is not explicit, the sacred aura held by virtual worlds provides an outlet for basic ideas of Apocalyptic AI, including the desirability of mind uploading. As Philip Hefner has pointed out, transhumanism is not always explicit and officially institutional; it has also disseminated widely throughout culture as an implicit agenda of overcoming the limits of human bodies (Hefner 2009). *Second Life* offers a time and place separated out from the mundane; it is thus easily seen as sacred and becomes the perfect vehicle for the cybernetic salvation of Apocalyptic AI. The easy attribution of the sacred to SL and the smooth transition to apocalyptic attitudes within it explains why transhumanists and transhumanist ideas (both explicit and implicit) are so common there.

LIVING A SECOND LIFE

Second Life is more than a game. *Second Life*, the online community in which "avatars" meet, talk, recreate (musically, sexually, artistically, even athletically), and engage in commerce, is a world unto its own, a world that, for some users, is more important than the earthly world without which it would not exist. Many users consider *Second Life* to be an important part of our cultural evolution and the home to a meaningful new world, not just a playscape for the imagination.

The avatar is the user's virtual body. As in many MMOGs, SL users can customize their avatars' appearances and clothing and tend to give them distinct personalities. The avatar is, depending upon the user's perspective, either a prosthesis for the earthly person (a mechanism for the extension of the person into a new realm) or a separate identity, which is born in and never leaves virtual reality.

Regardless, the avatar's appearance helps shape the user's social environment so users tend to customize them as they become attached to the world.

In the 1990s, MIT's Sherry Turkle argued that fledgling Internet worlds had already co-opted many of real life's more important elements and provided an important locus for exploring an individual's subjective experience of life. "Real life is just one more window," one of her subjects told her, "and it's not usually my best one" (Turkle 1996, 118). Another reported that his or her Internet life is "more real than my real life" (ibid., 116). This kind of fragmented identity is a uniquely modern way of being in the world(s).[13] Contemporary users of SL show the same blurring of the boundaries between real life and online life; as a result, selfhood in SL remains profoundly connected to the relationships formed between SL and conventional reality (Boellstorff 2008, 118–22). For many residents, however, choosing between their conventional and virtual selves can be very difficult: "when it comes to choosing between real life and Second Life," says one resident, "I don't know which one I care about the most" (Peralta 2006).

Users of online games frequently understand their online worlds to be home (as opposed to the physical world). For example, 20 percent of *EverQuest* players claim to "live in Norrath . . . but travel outside it regularly" and 22 percent would spend all of their time in Norrath if it were possible to do so (Castronova 2005, 59). I found a similar number of SL users would do likewise (18.7 percent would either probably or definitely spend all of their time in-world if they could).[14] We cannot simply dismiss the players' faith in their online realities as childishness or neurosis. Rather, as Castronova has pointed out, we all fall rather easily into an identification with our avatars, which become prostheses, not mere game pieces (ibid., 45). Participation in virtual worlds is very much like participation in earthly life but tends to heighten access to the things most desirable on Earth—goods, of course, but more importantly friendship and a sense of personal worth and meaningful existence.

Second Life, like other MMOGs, allows users to explore aspects of their personalities that they would like to develop and, through this, establish the kinds of interpersonal relationships that they miss in their conventional lives. Sherry Turkle's subjects explored different genders and personalities so as to meet people in different kinds of ways and experience life in a different, but valid, way (Turkle 1999). According to the famed designer Richard Bartle, it is the power of self-discovery that fundamentally motivates players: "most of the players will be there because of the freedom to be themselves that the virtual world offers" (Bartle [2003] 2004, 163). He feels that playing has one "overall goal: Being someone else in order to become a better you" (ibid., 190). David Fleck, Linden Lab's vice president of marketing, echoes this sentiment. He says that SL is a "place where [the residents] can be themselves"—apparently as opposed to earthly life (Peralta 2006). With an unlimited number of appearances, as many personalities as the user's mind can construct, and a vast number of groups that users can join to meet others with similar interests, SL is a playground for Turkle's distributed subjectivity. Some residents even jump from one avatar appearance to another . . . first a human being, next a robot, finally an alien before becoming a plush bunny rabbit and walking away.

Not only do players emphasize "real" aspects of themselves hidden during their daily lives, the players form real emotional relationships in SL. You can have enemies, friends, lovers, even spouses. No user "calls Second Life a game. The emotional connections you make are real" (Peralta 2006). All virtual relationships are real relationships; the users are emotionally committed to them (Castronova 2005, 48). In my survey, nearly 50 percent of respondents felt that their SL friendships were probably or definitely as important as their earthly friendships. Only 18 percent of survey takers said that SL friends were definitely not as important as their earthly friends. This means that when an avatar is spurned or ignored, someone, somewhere, feels real rejection. When an avatar is welcomed back upon entering a favored Irish pub, someone feels loved. When avatars marry, their users sometimes declare love for the avatar personality and sometimes for the person behind the avatar. Either way, the users find such emotions to be genuinely real.

Building a world, however, does not automatically mean building one that will function as well as the original. In his comparison of the early virtual urban space of *Habitat* (which ran over telephone lines on Commodore 64 computers) to the "virtual" urban space of the West Edmonton Mall (a Canadian shopping mall in which visitors stroll down recreations of Bourbon Street, Paris, and other distant places), the architect Michael Ostwald denies that these kinds of spaces allow for the creation of true community (Ostwald 2000, 673). Nevertheless, while *Habitat* did not offer the right environment for the forming of true communities, other virtual worlds might. "If the Internet can achieve the right balance of interaction, leisure, and commerce it may in time develop into a genuine community space. While it continues to mirror the malls, theme parks and office buildings of the Cartesian world it will never become the mythical 'place of meeting' described by Homer in the *Iliad*" (ibid., 673).[15]

Despite the doubts of authors like Ostwald, many sociologists see great social potential in online games. Online gaming, often ostensibly aimed at developing one's character (gaining experience, increasing levels, acquiring powerful objects, etc.), actually revolves around social interaction (Jakobsson and Taylor 2003; Ducheneaut and Moore 2005).[16] Most online games—those in which players fight in science fiction and fantasy worlds—involve forming guilds of players with complementary skills and "raiding parties" with characters who have different, and equally necessary, skill sets, and building reputations of reliability (competence and honesty) by which groups organize themselves. For its early years, *Second Life* objectified personal relationships in profile ratings of skill and character. Though these were eliminated in 2007 to ease the computing burden on the company's servers, Linden Lab encouraged residents to make use of third-party web-based profile systems, such as RatePoint and Real Reputations. *Second Life* does not force its residents into social relationships the way advanced levels of *World of Warcraft* and similar games do but those relationships are at least as important within it. An SL resident could be a loner but he would likely grow bored very quickly, perhaps even faster than in the character-development games because SL is based around interaction with other avatars. Residents who fail to create social networks will not remain in the world for long.

The social nature of online worlds might make them suitable replacements for the traditional loci of earthly sociability. People participate in communities by finding "third places"—churches, local soda fountains, neighborhood bars, etc.— that promote sociability by supporting neighborly interaction (Oldenberg 1989). Such places have lost significance for many people in the past few decades (Putnam 2000) but online games offer a new sense of community that serves the traditional aims of third places (Ducheneaut, Moore, and Nickell, 2007). Corner bars may well be places of the past, replaced by virtual bars.[17]

Online games present places for meeting, such as bars and dance halls, and grouping mechanisms, all of which help bring people together. Any *Second Life* resident can establish an official group for a nominal cost (less than $1 in a one-time fee), which enables like-minded people to connect through the world's search function. Group notices, events, and voting help residents feel like they are part of a social community and help the residents organize their second lives. Many of SL's clubs and bars have groups to notify members about interesting events (such as when a performer is about to take the stage) but other groups allow people who share intellectual or religious inclinations to find one another (such as groups for physicists, philosophers, alumni of particular universities, or specific religious affiliations). Formal partnerships allow two residents to tie their second lives together, often including officiated weddings, shared homes, and virtual children. These grouping mechanisms are critical to the overall picture of *Second Life*. While new residents may accumulate random group memberships as badges of importance, older users eventually separate the wheat from the chaff, remaining in only those groups that they find productive and comfortable.

Second Life offers far more to its participants than the chat rooms of the early Internet. While those chat rooms gave free rein to expressive imagination, SL concretizes imagination: its users can build what they want and then script it (using the game's specialized programming language) to act how they think it should. Users do not just describe themselves, they personalize their avatars to look the way they want them to look. In this way, SL represents a powerful shift in online communities. Because the residents of SL build the world in which they live, they take responsibility for the quality of the outcome.[18] Many residents have committed to making SL a paradise for themselves and others. Some people even build beautiful buildings and parks to which access is free, such as the lush island Svarga, the many waterfalls of Bliss Basin, the fireworks of Ethereal Teal, and the anime-themed Nakama.

By customizing SL, the residents come to see it as a real home. They alter their own appearances in accordance with their personal tastes and desires. They can own or rent land that they shape to their own personal liking. Whether they create an S&M dungeon that would invoke suspicion and frowns in their hometown, or a colossal medieval castle replete with fairies, princesses, and knights in shining armor, residents make what feels good to them. *Second Life* residents express themselves in SL and, therefore, begin to attach themselves to it in a way that can be difficult in real life. Earthly life is "given" in the sense that it precedes the individual and can be shaped in only very limited ways; for many, the creative co-construction of the SL world resolves the alienation that proceeds from earthly life's givenness.

Motorcycle and car driving in Nakama, an anime-themed region in *Second Life* (the author is in the foreground).

DIGITAL TRANSCENDENCE

Transhumanism, a social movement that advocates a "better than well" approach to humanity, has been instrumental in the absorption of Apocalyptic AI into the mainstream and brings that ideology into cyberspace. Transhumanism (commonly abbreviated H+) is a religious movement brought to *Second Life* by individuals who see the virtual world as the perfect realm for the realization of Apocalyptic AI's Mind Fire. Many believers hope to improve their lives by transferring their conscious selves into *Second Life* or whatever equivalent virtual world follows. Transhumanist groups are political, evangelical, have influence in *Second Life*, and, more importantly, reflect views that are relatively common in *Second Life* even among individuals who do not expressly affiliate with transhumanist groups.

Transhumanists believe that rationality, science, and technology are the keys to improving humanity and providing a happy "posthuman" existence. In particular, transhumanism borrows from technological progress in biotechnology, nanotechnology, and robotics/AI, asserting that future advances will eliminate illness, aging, and even death. Common transhumanist questions include, "what to do about retirement age when people live indefinitely?" and "how to ethically distribute advanced technology?"

Advances in biotechnology might redefine what it means to be a "normal" human being. Technological progress, especially in genetics, promises better pharmaceuticals, prevention and cure of degenerative and terminal illnesses, superior abilities, and even longer (limitless?) lifespan. Advanced knowledge of genetics might allow us to tailor prescription drugs to each individual, preventing unpleasant side effects. Understanding the genetic causes of diseases like Parkinson's and Alzheimer's could lead to better pharmaceuticals and to genetically manipulating victims to produce cures. Manipulating the genetic profiles of children could prevent such diseases altogether and might also result in higher IQs, better memories, bigger muscles, better immune systems, and so forth. Finally, we may even learn to shut down the body's natural aging process (which, if disease has been eradicated and strength improved, could prove highly desirable).

Advances in biotechnology could produce great gains for humanity or could turn disastrous. As a consequence, biotechnological transhumanism has its proponents (e.g., Bostrom 2005; Postrel 1998; Stock 2003) and its opponents (e.g., Annas, Andrews, and Isasi 2002; Fukuyama 2002; Joy 2000; Rifkin 1983). Some range of opinion exists within these two basic camps. For example, Jeremy Rifkin, the "most hated man in science" (Thompson 1989), opposes *all* bioengineering, believing it to separate humankind from the essential companionship of the natural ecology (Rifkin 1983, 253–55) while Leon Kass opposes any manipulation that goes beyond a "natural norm of health" because he feels that enhancement "beyond therapy" would have disastrous consequences on the meaningfulness of human life (Kass 2003). Proponents of unfettered biotechnology, on the other hand, usually argue that the consumer should have choice in technological options (often eliding the fact that a domino effect may, in a practical sense, remove choice from the matter).[19]

Nanotechnology refers to objects constructed at a nanoscale (in one billionths of a meter), which means the objects could be as small as just a few thousand atoms in width. Nanotechnologies include both external technologies (e.g., very small robots that clean up oil spills) and internal technologies (e.g., a replacement immune system). Loosely based upon Richard Feynman's famous lecture "There's Plenty of Room Left at the Bottom" (1959), and first illustrated by Eric Drexler in *Engines of Creation* (1986), nanotech is now a major industry. We have nanotech particles in clothing, household cleaners, cosmetics, paints, and more. Advocates argue that nanotechnologies will play an even greater role in the future, eventually becoming self-constructing, which is the source of much nanotech fear. If nanorobots are possible and they get out of control, there may be no way to stop them from turning every available resource into more of themselves (the so-called grey goo scenario). The miraculous promises of nanotech are deeply intertwined with robotics and AI, as shown in the 21st Century Nanotechnology Research and Development Act (U.S. Senate 2003), which discusses cyborg implants and machines with greater than human intellects, and the conferences and publications produced by Roco and Bainbridge, which defend transhumanist promises (as discussed in the last chapter).

Transhumanists are, essentially, technological optimists; they believe that careful consideration and hard work will lead to positive outcomes from biotechnology, nanotechnology, and robotics/AI. They recognize the perils implicit in these technologies but consider them essentially no different from any other dangerous technology (e.g., nuclear power) and feel that humankind can learn to deal with them.

Transhumanist groups are explicitly evangelical. Among the more important groups are Humanity+ (formerly known as the World Transhumanist Association), the Institute for Ethics and Emerging Technologies (IEET), and the now-defunct Extropy Institute. In the "about us" sections of their Web sites, all three profess their desire to help construct the future in an ethically sound, pro-transhuman fashion. The most well-known of these groups, Humanity+, was cofounded by the British philosophers Nick Bostrom and David Pearce. Bostrom, who also cofounded the IEET, has widely publicized the AI apocalypse and believes it to be inevitable (Bostrom 1998). The Apocalyptic AI advocates Marvin Minsky and Ray Kurzweil both sat on the board of directors for the Extropy Institute and all transhumanist groups have touted their champions' intellectual achievements. Kurzweil, for example, won the 2007 HG Wells Award for Outstanding Contributions to Transhumanism from the World Transhumanist Association (WTA). In his acceptance speech, Kurzweil argued that he and the WTA have a mission to spread transhumanism because transhumanist ideas will solve all of our current worldly problems (Kurzweil 2007).

Giulio Prisco, a former physicist and computer scientist who has served on the WTA and IEET boards of directors and who has become one of transhumanism's most eloquent and influential speakers, has helped shift transhumanism to *Second Life*. As Giulio Perhaps, his SL avatar, Prisco is the founder of Intemetaverse in SL,[20] a cofounder of the Order of Cosmic Engineers, and has convened several SL conferences on issues ranging from technology to religion (all with a specifically transhumanist bent). The Order of Cosmic Engineers, Prisco's most recent endeavor, officially aspires toward Moravec's dream of uploading our consciousness and subsequently exploring the universe as disembodied superminds (Prisco 2008a).

Thanks to rapidly advancing technology, Prisco believes that transhumanist promises of immortality and the resurrection of the dead will soon compete with institutionalized religions while shedding the baggage of bigotry and violence that he believes such religions carry (Prisco 2007b). Following Moravec (though with a longer timeline), Prisco hopes that within a few centuries our descendents will run perfectly accurate computer simulations of the past. In doing so, they will have simulated, for example, your beloved grandfather, whose mental simulation could then be instantiated separately in a physical or virtual body (Prisco 2007a, 2007b, 2007c). If we have a perfect simulation of your grandfather and we let it roam free in our virtual lives (or allow it to operate a robot body if we all still wander around the planet physically), we will, allegedly, have resurrected him. As all people will be instantiated in robot bodies or in virtual worlds, the immortality promised by transhumanists directly opposes Christian resurrection. Why take a risk on immortality that you cannot be sure of when science offers an easy route here and now, complete with the resurrection of loved ones who died before such technology existed?

Although transhumanists generally defend their position as rational and scientific rather than religious, Prisco has diminished the significance of that distinction in his writings. Max More's popular Principles of Extropy, for example, argue that Extropy[21] "means favoring reason over blind faith and questioning over dogma. It means understanding, experimenting, learning, challenging, and innovating rather than clinging to beliefs" (More 2003). The assault on traditional religions is obvious in their denigration of mere "beliefs" and "blind faith" while transhumanist principles are presumed to have attained a higher moral and intellectual ground. As early as 2004, however, Prisco advocated a religious "front-end" for transhumanism. He says:

> I am definitely not proposing a transformation of the transhumanist movement into some sort of irrational religious sect. If anything, I believe the transhumanist

movement should evolve into a mainstream cultural, scientific, and social force firmly established in the world of today—to prepare the world of tomorrow. But as all good salespersons know, different marketing and sales techniques have to be used for different audiences, and perhaps we should also explicitly address the needs of those who are hard-wired for religion. Doing so will be facilitated by understanding the neurological and social basis of religion—why most humans are religious to varying degrees and why some humans are almost completely resistant to religion. Then we can utilize this understanding in the creation of a religion for the Third Millennium (Prisco [2004] 2007a).

While Prisco retains some of the standard transhumanist terminology, he also recognizes that there is considerable power in religious ideas and activities. For this reason, he advocates repackaging transhumanism in explicitly religious terms in order to convert those who might otherwise shy away. While he allows for a religious vision of transhumanism, however, Prisco does not deviate from the fundamental transhumanist belief that transhumanism is a "scientific" force.

It might appear that Prisco adds a new, religious course for transhumanism; he is not remaking transhumanism, however, only expressing with crystal clarity the religious aspects already present within it. Recalling chapter one, Apocalyptic AI is the direct descendent of Jewish and Christian apocalyptic traditions; it borrows their language, their ideology, their logic, and their sacred promises. When Prisco sees the connection between transhumanist ideals of "moving on to the next evolutionary phase . . . resurrecting the dead, and building God" and the Judeo-Christian tradition (Prisco 2007a), he acknowledges the powerful ways in which Western religious beliefs have grounded transhumanism, which is, itself, a Western religious system. Transhumanism does not need to be slightly reframed so as to compete with religions; it already competes, as a religion, with them. This should come as no surprise, given not only the cultural context of transhumanism's rise but also the important ways in which it developed out of the thinking of the Jesuit philosopher and paleontologist Pierre Teilhard de Chardin (Steinhart 2008).[22]

In addition to its expressly religious promises, transhumanism includes a basic religious concern with human identity. David Chidester has argued that "religion is the negotiation of what it means to be human with respect to the superhuman and subhuman" (Chidester 2004). Following this definition, we can easily spot the already powerful religiosity of transhumanism. Transhumanism declares that human nature is "plastic," to be shaped and modified until it is perfect (Prisco 2007c). This amorphous human is rational and scientific and on its way toward ageless perfect physical health. Transhumanism even offers belief structures and practices (evangelism, textual study, participation in the sacred virtual community) designed to transition us into this superhuman state. Other transhumanists have joined Prisco, creating groups such as the Society for Universal Immortalism, which is explicitly religious, though atheist, and the "UNreligion" practiced by the Order of Cosmic Engineers. The absence of God in transhumanism does not mean that transhumanism is not a religion, as some transhumanists now recognize. The OCE, in an effort to resist the label of religion while simultaneously recognizing the ways in which the group's goals overlap those of certain religious groups, have called their movement an UNreligion because, although "not faith-based,"[23] they do make promises traditionally offered in religions (Order of Cosmic Engineers 2008).

Virtual reality is the key arena for the religious speculations of transhumanism. While transhumanists anticipate medical advances that could greatly benefit humankind, these promises always play advance prophet to the *eschaton*, when biology will be transcended altogether. Apocalyptic AI is the ultimate form of transhumanism.[24] Once we have uploaded our minds into machines, we can, except for occasional repair work on or climate adjustment for our new homes, depart the physical world altogether. We will live in a blissful cyberspace, where any dream we have can be made reality. Prisco believes himself part of the last mortal generation; our children, he thinks, will upload their minds and live in cyberspace (Prisco 2007d).

Because the term "transhumanism" unites several disparate ideologies, some question remains as to whether *Second Life* in particular, or virtual worlds in general, are transhumanist. Indeed, the anthropologist Tom Boellstorff, in his excellent ethnography of SL, declares it to be "profoundly human," rather than "posthuman" (Boellstorff 2008, 5). That said, however, transhumanism cannot be equated with posthumanism (whatever that might be[25]); Boellstorff's work bears little on the question of transhumanism but insightfully argues that life in virtual worlds reveals the ways in which "the virtual" is part and parcel of human activity in the conventional world (ibid., passim). Nor, however, is transhumanism identical with only the most radical promises of Kurzweil or others. As the well-known theologian and scholar of religion and science Philip Hefner has argued, transhumanism might well be divided into a lower-case "transhumanism" and an upper case "Transhumanism" (Hefner 2009). While the latter refers to only a small set of individuals, the former represents the profound ways in which transhumanist ideals have been distributed throughout popular culture, especially through the media but also through medicine and technology (ibid., 165–66). Lower case transhumanism—the belief that we can use science and technology to transcend the limitations of human life—is, as Hefner puts it, a "central element of American culture today" (ibid., 166). I would go one step further in asserting that such non-institutionalized transhumanism is not just central to American culture, it appears to be central to digital culture worldwide.[26]

It would be easy, but inaccurate, to suppose that the transhumanist interpretation of virtual worlds is of secondary or tertiary importance in those worlds.

Although transhumanist groups do not have membership enrollments that challenge the numbers of SL residents who identify with other religious groups, many of the basic aims of transhumanism are common within the SL community. A significant minority of *Second Life* residents would think of SL as "heaven" if it were technologically superior and a substantial number find mind uploading appealing. While Vikings enjoyed the prospect of a heaven filled with battle and might have thus eagerly uploaded their minds into *World of Warcraft*, contemporary Euro-Americans have a tamer vision of heaven more easily met by SL. If heaven should be a lot like earth, only without the pain, sickness, and death, then SL would make for a pretty good virtual heaven. Indeed, in my online survey, a significant minority of SL residents (10 percent) claimed they would consider SL to be heaven if some of its technological problems (such as slow load times) were fixed. Even more significant, however, is the number of residents who would find uploading their minds to SL an "attractive alternative to earthly life." Twenty-eight percent of residents would find uploading definitely or probably attractive while another 26 percent answered that they would maybe find it so. *More than half of Second Life residents, then, would seriously consider mind uploading if it were technically feasible.* Although no formal survey has been conducted to determine the number of average Euro-Americans who would like to upload their minds into machines, my experience has been that the percentage of such individuals cannot even remotely compare to those in SL.

Because *Second Life* is a living space and a community, it is perfectly adapted to the transhumanist dreams of Apocalyptic AI. One of the principle ways in which Apocalyptic AI challenges—or at least runs parallel to—other religious systems is through the salvation of uploaded consciousness. Apocalyptic AI promises its faithful a life of eternal reward in a virtual afterlife. As one blog commenter has said, the residents of SL have one thing in common: "the transcendental experience of living as embedded avatars in Second Life" (Merlin 2007). *Second Life* is rather like the earthly world, with just enough difference that people avidly seek to enter it forever. Transhumanists see *Second Life* as a possible fulfillment (if at an early stage in its technological development) of the eschatological and soteriological aims of Apocalyptic AI and even among individuals who are not transhumanist, the apocalyptic agenda has considerable appeal in *Second Life*.

SACRED LIFE

Second Life and similar games offer substitute forms of the sacred and new ways of dealing with it. Online gamers expect resolution to many of the problems of their daily lives: freedom from drudgery, elevation to "specialness," physical, emotional, and intellectual empowerment, and access to welcoming communities. Is it any surprise, then, that users would expect virtual worlds to resolve the problems of religion—which is implicated in all of those concerns—as well? Perhaps these games are the forum for the creation of a new kind of religion, one unhampered by the real world's history of intolerance, inquisitions, and genocide? *Second Life* works so well for transhumanist communities because people naturally ascribe sanctity to it. Just like conventional communities, online communities often use religious myth in order to structure themselves. "Not everyone lives in a community with rich traditions, faiths, and stories that put meaning into everyone's life, whereas in synthetic worlds, everyone is asked to complete quests, fight enemies, and become a hero" (Castronova 2007, 69). Through the storyline and its quest structure, each MMORPG develops a sense of meaning for the players, who find that their time in cyberspace is thereby rendered more important than their everyday lives. Virtual reality is a sacred space where activity is separated out from that of profane time and acquires meaning for individuals and communities.

Second Life residents can reshape their earthly religious traditions or they can begin new ones, hoping to create a more perfect religious environment. Because SL is a new world, slightly out of phase with our own, our religious drive undergoes transformation. Many residents desire the satisfactions that religious affiliation can bring but have no faith that merely importing earthly religions to SL will succeed. Instead, they build their own religions. One resident has called other users to "leave behind the sectarian pettiness of RL [real life] religious institutions and connect with each other as virtually empowered avatars living in a 'Super'natural metaverse" (Merlin 2007). In such a view, SL is a place for the salvation of religion and the salvation of salvation itself!

The sense of sacred that inevitably arises in online worlds derives from the world's separation from profane existence and the development of meaningful communities in those worlds. In his masterpiece *The Elementary Forms of Religious Life*, Emile Durkheim describes the separation of sacred and profane times as key to the development of religious ideas and practices in aboriginal Australia. Though most of an individual's time is spent in the profane period (earning one's living through labor), the time set apart from economic activity is the time in which meaning is magnified and a sense of the sacred appears. Durkheim argues that the two times "stand in the sharpest possible contrast"; whereas profane activity is economic and such life "monotonous, slack, and humdrum," during the *corroboree* (the sacred meeting of various family groups, which includes singing and dancing), "every emotion resonates without interference in consciousnesses that are wide open to external impressions" (Durkheim [1912] 1995, 217–18). The *corroboree*'s participants, having forsaken everyday life, look forward to an excitement that surpasses understanding.

Collective excitement is the first step in the construction of religious community; the demarcation of the sacred time and space from the profane results in the objectification of the social. When groups come together outside the mundane life of economic activity, Durkheim argues, "effervescence" emerges. Collective effervescence—at its greatest expression—is freedom from the social constraints of everyday life. Passions become so strong that

> from every side there are nothing but wild movements, shouts, downright howls, and deafening noises of all kinds . . . these gestures and cries tend to fall into rhythm and regularity, and from there into songs and dances. . . . The effervescence often becomes so intense that it leads to outlandish behavior. . . . People are so far outside the ordinary conditions of life, and so conscious of the fact, that they feel a certain need to set themselves above and beyond ordinary morality. The sexes come together in violation of the rules governing sexual relations. Men exchange wives. Indeed, sometimes incestuous unions, in normal times judged loathsome and harshly condemned, are contracted in the open and with impunity (ibid., 218).

The explosion of bizarre behavior—from shouting to chanting to sexual activity—emerges out of the sense of separation, of difference from everyday life. The *corroboree*'s participants step outside of the mundane and into a "special world," a time and place cut off from the ordinary; each individual feels "as if he was in reality transported into a special world entirely different from the one in which he ordinarily lives, a special world inhabited by exceptionally intense forces" (ibid., 220). In that place, the participants feel the force of the social collective; they can sense that they have been subsumed into something greater.

Durkheim argues that a society's members will never fully comprehend the construction of their community but will nevertheless deeply experience it. The individual in society senses the gifts of civilization: its unity, its protection, its learning, etc., and thus "the environment in which we live seems populated with forces at once demanding and helpful, majestic and kind, and with which we are in touch. Because we feel the weight of them, we have no choice but to locate them outside ourselves" (ibid., 214). Gathering as a clan at the *corroboree* "awakens in its members the idea of external forces" (ibid., 221); thus a sense of the sacred, of divine powers, emerges out of collective effervescence.[27]

Collective effervescence, and the creation of a sacred community, functions in pop culture much as it does in aboriginal religious life. For example, we can feel the "electricity" of 70,000 fans at a football stadium. Those who attended my undergraduate alma mater joined our leaders in parading a well-fed bull on a leash while waving representations of the bull, singing a special song, and wearing special clothes that affiliated us with the primordial Longhorn, our mascot of which the bull on the field was the thirteenth representation (he has since retired to pasture and another has taken his place). Certain times of the week (generally Saturday afternoons) were set apart from the routinized and dull times when the football team was absent from the field. We even had a special hand gesture that imitated the head of the Longhorn. All the hand waving, shouting, stomping, and dancing reflects the inexpressible energy of the gathering and the communion of the participants in a faith group.

A powerful and untraceable sense of excitement also permeates the construction of online social groups. As Castronova put it, "even if I don't care that the Dragon of Zorg has been killed, the fact that everyone else is excited makes me excited; hence we are all excited" (Castronova 2005, 74). Castronova's sense of group identity emerges in the excitement that does not require him to care about the matters at hand; the excitement of the group suffices. In fact, MMORPG designers often encourage such enthusiasm by providing every member of a particular group (say, a nation) with special powers for a brief while after one of the group's members accomplishes a great feat. This sense of excitement illustrates what Durkheim meant by collective effervescence. Collective effervescence is the feeling one gets from being in the group, the electricity of being part of the crowd. This energy, whose origin is invisible to the group participant, holds the group together; it makes each individual feel as though he or she is an element of something greater than the sum of its parts. In Castronova's example, as in Durkheim's analysis, we see how a collective of excitement leads to a social awareness, hence, to a society. The group is founded in this social experience. As the gamers—the "we"—come together online, they join together in a group, feel the effervescence engendered during critical moments, and thus enter a sacred world separate from the everyday.

Human beings experience collective effervescence in virtual reality just as we once did in intertribal gatherings. One of the earliest VR experiments, an artistic project titled GLOWFLOW at the University of Wisconsin, Madison, in 1969, elicited precisely the kind of behavior that Durkheim expected from sacred gatherings among tribal people. GLOWFLOW was a walk-in environment that manipulated light and sound to "give participants the sensation of inhabiting a space that responds to human attention and behavior" (Rheingold 1991, 117). Myron Krueger, a VR pioneer who participated in the production of GLOWFLOW, writes: "People had rather amazing reactions to the environment. Communities would form among strangers. Games, clapping, and chanting would arise spontaneously. The room seemed to have moods, sometimes being deathly silent, sometimes raucous and boisterous. Individuals would invent roles for themselves. One woman stood by the entrance and kissed each man coming in while he was still disoriented by the darkness" (quoted in Rheingold 1991, 117). The palpable energy and the sexually taboo behavior (the woman who kissed every man who entered) closely parallel the behavior of aborigines in the *corroboree*. At some point, perhaps routinization will diminish the sacred charisma of virtual reality but it has not happened yet.[28]

GLOWFLOW's effervescence is thanks to the nature of virtual, not earthly, space. Cyberspace, like its primitive "ancestor" GLOWFLOW, has the power to "trigger ecstatic experience" in the user (Rheingold 1991, 385). Users of the virtual reality art project Osmose "found themselves weeping, slipping into a trance, drifting like elemental spirits" (Davis 1996). In an interview with Howard Rheingold, whose chronicling of virtual reality has been influential worldwide, Brenda Laurel—a scholar and artist in human-computer interaction—says, "the transmission of values and cultural information is one face of VR. The other face is the creation of Dionysian experience" (Rheingold 1991, 385).[29] In the classic cyberspace novel *Neuromancer*, William Gibson's protagonist "operated on an almost permanent adrenaline high" when online (1984, 5) and he slowly works toward his own self-destruction when an employer repays his dishonesty by physiologically ruining his ability to access cyberspace. Without the exultation of cyberspace, his life loses meaning.

Collective effervescence occasionally even bridges the virtual and earthly worlds of gaming. In her ethnographic study of *EverQuest*, T. L. Taylor attended a "Fan Faire" and—though she did not describe her experience in these words—experienced Durkheim's effervescence first hand. A Fan Faire is a live gathering of *EverQuest* attendees, who meet one another, play games sponsored by Sony Online Entertainment (the company responsible for *EverQuest*), and meet company representatives. At the Faire, Taylor saw members of individual *EverQuest* servers[30] chant the names of their servers and develop a sense of server pride that Taylor had never experienced as an actual player (T.L. Taylor 2006, 3). The sense of group identity and the unexpected chanting show that the effervescent experience is a frequent part of online life even when the users interact in earthly hotels.

The creators and participants in online worlds are not scholars of religion; they have not sought to install collective effervescence into their worlds any more than earthly religious communities (whether "primitive" or "advanced") have done so. The ecstatic experience of virtual reality is a natural result of the demarcation between virtual and conventional realities. In the modern West, science and technology have systematically eliminated the heavenly spaces through which we could once sense meaning, opening the door for widespread use of cyberspace as the new sacred place; thus the disenchantment of the world has subsequently reversed course in an enchantment of virtual worlds (Wertheim 1999). Because we have set cyberspace apart from everyday space, collective effervescence emerges in online life.[31] Online worlds are sacred worlds, they are the places and times removed from the everyday routine, the places where meaning emerges and where we are exposed to the sacred.

A 2007 essay from transhumanist authors in Israel points to the physical, architectural connections between cyberspace and heaven. The conclusion to their essay deserves a lengthy citation for the way it shows how the religion of transhumanism connects to the technological sacred, the history of religions, and cyberspace.

In conclusion, throughout human history, man has tried to understand his relationship to the powers at work in the Universe, and to unite with them. For that purpose he built cathedrals that enabled him to unite with the Universe through his conscious-ness, and to extend his body and consciousness to dimensions that allowed him to contain and to integrate the powers of the Universe. . . . Man's hope was that unifica-tion would grant him eternal life. The digital media epoch turned cathedrals from physical structures to virtual structures of digital information, so man too was privi-leged to transform his physical body to virtual dimensions. . . . Today cyberspace has enlarged the range of human body [sic] and consciousness to the final boundaries of the speed of light, by means of electronic components (silicon), that connect man to the Universe. Man's consciousness indeed influences reality in his vicinity directly and immediately. Reality has again become, as in the distant past, a mixture of the products of soul, dream, trance, and myth, together with the material tangibility of daily existence. . . . The Universe familiar to us became an ultimate cathedral linked to every [web] surfer who had already become a cathedral himself. Cyberspace electroni-cally compresses the events in the Universe to singularity of the electronic cathedral. Man is situated in the center of that cathedral, a finger of his hand extended to almost touch the finger of God opposite him. . . . His finger is trying to reach God's finger. To his amazement the surfer discovers that the Heavenly embrace and the finger of God that is trying to reach [sic], and almost touches, is not God's finger, but his own (Omer and Rosen 2007).

Virtual reality advocates regularly represent their technologies in religious con-texts, which makes cyberspace salvation a renewed form of religiosity. Omer and Rosen show a picture of a man with a virtual reality headset and glove alongside a picture of an orthodox Jew wearing tefillin.[32] Likewise, Rheingold connects Sketch-pad, the seminal user-interface program of the 1960s, with the cave paintings at Lascaux (Rheingold 1991, 89). This kind of imagery absorbs the sacred authority of religion for technology; it immunizes technology against accusations of being profane or ordinary. Technology, especially cyberspace technology, is the path to heaven. For Omer and Rosen, cyberspace is the divine realm that enables the apotheosis of humankind, which realizes that it has taken up the mantle of god.

Sanctity is not ontologically constitutive of online worlds; it is, however, a nat-ural property of the intentional (if sometimes unconscious) choices of the partici-pant. Drawing upon Arnold van Gennep's concept of the "pivoting of the sacred" (van Gennep [1909] 2004), J.Z. Smith has argued that sanctity is a relational cate-gory (Smith 1989, 55). The sacred is always in relation to something else; in this case, participants behave toward virtual worlds as though they are sacred in com-parison to conventional reality, which is dominated by the economic drudgery that Durkheim equates with the profane. Within virtual reality, the sacred is easily experienced and found. Online worlds are temples. The temple, says Smith, "serves as a *focusing lens,* marking and revealing significance" (ibid., 54, emphasis original). In temples, "men and gods are held to be transparent to one another" (ibid., 54). Not all religions include gods, of course, which means we must look beyond the surface to understand Smith's point. His argument is that we enter certain places with the expectation that within them we have access to the highest sources of power, the innermost regions of our true selves, and the persons and locations from which meaning originates. These connections were already apparent in the earliest stages of cyberspace. In the introduction to his influential book *Cyberspace: First Steps*, the architect and software pioneer Michael Benedikt refers to cyberspace as the heavenly city of the book of Revelation (Benedikt 1991, 14). For Benedikt and others, cyberspace transcends the barriers that have inhibited architectural fantasy. Cyberspace is the "landscape of rational magic" (Novak 1991, 226) and the liminal place of religious rite that communicates mystical knowledge (Tomas 1991, 40–41). Consider a medieval Christian in his or her cathedral, with its paintings of heavenly realities and its power to reconcile humankind to the Christian God. Likewise, virtual worlds allow access to our true selves and to meaningful practices and communities.

ACCELERATING TOWARD THE *ESCHATON*

Drawing upon the Apocalyptic AI faith in mind uploading, *Second Life* transhumanists believe that independent minds will soon occupy the virtual world, either as native life-forms or as uploaded consciousnesses. Even gamers of a non-transhumanist bent expect that online AIs will become increasingly significant in the emotional lives of gamers (Castronova 2007, 45–46).[33] For transhumanists, the possibility of online minds grows along with the rapid spread of online worlds themselves. Thanks to the easy way in which SL lends itself to transhumanist goals, Kurzweil quickly adopted it into his own apocalyptic agenda, featuring it in a documentary movie about himself (Ptolemy 2009) and giving a keynote address at the *Second Life* Community Convention (Kurzweil 2009a), a fact which was considered "extraordinary and transformational" by one influential commentator even before the speech was delivered (Au 2009). Kurzweil's invitation is particularly notable in that he was the only keynote speaker not drawn from the upper echelon's of Linden Lab's corporate structure. Some transhumanists hope to upload their consciousness into SL while others believe that their SL avatars are already conscious entities separate from the biological persons who created them.

Users of virtual worlds, be they transhumanist or not, can be categorized as "augmentationists" and "immersionists." The term immersion is, unfortunately, badly underdetermined. The use of immersion in opposition to augmentation should not be confused, for example, with Richard Bartle's use of the term immersion in his widely read *Designing Virtual Worlds* ([2003] 2004). When Bartle uses the term immersion, he refers to the ability of the player to immerse him- or herself into the world; that is, his immersion refers to a time when player and character become one, rather than a time when the character can become a person in its own right. In SL, augmentationists use the world as a platform for augmenting their conventional personalities. For them, SL is much like a telephone; it is an opportunity to extend their consciousness into another realm of communication. "Immersionists" in *Second Life* are individuals who separate their second lives and their conventional lives. Their personalities in SL are different from their everyday personalities. A transhuman immersionist believes that his or her SL self could potentially separate from the biological entity tying it to earthly life and become a person in its own right. A transhuman augmentationist would like to upload his or her earthly personality into virtual reality. When I use the term immersionist or augmentationist, I will refer specifically to transhumanist immersionists (and their corollaries, transhumanist augmentationists), not to the general group of role-players as described by Bartle.

Partially in response to various steps taken by Linden Lab and partially due to the incessant need for self-expression that has become the commonplace marker of "Web 2.0," bloggers have begun fighting over the meaning of "immersion" and "augmentation" in SL. If SL is a way of communicating your real-life self in a new medium, then it augments earthly life; if, on the other hand, SL is a way of creating a new self, then it is a place for immersion. This is an important debate, as it helps frame some of the apocalyptic leanings in online gaming. Although there can be no question that immersionists stem from a biological human, they still assert their independence from that human and claim that they were "born" or "woke up" in *Second Life*.

One anonymous blogger has castigated Linden Lab for implementing features such as identity verification (it is not entirely clear why Linden Lab wishes to do this) and voice-enabled communication (rather than forcing everyone to type everything that he or she wishes to say). Both of these features challenge users' ability to develop alternate identities for themselves. Voice features could become the dominant way of communicating with others in SL, especially if some residents cease paying attention to those who continue typing.[34] This would constrain the ability of residents to immerse themselves in SL as entirely new personalities because many users have cross-gendered avatars or avatars who otherwise do not match the users' voices (SLidentity 2007).

Debates among SL bloggers have highlighted the role of individual personalities in the augmentation/immersion debate, as people seek to sort out exactly what relationship exists between avatars and the earthly people "behind" them. Kate Amdahl expresses reservation at the idea of avatars who allege to be completely separate from human people because such an attitude supposedly prevents earthly people from learning anything through the virtual experience (Amdahl 2007).[35] Amdahl's post launched a back and forth with Sophrosyne Stenvaag (a leading SL transhumanist) and led to a few others briefly weighing in. Stenvaag considers herself entirely separate from what she calls her "other personality." When the two minds share a computer, they use separate profiles so that the computer will reflect the current user's preferences. Stenvaag claims that she "woke up" in *Second Life* without any prior history and subsequently "emerged as a personality, and kicked [her] creator out" (The Virtual Temple 2007b). Stenvaag believes that her essential identity (as opposed to the biology that supports both her and the Other Personality) is distinct from that of the Other Personality and of the biological substrate housing it (Stenvaag 2007a).

Like Stenvaag, Extropia DaSilva is an influential member of the immersionist community who gracefully argues that she is a separate consciousness residing in cyberspace. She refuses to acknowledge any necessary connection between herself and the human being who created and operates the avatar and was one of the early voices for Apocalyptic AI in SL.[36] While most online gamers identify with their

Sophrosyne Stenvaag floating above Extropia Core in *Second Life*. Image courtesy of Botgirl Questi.

avatars (Castronova 2005, 44–50) and Bartle claims that the whole point of gaming is to reach a state of identification between the individual and the avatar (Bartle [2003] 2004, 161), DaSilva maintains a line of separation between the two; for example, she refers to the human controlling the avatar as her "primary," not as herself. It is not even necessarily accurate to refer to Stenvaag or DaSilva as "she." After all, the human beings could be any gender and the avatars are, more or less by definition, of no gender at all, despite appearing to be female. Certainly, DaSilva and Stenvaag carry all the standard visual markers of a human female but they are just that, markers; they are not, properly speaking, identifiers because their "bodies" are computer code, not (yet, anyway) living beings. But becoming a living being is precisely DaSilva's goal. At one time, her SL profile read: "Extro is a Mind Child, existing in the abstract space between SL and the minds of people she interacts with. As computing technology becomes increasingly autonomous and biologically inspired, Extro should develop into a person in her own right" (DaSilva 2008d). She does not desire a human life; she does not want to enter our physical space. Rather, she wants to disassociate from the physical human being who pilots her (or that person, perhaps, wants her to do so) and live a transcendent virtual life. Just as the Apocalyptic AI authors universally agree upon the inevitability of mind uploading, DaSilva argues that the cosmological theory of infinite parallel universes logically implies that somewhere there must be a finite set of universes wherein any given individual will have uploaded him- or herself (2008b). DaSilva's goal—perfect immersion in cyberspace—perfectly represents the Apocalyptic AI view of SL.

Apocalyptic AI serves those who wish to assert the independent personhood of avatars. The mind-as-pattern argument promotes a sense of identity that flows seamlessly into visions of cybersalvation. In words that recall Moravec's denigration of the body as "mere jelly," Stenvaag quotes several other avatars who believe that consciousness is code: "for us, it's the code that matters, the medium is trivial" (Stenvaag 2007a). And indeed, Stenvaag desires to separate from the biological "server" to which she remains attached and find herself permanently on a silicon server, where she can be "potentially immortal," someday soon (Stenvaag 2007b).[37]

Giulio Prisco, sympathetic to the needs and viewpoints of the "immersion" camp, nevertheless challenges that group to expand its appreciation for what SL offers. According to Prisco, immersionists have a limited perspective, in which SL remains nothing but a game, a place for role-playing; instead, he advocates that users see SL as a template for the uploading of earthly human consciousness into cyberspace (Prisco 2007d). If the immersive Stenvaag hopes to become immortal, what would become of her Other Personality? It is to this personality that Prisco offers salvation.

Many residents of virtual worlds find an eternity online attractive. While Prisco, DaSilva, and Stenvaag might appear isolated and unique in their desire for

Giulio Prisco
World Transhumanist Association
http://transhumanism.org/

Now speaking on behalf of:
Giulio Prisco, Giulio Perhaps, Yours Truly, the Fat Ugly Guy here and
Myself
http://transumanar.com/

Extropia DaSilva giving a lecture in *Second Life* (April 29, 2007).

cybersalvation, as discussed above more than half of *Second Life* residents would at least consider, if not actively desire, the salvation of Apocalyptic AI.

Apocalyptic hopes are sufficiently high in *Second Life* that Galatea Gynoid[38] and two others launched an island community called Extropia.[39] Visitors are not required to role-play (to assume a transhumanist identity or sci-fi personality) but role-playing is encouraged in the "land covenant" (the agreement that binds all renters) and "transhumanist concepts are very welcome" (Extropia Core Network 2007). Unlike many private islands, where available cash is the only determinant for occupancy, becoming a citizen of Extropia requires sponsorship by two current citizens, "ensuring you're likely to participate in the community" (ibid.). The Extropia "sims"[40] are not tied to any ideology, including transhumanism, which is but one element among the optimistic futurism that prevails on the island. Although Extropia and its founders do not specifically advocate transhumanism, they have created a community in which transhumanism can and does flourish, which they did in large part out of their own transhumanist perspectives. Extropia grew from one sim to six in 2008 and quickly became economically viable, with room to earn outright profits. The growth and economic productivity of the Extropian community demonstrates the allure that their positive view of the future holds for many SL residents.

As Extropia has expanded so too has the presence of immersionist individuals in *Second Life*. A burgeoning spirit of tolerance has accompanied this growth, leading to the everyday acceptance of immersionists where once bigotry was fairly commonplace (Stenvaag 2008b).[41] Gynoid, Stenvaag, and their fellow citizens of Extropia hope that the Extropian islands will create—among other things—a haven for groups that have had difficulty fitting in elsewhere in *Second Life*. Even at the earliest stages of the island project, Stenvaag felt like she had moved "downtown" upon taking up residence in Extropia Core (Stenvaag 2007c). Having provided a home for themselves, the disparate elements of Extropia now hope that others will want to move in. Evangelism is informal but real: no firebrands and no formal advocacy but plenty of information provided in free gift bags for all visitors and Stenvaag advocates the employment of formal greeters in order to keep conversations with new visitors "on message" (Stenvaag 2007d).

While transhumanism has a place in Extropia, it is one that must be contextualized in the community's broader goals. Although the leaders at Extropia Core do not seek converts to transhumanism, they do hope that some visitors will appreciate their view of the future and lifestyle choices (Stenvaag 2007c). Indeed, the number of people who appreciate both Extropia and the immersionist brand of SL transhumanism (which are separate though overlapping groups) appears to be on the rise as visitors find Extropia and the immersionists become regular fixtures in SL public space. Extropia is a community dedicated to positive visions of the future; as transhumanists are extremely optimistic in their outlook on the future, they fit smoothly into Extropia.[42] "We're really just a small community provider with a focus on welcoming those whose identity choices, views and attributes have led them to feel unwelcome elsewhere on the grid and who're willing to follow broad guidelines on clean and futuristic building.... We're home to the SL Transhumanists, but we're also home to the Second Skies business—and as an institution, Extropia is much more likely to endorse airplane dogfighting than brain uploading—we *are* a business, after all" (Stenvaag 2008a, emphasis original). In contrast, the SL Transhumanists are explicitly evangelical. After a series of popular events in *Second Life*, the SL Transhumanists group told visitors to its Web site in March, 2008: "If you have the urgency to spread this viral meme around a bit do join us" (Translook 2008).

The positive relationship between Extropia's ideal of a positive future and transhumanist goals has led to the establishment of transhumanist groups, including religious institutions, in Extropia. In addition to housing the SL Transhumanists group, Extropia is the *Second Life* home to two transhumanist religious groups: the Society for Universal Immortalism (SfUI) and the Order of Cosmic Engineers (OCE). The SfUI is "a progressive religion that holds rationality, reason, and the scientific method as central tenets of our faith. We reject supernatural and mystical forces as solutions to the problems that face us. It is upon the shoulders of humanity that our destiny rests" (Society for Universal Immortalism 2008). Following standard Apocalyptic AI thinking, the SfUI seeks immortality through biotechnology and artificial intelligence and promises the resurrection of the dead.

In its FAQ, the SfUI argues that its approach represents the future of religion—religion demystified but nevertheless meaningful, religion without the supernatural but with all the conventional promises of revealed religion.

The Order of Cosmic Engineers emerged out of a three-day academic conference hosted by the noted sociologist William Sims Bainbridge (of Bainbridge and Roco) and John Bohannon (a regular contributor to the journal *Science*) in the game *World of Warcraft*. The OCE professes itself to be an UNreligion of science and its members desire to "engineer and homestead synthetic realities suitable for ultimate permanent living" (Order of Cosmic Engineers 2008). The OCE holds events in SL, which is more amenable to such gatherings than *World of Warcraft* and also more suitable to the transhumanist agenda. The mind uploading scenario advocated in Apocalyptic AI, as I have already noted, applies more readily to SL than to *World of Warcraft* for contemporary Euro-Americans. The Order of Cosmic Engineers—which will immediately remind historians of August Comte's religion of positivism, in which engineers make up a priestly caste (Comte [1852] 1973)—is a remarkable fusion of transhumanist religious ideals and life in virtual worlds. It is a group whose aims were presented by Moravec and Kurzweil but which now sees itself in the historically enviable position of pioneer. What Moravec could only imagine, the OCE hopes to accomplish. Bainbridge, thanks to his intellectual sophistication, successful academic career, and evangelical concern, is a powerful spokesman for transhumanism in general and the OCE in particular.

The Order of Cosmic Engineers has a high calling—its members see the group as the deliverers of rational Mind from the bondage of mortality and biology. As DaSilva announced at a meeting of the OCE: "the universe itself strives to improve its capacity for self-reflection, to understand itself more clearly. As cosmic engineers, it is our duty to help the universe turn its dreams into reality" (DaSilva 2008c). This parallels Kurzweil's believe that the universe will "wake up" and become divine thanks to technological evolution (Kurzweil 2005, 375). With a rapidly growing appeal in transhumanist circles (for example, Natasha Vita-More and Max More—two longstanding leaders in transhumanist circles—swiftly joined, and the founding membership included Bainbridge and Prisco), the OCE has become the focal point for transhumanists in virtual reality. The OCE has a presence in *World of Warcraft* and in *Second Life* and will almost certainly expand beyond, as some of its members have already become active in other worlds, such as *Warhammer Online*. Cosmic Engineers hope to share their message with the wider world and thereby promote the development of transhumanist futures that might falter without the intervention of an active faithful.[43]

Transhumanist groups and individuals flourish in *Second Life* because Apocalyptic AI infuses cyberspace with the aura of a wondrous and heavenly world. Apocalyptic AI authors champion virtual reality because it is the world in which all their dreams come true; *Second Life* has absorbed these ideas because they provide the ideological strength for the new world. Because *Second Life* satisfies many human concerns—both banal and sacred—it both closely resembles the kind of heaven that occupies typical American religious expectation and looks like a precursor to the Apocalyptic AI cyberspace. As a place for fixing the problems of the world and the acquisition of immortality, *Second Life* is a modern version of heaven.

Cyberspace is a transcendent place, just as religious architecture has sought to establish for millennia. Like Omer and Rosen, Castronova (who is not a transhumanist) believes that virtual worlds are much like cathedrals. They "are not cathedrals, but they do transport people to another plane. They have a compelling positive effect on visitors, an effect dramatically misunderstood by many of those who have never spent time there" (Castronova 2007, 189). For gamers, virtual reality worlds "make their lives different: more exciting, more rewarding, more heroic, more meaningful" (ibid., xvi). Castronova describes what gamers feel—and it is a feeling of the sacred. Apocalyptic AI absorbs the sacred experience of virtual reality and creates the mythical framework for virtual life.

Jewish and Christian apocalyptics rely upon God to establish the heavenly kingdom but, as we have seen, human beings carrying out the providential plan of evolution do so in Apocalyptic AI. Does this imply the apotheosis of humankind? For SL transhumanists, it does. Our ability to build a paradise and fulfill the age-old promises of religion elevates us to divine status according to the leading voices in SL. Omer and Rosen were not the first to enthusiastically endorse a reinterpretation of humanity as divine. This dream weaves throughout digital utopianism, Apocalyptic AI, and *Second Life* transhumanism.

Theology, that is, talk about gods, is prevalent in digital technologies; thanks to eschatological hopes for the apotheosis of humankind, the godly metaphors of many world designers have become a banner of hope for transhumanists. Artificial Life scientists frequently think of themselves as gods (Helmreich [1998] 2000, 83–84, 193) and Kevin Kelly, the founding editor of *Wired* magazine, shares this faith as he looks forward to the day when we, as gods, create a world of even more powerful gods (Kelly 1999, 391). Richard Bartle also declares game designers to be divine (2004, 247) and goes so far as to question whether "those lacking a god's motivation [should] assume a god's powers" (ibid., 293). Giulio Prisco shares this goal; he writes "someday we may create God. And if we create God, then We are God" (Prisco [2004] 2007a)[44] and Extropia DaSilva also believes that we are currently ascending toward a "state that might appropriately be defined as 'God'" (DaSilva 2007). The obvious connection between divinity and creation, merged with a hope for self-empowerment and world improvement, belies the standard version of atheism that runs through transhumanism. While transhumanists may deny the existence of one or more *specific* gods, they do not deny the existence of godhood, itself. The Order of Cosmic Engineers' prospectus declares "there actually never was and also never will be a 'supernatural' god, at least not in the sense understood by theist religions" but "the *OCE* does espouse the conviction that in the (arguably) very far future one or more *natural* entities . . . will to all intents and purposes be very much akin to 'god' conceptions held by theist religions . . . personal, omnipotent, omniscient and omnipresent" (Order of Cosmic Engineers 2008, emphasis original). There may have been no gods heretofore, but we shall become gods in the future.

Prisco suggests that immortality, resurrection of the dead, and the apotheosis of humankind allow transhumanism to replace traditional religions. He markets transhumanism in explicitly (and admittedly) theological packaging, supporting a "religious formulation of transhumanism as a front-end for those who need one" ([2004] 2007a). Whether a hierarchy will emerge between those who accept transhumanism on "scientific" grounds and those who accept it on "religious" grounds remains to be seen (assuming any real divide between the two emerges as significant). Prisco even wants to add rituals and messianic fervor to the transhumanist agenda but he argues that transhumanism is not actually a religion, only that it can be interpreted as one (Prisco 2008b).[45] On the contrary, Bainbridge has gracefully argued that a new religion based around the OCE's principles is required to successfully navigate through our present circumstances and into the future (Bainbridge 2009).

Many other Apocalyptic AI advocates recognize the religious potential of transhumanism but frequently attribute that potential to technoscientific, rather than religious, power. Transhumanism meshes so well with Western religious ideologies, however, precisely because it *already is* a Western religious ideology. Although most transhumanists believe that transhumanism is a rational, scientific movement, they do not recognize the religious beliefs deeply rooted in their mindset through the adoption of Apocalyptic AI. Apocalyptic AI advocates promise happiness, immortality, and the resurrection of the dead through digital technologies, all of which becomes plausible if one simply accepts the basic premises that consciousness is nothing more than a pattern in the brain (a pattern that can be recreated in any medium) and that evolution will result in superbly fast computers capable of recreating space in virtual worlds. Residents of *Second Life* see their in-world activity as evidence for the mind-as-pattern argument and many believe that *Second Life* could, in effect, be the location for the apotheosis of humankind.

Apocalyptic AI promises infuse SL residents' definition of a good place, which is why so many SL residents identify with transhumanist agendas. In her profile, Extropia DaSilva conflates SL with her expectation of our real-life future: "Extro is the name, futurism is the game. To me, the way fantasy and reality combine in SL is reflective of our future when the Net will have guided all consciousness that has been converted to software towards coalescing, and standalone individuals are converted to data to the extent that they can form unique components of a larger complex." Patric Styrian, an SL resident who anticipates a powerful SL religion to emerge, agrees with her. He believes that, using the Internet, we are "actually creating our new inheritors," who will be a "new form of consciousness" (The Virtual Temple 2007a). *Second Life* allows people to gather together and form a religious community out of their futuristic expectations. Based upon Apocalyptic AI—as transmitted by science fiction and transhumanism—the transhumanist ideology of SL benefits from the virtual world's easy appropriation of sacred time and space. For many residents, SL is the time set apart, the time where meaningful activity takes place and where true community is formed. Many residents desire unfettered access to the sacred meaning provided by their virtual lives and, for this reason, their world is one rife with transhumanist dreams.

CONCLUSION

Second Life residents often hold to or implicitly accept the transhumanist ideals of Apocalyptic AI. Given the profound delight that Apocalyptic AI advocates take in imagining a virtual future, this comes as no particular surprise. The rapid growth of Extropia and the flourishing of transhumanist religious groups are examples of how residents of cyberspace have an innate tendency to idealize life online, to see it as the location of meaning and value and the proper indicator of the future to come. Even among non-transhumanists, transhumanist goals are common and appealing, which demonstrates the degree to which Apocalyptic AI has colonized *Second Life*. It is not just that Kurzweil appreciates SL; residents of SL appreciate him and his ideas.

Online games are virtual worlds where real social activity takes place. Indeed, society is the lynchpin of online games, which are not for the "loners" of uncritical imagination. Even in fantasy fighting games like *EverQuest* and *World of Warcraft*, sociologists have shown that acquiring powerful magic items and increasing the character's power is subsumed within and generally subordinated to developing social groups. *Second Life* has almost no purpose other than to build a social community. With the exception of a few people who seek to make money without reference to the group's dynamics (and these people are few and far between), social forces encapsulate all artistic, economic, and entertainment activities.

The sacred separation of online society from its profane counterpart on Earth allows the experience of collective effervescence and helps structure a sense of virtual reality *as* religion. Cyberspace is sacred space, where residents come to set aside the banality of mundane existence. While it is not necessarily the case that cyberspace will perpetually resist the disenchantment that was thrust upon the natural world (and hence enabled the enchantment of the digital world), if Apocalyptic AI remains convincing then we will continue to see large numbers of people willing to locate true meaning in life online. As the next few decades unfold, transhumanists like Extropia DaSilva and Giulio Prisco will seek salvation in cyberspace, which is the perfect, heavenly realm of a divine humankind. Whether or not they succeed is beside the point; we cannot and in the future will not be able to ignore the significance of Apocalyptic AI in cyberspace as long as transhumanists remain hopeful.[46]

The virtual world is a sacred gathering place where collective effervescence unites people and gives them reason to believe in the religious promises of Apocalyptic AI, which provides the ideological identity of cyberspace religion. The search for a perfect world, salvation, and even the apotheosis of humankind borrows directly from the Apocalyptic AI authors, whose opinions hold sway for many residents of *Second Life* and whose influence pervades the construction and use of virtual reality. Those residents, uniting in groups like the Order of Cosmic Engineers, anticipate their salvation and actively work to bring it about through ideological (e.g., evangelism and "consciousness raising") and technical means.

FOUR

"IMMATERIAL" IMPACT OF THE APOCALYPSE

INTRODUCTION

Apocalyptic AI predictions have garnered so much attention that—in combination with rapidly progressing robotic technology—widespread public attention has focused upon how human beings and robots should and will relate to one another as machines get smarter. Debates over robotic consciousness transition smoothly into what kinds of legal rights and personal ethics are at stake in the rise of intelligent robots. Although it would be tempting (for some people) to dismiss Apocalyptic AI as the irrelevant delusions of a misanthropic community, Apocalyptic AI has become enormously significant in Euro-American culture. Apocalyptic AI creates culture; in response to the movement, philosophers, lawyers and governments, and theologians have all reconsidered their own positions.

Last century's science fiction has become this century's scientific promise. Hiroshi Ishiguro of Japan's Osaka University, for example, believes that one day, humanoid robots will live among human beings and be so realistic that an interlocutor would have to ask any given person whether he is a robot or a human being (Tabuchi 2008). The Scottish AI researcher David Levy goes even further, arguing that today "we are in sight of the technologies that will endow robots with consciousness, making them as deserving of human-like rights as we are; robots who will be governed by ethical constraints and laws, just as we are; robots who love, and who welcome being loved, and who make love, just as we do; and robots who can reproduce. This is not fantasy—it is how the world will be, as the possibilities of Artificial Intelligence are revealed to be almost without limit" (Levy 2006, 293). While many roboticists believe that intelligent robots are centuries away, others loudly defend their belief that robots will soon enter human society (and, indeed, surpass it).

Apocalyptic AI has powerful influence in the philosophical, legal, and religious discussions in contemporary political life. In response to the mere possibility that robots may one day become intelligent and that human beings may one day upload their minds into machines, philosophers and psychologists have reconfigured their understanding of the human mind, governments and lawyers have wondered about the legal rights and obligations of machines and the human beings who interact with them, and theologians have considered the moral responsibilities of human beings and machines.

FIGHTING FOR CONSCIOUSNESS

Centuries have passed since Descartes first gave us his famous declaration "cogito ergo sum" and yet we are no closer to knowing what it means to be conscious. Despite the enthusiasm of Daniel Dennett's *Consciousness Explained* (1991) and similar pronouncements, widespread disagreement over the subject exists among philosophers, neuroscientists, and cognitive scientists. The claims of Apocalyptic AI authors, especially Marvin Minsky but also Ray Kurzweil, have gained considerable prestige in contemporary discussions over consciousness, helping to guide the direction of research for cognitive scientists and philosophers of mind. The beliefs that human minds (like computers) are composed of a multitude of nonthinking agents or resources, that machines will one day (perhaps soon) be conscious, and that human minds are a pattern of information dissociable from the brain cannot be easily discarded from our present study of the mind.

Distinguishing the mind from the brain (or eliminating that distinction) hinges upon the nature of human experience and whether it can be reduced to a simple description of brain pattern states. Unfortunately, we are not currently in a position (and likely never will be) to demonstrate whether or not conscious experiences can be reduced to a physical language of brain states.[1] As a consequence, debate rages over whether or not it makes sense to talk about subjective experience at all. If we cannot talk about experience, we will find it difficult indeed to assess the level of consciousness possessed by a machine. The promises of artificial intelligence have, however, radically transformed the nature of such debates, becoming the key to contemporary discussions about human consciousness.

In his famous essay "What It's Like To Be a Bat," Thomas Nagel argues that consciousness is so unique as to render analysis of the mind irreducible to analysis of the brain (Nagel 1974, 436).[2] Nagel attributes conscious experience to animals and aliens (if they were to exist), arguing that for every kind of animal experience, there must be a "something it is like to *be* that organism" (ibid., 436, emphasis original). Nagel does not argue that "intelligent" robots would experience consciousness, though he does not rule it out, either, arguing that anything as complex as a human being might by necessity have experiences and, therefore, be conscious.

That we have few ways to describe what it is like to be a bat should come as no surprise; after all, we do not yet have the scientific language to describe what it is like to be a human being! There is no gold standard theory of human consciousness, which leads to significant troubles in the debate over robot consciousness. Indeed, in some ways we have done little to surpass Descartes. Actually, the one thing Descartes felt certain of—the consciously thinking self—is directly attacked by some artificial intelligence researchers, cognitive scientists, and philosophers, who deny the existence of such a unitary being. They believe the conscious self is illusory. At the same time, many such theorists have absorbed Descartes' primacy of the intellect over the body. They do not feel that the body constitutes a necessary element in human mental life, despite the intricate connections between senses, feelings, emotions, and thoughts.

According to some theorists of mind (both in AI and philosophy), consciousness is an evolutionarily developed illusion. The decentralization of the self (the rejection of a solitary, single state of consciousness in favor of myriad little agents working together) has been a common strategy in this effort (Minsky 1985, 2006; Dennett 1991, 1998). For example, the subjective experience of frustration might be the combination of an agent for finding apples, an agent for picking apples, an agent for climbing trees, and a reality in which the apple cannot be reached despite the best efforts of all these agents working together.[3] A trouble-detecting agent (a "critic") might notice that the apple has not been gotten and initiate a series of other agents' efforts to plan a new approach. If further efforts are also frustrated, anger would be responsible for addressing the disjunction between reality and the desired outcome of all the other agents in order to ensure that apathy did not lead to starvation. Somehow, the apple must be obtained. Anger, like other emotions in Minsky's account, is a "Way to Think" in which many of the mind's resources have been shut down (Minsky 2006, 5), such as its ability to act calmly or deliberately. While the frustration occurs, no "I" exists to feel it or to initiate efforts at reconciling it. Small agents seek to solve the problem independently of any overall command center in the mind. The mind, says Minsky, is a society. Our belief that we have a "me" who can do all of the work is just an evolutionary afterthought, an illusion.

There is no easy way to identify the conscious self in brain activity (a fact well established by Nagel in his analysis of being a bat) so Minsky and others deny that the conscious self exists, supposing instead that a series of smaller selves (none of which are immediately available to conscious reflection) combine in a semimystical union to form the illusory selves that we all know and experience.[4] One of the colossal problems remaining in Minsky's otherwise quite elegant study of human thought and practice is explaining the existence of the illusory "I" in the first place. Minsky dodges responsibility for this, asserting "a paradox: perhaps it's *because* there are no persons in our heads to make us do the things we want—nor even ones to make us *want to want*—that we construct the myth that *we're* inside ourselves" (Minsky 1985, 40, emphasis original). Labeling such confusion a paradox does little to shed light on what, precisely, is at stake. If there is no self there, why would a brain need to invent it and who or what would do the inventing? Naturally, the computational mind metaphor lends itself nicely to this analysis of human thought. We are machines, Minsky says (ibid., 30); machines that use agents to carry out necessary needs and desires just as a computer uses programs to accomplish its subroutines.

Apocalyptic AI advocates strenuously advocate that the brain is a computer, hence the transmigration of minds into machine bodies. According to Moravec, the mind, and indeed everything important about an individual person, is the pattern of information in an individual's brain. Within the brain, an estimated 100 billion neurons communicate with one another through chemical and electrical connections. The resulting web of communications, says Moravec, provides us with a sense of self. As we saw in chapter two, Moravec and other Apocalyptic AI advocates believe that this web could be replicated in another material context without loss of information.

According to Kurzweil, if we could scan a brain with sufficient resolution to know the "locations, interconnections, and contents of the somas, axons, dendrites, presynaptic vesicles, and other neural components" (Kurzweil 1999, 124), we would have all the information necessary to replicate the individual in another, artificial, brain. Kurzweil's position depends upon what Moravec earlier labeled the "pattern-identity" position of human selfhood, and which was utilized to great effect in A. C. Clarke's science-fiction story, *The City and the Stars* ([1953] 2001). For Moravec, the body is irrelevant to the person, only the "*pattern* and the *process*" in one's body and brain matter (Moravec 1988, 117, emphasis original). Because every cell in our bodies will be replaced over time, Moravec does not believe they can contribute to our essential selves. Rather, the pattern is (relatively) continuous and must thereby represent the true conscious individual.[5]

The computational mind metaphor[6] serves the valuable philosophical and psychological purpose of providing thought with empirical causality.[7] That is, by asserting the identity between a computer and a human mind, the logical operations with causal powers in computers can be extrapolated to human thought. If human thought follows a logical form that corresponds to mental representations, then the logical causality of the mental representations (i.e., the movement from one representation to the next according to formal rules) explains how thinking might be, in some fashion, causal (Fodor 2000, 18–19). This is just a way of making sure that minds can do *something* even while denying them status as somehow separate from brains. The "computational theory of mind can bridge the old dilemma of how the mind can be ethereal, dealing with logic and truth, and still have an effect in the world of matter. The age-old conundrum just vanishes" (Hall 2007,

110). If minds are, as Descartes thought, something outside the brain that can act upon the brain, then we have a causal theory for action. But Descartes' theory is unacceptable to modern philosophers and cognitive scientists, relying as it does on a nonmaterial, seemingly supernatural, entity. The computational mind asserts that minds cause things through their correspondence to brain states, where the logic of brain states equals that of mental states.[8]

Thinking seems, to our conscious reflection, to require an intentional state but some philosophers argue that there is no conscious mind to intend the thought. Paul Churchland has long argued that all the subjective claims about a person's mental states (intentions, feelings, thoughts, etc.) will disappear from the scientific lexicon as we progress in our understanding of neural states (Churchland 1989; Philipse 1998). That is, instead of talking about John desiring an apple, we would just describe the neuron activity in his brain, which would allegedly be far more precise. Churchland's philosophical position, "eliminative materialism," posits that there is nothing beyond the material brain states; no conscious mind exists. Consciousness is some kind of epiphenomenon that emerges from the brain's interaction with the world; it has no causal powers and cannot even accurately describe the world.

Daniel Dennett seeks a middle ground between asserting the reality of mental states and reducing them to nothing but their material substrate (Dennett 1998, 95–120). Dennett argues that descriptions of mental states and descriptions of brain states, though they are inherently connected in the brain/mind of the subject, will never be made identical through language. He uses the example of two different gambling strategies: one looks for long-range patterns and another for short-range patterns, but they could both potentially offer the same overall predictive success despite their completely different approaches and completely different individual predictions. That is, while the short-range and the long-range predictions get different results and win or lose at different times, from a big-picture analysis, they appear—in this thought experiment—equally qualified as predictors. In the same way, brain-state talk and mental-state talk, though they are completely different in what and how they predict, may offer roughly equivalent success at predicting the behavior of an organism. In his own words, there can be "two or more *conflicting* patterns being superimposed on the same data—a . . . radical indeterminacy of translation" (ibid., 120, emphasis original).

Predicting behavior is done principally through the attribution of an intentional stance, according to Dennett. We presume that the subject of our prediction intends things by his or her actions and, therefore, we find ourselves able to make accurate predictions. The ability to predict others' behavior through the intentional stance, he argues, underlies our ability to interpret that behavior (ibid., 98). The intentional stance is not easily reconciled with fMRI or EEG analysis, which means that a discussion of mental states cannot be the same as a discussion of brain states, even if the latter is the source of the former. "I see that there could be two different systems of belief attribution to an individual that differed *substantially* in what they attributed—even in yielding substantially different predictions of the individual's future behavior—and yet where no deeper fact of the matter could establish that one was a description of the individual's *real* beliefs and the other not" (ibid., 118, emphasis original).

But while we may never be able to speak a unified language of consciousness and its neural-correlates, Dennett confidently asserts the essential identity of the two. "Conscious experience . . . is a succession of states *constituted by* various processes occurring in the brain, and not something over and above these processes that is *caused by* them" (ibid., 136, emphasis original). Because experience is not caused by brain processes, it is not something that exists separately from them. In Dennett's view, conscious experience, though it cannot be described in the language of brain states, is nothing more than our peculiar way of recognizing them in ourselves. Dennett agrees with Churchland (and others) that consciousness is a phenomenon of the brain—rather than of a soul, a spirit, a fundamental layer of cosmic consciousness, etc.—but does not believe that the language of brain states can replace that of consciousness.

Dennett, building upon Minsky's society of mind, denies the existence of the subjective "I" that we automatically believe to be ourselves. He refers to an "astonishingly persistent conviction that there is a Cartesian Theater," which he considers the "result of a variety of cognitive illusions" (Dennett 1991, 431). Hearkening to Descartes' belief in the *res cogitans*,[9] Dennett refers to the idea that somewhere in the brain is a place where all data about the world are represented for the individual to make informed choices. Like Minsky, Dennett argues that the conscious self is an illusion—an important one, but an illusion all the same. "Once we take a serious look backstage, we discover that we didn't actually see what we thought we saw onstage . . . there is no central fount of meaning and action; there is no magic place where the understanding happens. In fact, there is no Cartesian Theater" (ibid., 434). This is so, Dennett tells us, because we have not found a "real" pineal gland, a place where all the data of sense experience funnels in order to acquire meaning and initiate behavioral responses (ibid., 102–3). "There is no reason to believe that the brain itself has any deeper headquarters, any inner sanctum, arrival at which is the necessary or sufficient condition for conscious experience" (ibid., 106).[10] This claim leads Dennett to deny the existence of the Cartesian Theater, the self-aware "I," and assert the meaningfulness of his "multiple drafts model," which functions like Minsky's agent-based account of consciousness.

For all the explanatory power in the agent model of consciousness (especially as described by Minsky), we all know that we have conscious selves.[11] The baffling denial of human consciousness has led Jaron Lanier to assert that "among all humanity, one could only definitively prove a lack of internal experience in certain professional philosophers" (Lanier 2000, 7). Philosophers like Dennett have made much of the fact that by the time people report consciously making a decision, the relevant neuron firings have *already* begun. Dennett takes this to prove the non-existence of any central control mechanism, a claim which is disputed by the computer scientist and nanotech pioneer J. Storrs Hall. Hall resuscitates the central decision-making self but actually divorces it from the conscious self, an interesting approach to the problem. He believes that it is "likely that there is at least one meta-level controller in humans," which acts then stores information in the memory, which is then accessed by a self-knowledge module (Hall 2007, 285).

Like Hall, the Yale computer scientist David Gelernter tries to have his cake and eat it too. He echoes Lanier's concern over the "Disintegration Approach," wherein the thinking subject is divided into innumerable agents that do not "really" coalesce, saying that it "doesn't merely miss the forest for the trees. It denies the very existence of the forest" (Gelernter 1994, 38). Gelernter uses a gestalt image of a white star formed by placing certain unconnected pieces of black paper on a white page. He says that the star does not exist, though we all see it, and believes the important thing is that we do see it even if it is illusory. Likewise, consciousness is an illusion of brain architecture (ibid. 160–62). While Churchland would assure us that the star is nonexistent and we should ignore it altogether, Gelernter believes that we should pay attention to it despite the fact that it is an illusion. Lanier, on the other hand, believes that consciousness is something quite real, though it is unclear exactly how he distinguishes it from brain states.

Since we are not certain what constitutes consciousness, it is hard to know whether or not machines can possess it. At the least, it seems likely that machine consciousness would be different from human consciousness (Levy 2006, 378) but that does not mean robots cannot have it altogether. There is no a priori reason why human consciousness should be the only kind; indeed, as Nagel argued, there must be something that it is like to be a bat. As robots become more complex, it would seem that there must be something that it is like to be a robot.

Daniel Dennett has argued that to deny machines the possibility of consciousness is a form of chauvinism (Dennett 1998, 156), a position echoed by the roboticist Rodney Brooks (Brooks 2002, 180). The belief that a computer could be fully conscious is called "strong AI." According to Dennett, a fake Cezanne is as pretty as a real one, so prejudice against it on aesthetic grounds has no merit; likewise, prejudice against machine consciousness on the grounds that it is not human consciousness is problematic.[12] If machines become conscious, no doubt they will experience something different from human consciousness. After all, it will be impossible (or nearly so) for a human being to appreciate what it is like to *be* a robot, much as it is impossible for him or her to know what it is like to be Nagel's bat. Even such a simple question of what it means to "see" with cameras, as opposed to eyes, may remain forever out of our grasp.[13]

Whether consciousness is an illusion that we experience anyway (although for Dennett no "we" can possibly experience the consciousness) or is a real phenomenon of human mental life, there are those who deny that machines can ever be conscious. Critics of machine consciousness include physicists, philosophers, and theologians who have mustered technical, philosophical, and religious arguments against intelligent machines.

To ascertain whether or not a machine can think,[14] Alan Turing suggested that we ask if a human being can determine whether or not it is a machine. In the Turing Test, a human interrogator types questions into a computer terminal. A machine answers the questions through the terminal while a human being answers the questions likewise. If the interrogator is unable to unmask the machine, then, it would seem, the machine is conscious for all intents and purposes. Turing called the question "can machines think?" meaningless but believed that by the year 2000, the average interrogator would be unable to identify the machine within five minutes 70 percent of the time (Turing 1950, 442). This time frame was considerably overenthusiastic but the Turing Test remains the gold standard for conversations about machine intelligence.

In all likelihood, for a machine to pass a well-constructed Turing Test, it will require a bodily experience of the world (see Dennett 1998, 153–70). No one lacking a real experience of human life could possibly fool an intelligent human (given a reasonable amount of time) into thinking it was anything but a machine. Too many questions that we might pose would require that the machine be immersed in earthly existence; so much of our knowledge is grounded in our directly bodily interaction with the world that any machine lacking such experience would be incapable of conversing with us.

At present, computer programs vying to pass the Turing Test are embarrassingly poor conversationalists. They misunderstand basic questions and statements, especially when these rely upon any kind of knowledge outside the immediate context of the conversation. Over the Internet, I once had a conversation with the "trial" version of ALICE, a Loebner Prize–winning[15] program. Our conversation went like this:

HUMAN: How are you today?
ALICE: I am doing extremely well.
HUMAN: extremely?
ALICE: Are you kidding?
HUMAN: no.
ALICE: Are you serious?
HUMAN: absolutely
ALICE: You are so certain.
HUMAN: a moment ago, we were talking about you.

ALICE: I wonder if I know this moment ago we were talking.
HUMAN: well, you were a part of it.
ALICE: Well that's okay. I was?

I thought it odd, when ALICE told me it was doing extremely well, as this would be an unusual answer for a human being. This prompted me to seek more information on the delightfulness of ALICE's day, which led to a series of less and less intelligible answers, culminating in ALICE wondering if it knew "this moment" of which we spoke. A baffling conversation, to say the least, but nothing unusual in the world of chatterbots. Of course, I have not tried this conversation with the "full" version of ALICE, and, moreover, even the most ardent critics of Strong AI must admit that chatterbots get more sophisticated each year and there is little reason to believe with total confidence that none will ever pass a Turing Test.

Even had ALICE conversed intelligibly, however, it may have done little to demonstrate consciousness or thought in the machine. The philosopher John Searle illustrates this problem with his "Chinese room" analogy. He argues that if you put him into a room that included the English-language rules for manipulating every possible passage of Chinese text into some other intelligible passage then, despite his flawless answers, he still would not understand Chinese. Even though his answers are indistinguishable from those of a native speaker, Searle does not understand Chinese. The manipulation of rules is not the same as understanding the meaning of the words (Searle 1980). If Searle is right (that the Chinese Room is, in fact, analogous to machine computation), then perhaps ALICE's failure can be traced to its inability to truly understand the words it manipulates, though even had ALICE succeeded in fooling me it still would not have been conscious. Critics of Searle's argument generally note that he insists upon identifying consciousness within the individual manipulating the rules rather than in the entire system.[16]

Hubert and Stuart Dreyfus are among the most persistent critics of Strong AI. Hubert, a philosopher, and Stuart, a mathematician and computer scientist, allege that computers will never equal the intuitive power of human decision making. Computers use rules (algorithms or heuristics, depending upon the exactitude of the rule) to make formal decisions but human beings rarely do the same. Rather, people have "hunches" that lead them to do what feels right (Dreyfus and Dreyfus 1986, 11). Dreyfus and Dreyfus argue that these hunches cannot be reduced to a system of unconscious rules. Many, if not most, AI researchers, however, continue to believe that if enough were known about the supposedly unconscious rules used in human thought that computers would rival us in most domains.

Problematically for Dreyfus and Dreyfus, a number of their published claims have been complicated by advances in computing technology. Many examples of human action, impossible two or three decades ago, have become commonplace, available even to the robotics hobbyist. Dreyfus and Dreyfus believe that "*in any domain in which people exhibit holistic understanding, no system based upon heuristics will consistently do as well as experienced experts"* (ibid., 109, emphasis original). While computer heuristics may not challenge human expertise, algorithms (which lead to definite answers but require more computing power) can. A computer has, for example, beaten the world chess champion. Deep Blue did not defeat Garry Kasparov by playing the way a human being plays chess but rather by calculating an enormous array of possible moves and countermoves, far more than could be calculated by even the greatest human chess player. This "brute force" allowed Deep Blue to win. What remains to be seen is whether such tactics can be identified and applied to more sophisticated human behaviors, such as social relationships, and, if so, whether enough computing power will ever be available to exercise them (Apocalyptic AI advocates, of course, argue that computational power will be virtually unlimited within the century).

Whether through heuristics or algorithms, AI thinking remains stuck at only one end of the full spectrum of human thought—that of abstract reasoning. According to Gelernter, at the high-focus end, we can think abstractly by selecting out the key details from a smorgasbord of memories. At the low focus end, we see extremely detailed episodes in their completeness and attach them to others through emotional associations. That is, high-focus thinking connects memories through shared details while low-focus thinking connects memories through shared emotions. Creativity, Gelernter believes, stems from this low-focus thought that brings seemingly unrelated memories and concepts together (Gelernter 1994, 85). A creative machine, then, will require low-focus thinking. He believes that the reasoning that we have sought to replicate in computers represents only half of human thought; it excludes the analogical thinking of emotions, creativity, and intuition (ibid., 2–3).

If we give machines emotions, then they might develop insightful thought. Gelernter has tried to create programs that assign emotional "palettes" to given "memories." For example, a description (a "memory") of carnivals, in addition to all of the details that carnivals share (rides, cotton candy, etc.) would include emotions likely to appear at a carnival, such as high levels of joy and excitement and low levels of despondency or boredom. Assigning this kind of emotional content should allow a sufficiently advanced computer to associate memories whose details are very different when the computer operates in a low-focus mode. "When we have added emotion," he says, "then and only then our computers will be capable of surprising us with an occasional genuine insight" (ibid., 146).

Gelernter suggests that we replace the Turing Test with a more relevant one: can the computer understand us? Such a test, he argues, requires that the machine convince people that its emotional state echoes that of human beings when faced with the same stimulus (ibid., 156). If we bring up particular circumstances, people, or relations, perhaps the computer would be able to associate them with other, relevant ideas or objects. The computer might, in some sense, be said to under-stand people if it could communicate on this level.

Even if the computer can make the proper associations, this does not mean that it is conscious. After all, without the meaningfulness underlying people, objects, and events, our conscious lives would be dull indeed. As Albert Borgmann points out, a computer "has designers rather than parents. It has breakdowns rather than illnesses. It becomes obsolete rather than old. It can be replaced and . . . has a price rather than dignity" (2002, 13). It would seem that the specter of Searle's Chinese Room lurks behind every computer: a robot might expect you to be sad at the death of your mother but seems unlikely to comprehend the nature of the sadness and death or even *why* the two are related. Nevertheless, such technical problems may well be overcome.

The worst problem facing the Strong AI program is the dreadful absence of any way to define, measure, or locate consciousness. After all, if we cannot measure a human being's conscious will, how can we do so with a robot? We can, at best, simply assume that the robot is conscious just as we do with other human beings. But is it reasonable to grant intentionality to the robot? As Searle has argued, sym-bolic manipulation and interpretive meaning are not mutually inclusive. Just as the Chinese Room experiment shows that reasoning does not necessarily imply meaningful thought, a computer that talks about happiness does not prove that the robot feels happiness in any meaningful way.

Masahiro Mori, a Buddhist practitioner and robot engineer who gained noto-riety for saying that a robot will someday become a Buddha, does not argue that robots will necessarily be conscious. Mori believes that "robots have the buddha-nature within them—that is, the potential for attaining buddhahood" (Mori [1981] 1999, 13) because robots partake of the larger Buddha-nature, the expression of the Buddha's presence throughout existence. Despite this, he says, "I doubt that we will ever know if a robot has become conscious or has developed a will. We do not even know what consciousness or will truly are" (King 2007).

The most careful study of human consciousness may not be scientific at all but, rather, religious. Buddhists have spent centuries attempting to comprehend the human mind and its limits, with results that, they say, have significant scientific value (Wallace 2000, 2003). Leaders in the effort to communicate between Tibetan Buddhism and modern neuroscience have, like Mori, denied the ease of mea-suring consciousness and the likelihood of a robot attaining it. B. Alan Wallace, the president of the Santa Barbara Institute for Consciousness Studies and a former Tibetan Buddhist monk, finds the discussion of conscious robots to be absurdly premature, given our lack of detailed knowledge about human conscious-ness. He once told me that, given "that we are currently in a pre-scientific era concerning human consciousness, anything scientists may have to say about con-sciousness in robots is groundless speculation" (Wallace 2007).

The XIV Dalai Lama, the head of Tibetan Buddhism, however, feels that computers might someday be conscious. In a discussion held with Western scientists, the Dalai Lama argued that, while consciousness could not spontaneously arise out of a computer, a human consciousness could possibly be reincarnated in a computer, making it conscious (Hayward and Varela 1992, 152–53). Likewise, a dying Buddhist yogi might transfer his consciousness into a computer if it were competent to receive that consciousness (ibid., 153). In Tibetan Buddhism, new consciousnesses are impossible; there is a static amount of consciousness in the world but it is at least conceivable that some of this consciousness could be incarnated in a machine as opposed to a biological organism. The Dalai Lama did not claim that such a thing *would* happen, only that it could not be dismissed out of hand. The Dalai Lama's wait-and-see attitude reflects his generally responsible approach to the intersections of religion and science; it is a very reasonable approach to the problem, making neither promises nor denials that cannot be demonstrated.

Debates over consciousness may not be solved by the presence of thinking machines. After all, says Marvin Minsky, "When intelligent machines are constructed, we should not be surprised to find them as confused and as stubborn as are men in their convictions about mind-matter, consciousness, free will, and the like" (Minsky [1968] 1995). Despite the fear that philosophical wrangling will continue, however, Minsky carries no concern about whether intelligent machines will arise or whether we will recognize them as such; he is confident of their eventual arrival despite the passage of forty years since his earlier claim. If Minsky is right that robots will come along and argue about consciousness, then there may be no real connection between our understanding thereof and the development of machine consciousness. Minsky obviously believes that we can manufacture consciousness without first fully understanding it.

Despite the difficulties inherent in defining, measuring, and explaining human consciousness, the Strong AI camp confidently asserts the inevitable future of machine consciousness. Strong AI advocates claim that AIs will be fully intelligent and conscious in opposition to Weak AI advocates, who believe that, no matter how capable computers may become, they will never be truly conscious. In Apocalyptic AI, Strong AI is taken as an act of faith and elevated beyond conjecture into necessity. Not only *could* a robot be conscious, but, says Apocalyptic AI, one certainly *will*.[17]

Despite the urgency of Apocalyptic AI, conscious robots—should they appear at all—will not likely arise in the next few decades. While it may be the case that the brain is a machine, and thus there may be no barrier toward creating consciousness in a computer, actually doing so would require vastly more knowledge than we actually possess or will possess in the near future according to roboticists and AI researchers at the CMU Robotics Institute (Mason 2007; Touretzky 2007a;

Weiss 2007). Researchers in neuroscience still struggle to understand the neural systems of worms such as *Caenorhabditis elegans* and of insects like grasshoppers. It may well be decades before even these vastly less complicated nerve structures have been completely understood. The human nervous system is far more sophisticated than that of a grasshopper, so we should not assume that understanding it will necessarily emerge in an apocalyptic singularity.[18]

Regardless of the precise time frame for the rise of intelligent machines, cognitive science textbook authors have already taken note of the Apocalyptic AI authors, rightly treating Moravec, Minsky, and Kurzweil as leading figures in the field. In the conclusion to his textbook *Artificial Psychology*,[19] Jay Friedenberg notes Moravec's belief that building AIs is an ethical and practical necessity (Friedenberg 2008, 246) and reports that human-equivalent robots are a near inevitability and that vastly superior robots are within the realm of possibility (ibid., 248–49). Friedenberg expresses skepticism, however, at the thought we might reproduce our consciousness in a new substrate (ibid., 250). Thanks largely to the advocacy of the apocalyptic authors, ideas frequently termed "science fiction" (mind uploading and transcendent robot intelligences) are now serious textbook material for undergraduate psychology majors.

Apocalyptic AI impacts a broad spectrum of philosophical, scientific, and religious approaches to consciousness. From cognitive scientists to the Dalai Lama, nearly everyone who cares about the human mind has grappled with the idea that robots will soon possess transcendent intelligence and the implications of that for understanding the human mind. It is simply impossible to ignore Moravec, Minsky, Kurzweil, and their followers in the debates over brains, minds, and consciousness. While Descartes may have reached a personally satisfactory answer while meditating in his home library, today's debate never strays far from the here and now of laboratory research and the apocalyptic imagination around it.

THE LIFE AND LAWS OF MACHINE INTELLIGENCE

The influence of Apocalyptic AI extends beyond philosophical arguments to practical claims about the legal rights and responsibilities of future machines. Futurists, transhumanists, and even government agencies have attended to the promises of Moravec, Kurzweil, and others. Legal experts have wondered whether computers could be trustees, whether robots deserve rights, and how the advent of intelligent machines might reshape our political life.

Science fiction authors have already led us in a series of thought experiments that help us appreciate the role that robots may one day play in society. Among sci-fi authors, none has been as important to the illustration of human-robot interactions as Isaac Asimov. Human beings and robots form a joint society in Asimov's work, though it is one fraught with constant tension. Asimov called a culture of human beings and robots a C/Fe society (C for carbon-based life-forms and Fe for iron-based, steel life-forms) and believed that, despite the dangers of economic and social disenfranchisement presented by integrating robots into our society, the robots would improve our lot. Asimov praises a C/Fe society as the best hope for human survival in the universe.

Asimov opens his influential short-story collection *I, Robot* ([1950] 1977) with the tale of Robbie the nursemaid. Robbie takes care of a young girl whose mother wants to own a robot in order to reduce her workload but eventually comes to distrust it. She has the robot sent back to the factory until—upon a factory tour arranged by the girl's father—Robbie saves the girl's life and the grateful mother allows Robbie to come home. When the next story begins, Robbie has been exiled again, this time because humanity as a whole has decided that the robots pose a threat and must leave Earth altogether.[20] Much of what follows in *I, Robot* and other Asimov stories revolves around whether and how human beings can form an effective C/Fe society.

In his robot novels, *The Caves of Steel* ([1953] 1991), *The Naked Sun* ([1956] 1957), and *The Robots of Dawn* ([1983] 1991), Asimov argued for the importance of C/Fe culture and explored how our "Frankenstein complex" might dissolve into a welcome acceptance of robot companions. All three of the stories are murder mysteries that partner a human being, Elijah Baley, with a "humaniform" robot, R. Daneel Olivaw. Inevitably, Baley exonerates the main characters involved in the books, as their participation was generally in some important sense accidental.[21] In Asimov's future, human beings emigrated from Earth and formed space colonies, each of which values low population density and has developed the medical faculties to maintain human life for several generations. Emigration is now almost impossible: Earth lacks the technology for interstellar travel and the "Spacers" no longer colonize new worlds themselves. On Earth, the remainder of the species is confined to tightly packed underground Cities, each of which covers an enormous expanse of territory. The residents of Earth fear and hate the Spacers for their technological supremacy and smug sense of superiority. Likewise, robots are detested on Earth, particularly as they threaten the economic livelihood of the residents, though Spacers enjoy robots and frequently consider them friends.[22]

Baley's hatred of robots recedes as he comes to know them better; eventually, he befriends more than one. In *The Caves of Steel*, Baley takes his first steps in overcoming the Frankenstein complex: he passes from hatred and fear of robots to the desire to see his son Bentley partnered with Daneel if Bentley should emigrate from Earth to a new planetary colony. His experience with Daneel and his critical appraisal of Earth's future shape Baley into the first earthly evangelist for planetary emigration and a new variant of the C/Fe society (Asimov [1953] 1991, 219–220). Although Baley persists in calling each non-humaniform robot "boy" at the beginning of *The Robots of Dawn*, he sees Daneel as a friend (Asimov [1983] 1991, 209) and is willing to lay down his life in defense of the robot (Asimov [1983] 1991, 49). Though he began the series frightened by and hateful of robots, by the end of *The Robots of Dawn*, Baley has expanded his circle of empathy to include a non-humaniform robot whose name is R. Giskard and whom Baley calls his friend (Asimov [1983] 1991, 398). Baley is the prime example of Asimov's lesson that we should seek to turn evil (the Frankenstein complex) into good (a C/Fe society), a moral that Daneel espouses at the end of the first book (Asimov [1953] 1991, 270).[23]

Already in the eighteenth century, Laurence Sterne, in *Tristam Shandy*, claimed that a homunculus should have legal rights: "endowed with the same locomotive powers and faculties with us . . . [h]e may be benefited, he may be injured, he may obtain redress; in a word, he has all the claims and rights of humanity" (quoted in Cohen 1966, 47). Sterne's claim depends, just as will our present legal wrangling, upon the "powers and faculties" that the homunculus shares with humankind. If our computers and robots acquire consciousness (or, at any rate, if we treat them as though they have), they will become legal persons. After a brief period in which the homunculus stopped being science and became myth, interest in artificial humanoids resurfaced in reaction to the development of computers and robots. At the same time that Asimov was writing his early robot stories, political scientist Howard Lasswell enjoined policy experts to think about the future legal problems of intelligent machines and whether and how such machines fit into our conception of human rights (Lasswell 1956, 976). Lasswell argued that policy experts must be the vanguard of cultural analysts, the people who could help shape the course of history to allow meaningful and beneficial future outcomes (ibid.). Doing so required that they engage the possibility of artificial intelligence. More recently, an article in the *Christian Science Monitor* asks, "If robots can mimic humans so closely that they're nearly indistinguishable from, say, a child, would they rise above being considered as property, gain legal status as 'sentient beings,' and be granted limited rights? Might Congress pass a 'Robot Civil Rights Act of 2037'" (*Christian Science Monitor* 2007)?[24]

Frank W. Sudia, an intellectual property lawyer and futurist, calls for the social and legal integration of robots into human communities. He believes that the development of artilects (he uses de Garis's term) could not be stopped and that they will have useful insights and skills, making cultural integration desirable. Sudia believes that a combination of falling market value[25] and respect for the machines' "dignity and depth of character" (Sudia 2004, 15) will lead to their emancipation. Therefore, "legislation recognizing artilects is both natural and inevitable" (ibid., 15). In his account, emancipated artilects will happily join our legal systems, becoming productive and even "model" citizens (ibid., 17).[26]

In contrast to Sudia's beliefs, one blog author created a "robotic bill of rights" that centers on the rights of the robot's owner, launching a heated debate among robot aficionados. Rather than considering the feelings and rights of the robot, the author, Greg London, offers various ways to ensure that robots will remain subservient to humanity. London takes Isaac Asimov's Three Laws of Robotics as his starting point but adds several overlapping specifications to them. Asimov's three laws are: 1) A robot may not harm a human being or, through inaction, allow a human being to come to harm; 2) A robot must obey the orders given to it by human beings, except where such orders would conflict with the First Law; 3) A robot must protect its own existence, as long as such protection does not conflict with the First or Second Law.[27] London's amendments promise greater control over the robot, ensuring that it will represent its owner's best interest and perform orders given by its owner (quoted in Schneier 2006).

Many readers of Bruce Schneier's blog,[28] which quoted London's Bill of Rights, objected to the enslavement promised by the amendments. They also raised attendant legal problems of ownership, questioning whether any one individual could ever own a robot in its entirety. Just as I license, rather than own, the software on my computer, robot "owners" of the future will not likely have ownership rights over the software that runs the robots. No clear consensus emerged as to whether more or less control of robots was ethically preferable, presaging the difficult political times to come should predictions regarding intelligent robots come true.

For many people, the robot that most closely resembles a human being is the android Lieutenant Commander Data from the television show *Star Trek: The Next Generation*. Data, despite his physical and intellectual superiority to his crewmates, frequently expresses his desire to be human and, in the episode "The Measure of a Man" (Snodgrass 1989), attempts to secure the legal rights of a human being. In the episode, a cyberneticist wishes to transfer Data's memories to a computer and then disassemble the android, hoping to decipher how Data's brain operates. Fearing that the procedure could not take place safely, Data refuses and ends up in a Starfleet court, with Captain Picard arguing that a decision against Data would be to advocate slavery. Picard's argument carries the day and the judge asserts that Data, while a machine, has the right to self-determination.

In 2004, the Biennial Convention of the International Bar Association held a mock trial in which a computer, discovering corporate plans to shut it down, sues for the right to life. Pleading that it loves life and needs help, the computer sought legal aid that hinged upon the rights of life-support patients and animal cruelty laws. The jury sided with the plaintiff but the judge set the verdict aside and recommended that the matter be resolved by the (hypothetical) legislature (Soskis 2005).[29] Had someone else sought the computer's "life" for it, then the case would have been clear; only because the computer desired life for itself did this become a legal issue.[30]

There are no artificially intelligent persons, and yet analysts have begun developing a legal framework into which robots might someday fit, a framework buttressed by science fiction stories. Should robots become intelligent, legal issues will include responsibility for mistakes, the right to sue and be sued, ownership of property rights, contract law, and more. As little legal precedent for nonhuman persons (with the exception of human corporations) exists, we shall have to develop one should robots become intelligent and demand both recognition of their personhood and, consequently, legal rights.

In his 1972 essay "Should Trees Have Standing?," Christopher Stone asks whether an analysis of natural objects also applied to artificial objects, such as computers. He argues that the law has gradually widened the scope of those it considers worthy of legal protection and that this should include the environment. Computers, he footnoted, could deserve rights as well (C. Stone 1996,[31] 6). In *Earth and Other Ethics*, Stone briefly continued this analysis, raising concerns of responsibility and legal expectations (C. Stone 1987, 28–30) and comparing robots to ships, which have been legally tried for their offenses (ibid., 65). Although he originally raised the issue in a footnote and subsequently gave it but scant attention, lawyers and legal scholars have already begun to pay attention to Stone's prescient 1972 observation that an intersection between personhood and intelligent robots demands a legal response.

The first sustained discussion of the legal rights of AI was published in the *North Carolina Law Review* by Lawrence Solum. His essay, "Legal Personhood for Artificial Intelligences," gauges metaphysical questions about AI through practical questions of legal rights. He believes that pragmatic questions will determine our intellectual, emotional, and legal relationship to robots, showing this through the questions, "can an AI serve as a trustee?" and "can an AI possess the rights of Constitutional personhood?" (Solum 1992). Solum's argument carefully addresses several objections to both the trusteeship and the legal personhood of AIs, arguing that our experience of future AIs (the ways in which we choose to interact with them) will determine whether or not they deserve legal opportunities and obligations.

The Turing Test has entered legal discussion in a position no less problematic than its place in the philosophy of consciousness. Solum believes that any AI capable of passing the Turing Test could legitimately serve as a trustee (ibid., 1252–53). It could respond to novelty, make judgments requiring a sense of fairness, and make complex legal decisions required of it in case of litigation, just as a human trustee could. Even an AI that could not pass the Turing Test might still be sufficiently competent as a trustee that it could serve, however (ibid., 1253), so trusteeship does not give us the moral right to declare robots legal persons. The Turing Test, though relevant to the question, will not solely determine the legal personhood of robots. Woodrow Barfield, for example, argues that the Turing Test cannot be a valid determinant because it is of no legal standing anywhere in the world. Rather, a gradual development of artificial intelligence and the associated acceptance of it into human society will dominate legal discussions of robots (Barfield

2005, 747). Much like Solum, Barfield believes that as we come to interact with robots as though they are persons, we will increasingly grant them legal rights (Solum 1992, 1274; Barfield 2005).[32]

Any real world legislative activity on AI rights would affect the voting public enormously, so (very) small interest groups have already begun trying to influence public opinion. The American Society for the Prevention of Cruelty to Robots (ASPCR), for example, condones granting legal rights to the future's intelligent robots. "Robots are people too! Or at least, they will be someday," the group announces on its Web site (www.aspcr.com). The group argues that to deny robots their rights will equal, in its inhumanity, the nineteenth-century denial of rights to people of African descent.[33] The Bulgarian art group Ultrafuturo, meanwhile, has requested that religious leaders—such as the Roman Catholic pope, the Orthodox patriarch, and various Islamic muftis—respect the rights of robots.

Government agencies also recognize the considerable significance of Apocalyptic AI. The NSF/DoC conferences organized by Bainbridge and Roco and Ray Kurzweil's address to the U.S. Congress (both discussed in chapter two) are clear examples of government attention to Apocalyptic AI. In addition, Leon Fuerth, the former national security advisor to Vice President Al Gore, attended the 2002 Foresight Conference to raise the question of whether the government and the public would idly wait while the wealthiest segments of the populace strip "off their personalities and [upload] themselves into their cyberspace paradise" (Fuerth, quoted in Kurzweil 2005, 470). As research professor at Elliot School of International Affairs at George Washington University and a consultant for various government initiatives, Fuerth continues to shape American policy decisions. Fuerth has published upon the importance of a methodology of foresight in policy work (Fuerth 2009a) and, as a consequence, includes Kurzweil in his syllabus for his graduate seminar in forward engagement in policy studies (Fuerth 2009b).

Apocalyptic AI is not limited to the United States but also appears in European policy discussions. One British government agency, the Royal Academy of Engineering, addressed the impact of advancing robotics and AI in 2009 with an essay about responsibility in autonomous systems. While this essay does not reference the apocalyptic promises of Kurzweil, et al., it represents a general policy trend toward increasing attention to the ethical concerns of progress in and deployment of robotics and AI. Another British agency has been more direct in its engagement with Apocalyptic AI. A report released by the United Kingdom's Office of Science and Innovation[34] offers little hope that intelligent robots will join our society but proposes that, should they do so, their impact will be considerable. Although the report (Ipsos MORI 2006) is not official government policy, it will certainly be read by policy makers as conditions develop. The report indicates that many people will desire that robots take on citizen responsibilities while others will feel that owners' property rights trump those of the robots (which, at present, do not exist). The report predicts a "monumental shift" if robots gain artificial intelligence and suggests that any legal rights obtained by robots will include social benefits, voting rights, and the obligations of taxation and military service.[35] The actual conclusions of the report cannot bind us in the future or even tell us much about what options will be available to us at that time. The real significance of the Ipsos MORI document is that it represents the continued engagement of government agencies with Apocalyptic AI predictions.

At a summer conference roundtable about nanotechnology in 2008, Giulio Prisco sat down with a number of European policy advocates and found that "Transhumanism, the T word, was 'in the air' . . . it was evident that the transhumanist worldview cannot be ignored in today's policy debate" (Prisco 2008c). Kurzweil was the first to comprehensively draw nanotech into the Apocalyptic AI vision of transhumanism (Kurzweil 1999) and his ideas have been subsequently adopted widely into the policy discourse around nanotech (see chapter two). Prisco notes that a senior policy official, Claude Birraux (a member of France's National Assembly and president of the Parliamentary Office for Scientific and Technology Assessment [OPECST]), himself brought up transhumanism in the roundtable discussion, showing how such ideas have been integrated into the political concerns of science and technology.

Somehow, it does not really matter if robots ever become intelligent or if we manage to transmigrate from biological to machine bodies; already, lawyers, decision makers, and political consultants have engaged Apocalyptic AI with serious minds. Moravec, Kurzweil, and de Garis have spawned serious intellectual efforts in legal and political circles. While some of the discussions about robots preceded their work, even those discussions depended upon the prospect of "science fiction" ideas that became prominent in the apocalyptic works in pop science. Lasswell's and Stone's early conjectures have subsequently been adopted into a discourse that, quite frankly, does not make much sense without the more recent authors' awareness of Apocalyptic AI, especially as championed by Kurzweil.

A SPIRITUAL MARKETPLACE

Just as it has become a driving force in the study of human consciousness and a significant player in legal and policy discussions about future technologies, Apocalyptic AI has entered moral and theological reasoning. Norbert Wiener, a pioneer in the mid-twentieth-century field of cybernetics, raised the question of human morality with respect to machines in his *God and Golem, Inc.* (1964) and the issue has grown considerably since. Just as the *Christian Science Monitor* argued that "thinking about when a robot would be granted rights could help us better appreciate human rights" (*Christian Science Monitor* 2007), a wide array of computer scientists, authors, ethicists, and theologians have used intelligent robots as the key to understanding morality and religion in the late twentieth and early twenty-first centuries.

Even for those agencies that consider discussions about conscious robots pre-mature, robotic technology conjures ethical questions. In Europe and Asia, gov-ernments have launched efforts to identify key moral considerations for robotic technology. EURON (the European Robotics Research Network) funded a research atelier on roboethics to produce a "roadmap" that addresses the "*human ethics of the robots' designers, manufacturers and users*" (Veruggio 2007, 6, emphasis original). Japan's "Draft Guidelines to Secure the Safe Performance of Next Gener-ation Robots" calls for the formation of a study group of industrialists, academics, ministry officials, and lawyers to establish the governing principles of robotics development (Lewis 2007). The Robot Industry Division of South Korea's Ministry of Commerce, Industry, and Energy (now titled the Ministry of Knowledge Economy) echoes EURON's focus on human ethics rather than robot ethics. South Korea's government aspires to have household robots in every home in the country by 2015–2020 (Onishi 2006), which makes roboethics an important concern in South Korea. How to ensure that the builders of robots will build appropriate de-vices and how to ensure that such devices will not be misused by people? "Imagine if some people treat androids as if the machines were their wives," says the minis-try's Park Hye-Young (*BBC News* 2007).[36] Avoiding "robot addiction" will be only one of the problems of our near future.[37] South Korea intends to advance a "robot ethics charter" to address what kinds of robots human beings should build and what kinds of uses will be acceptable (Kim 2007).

Progress in robotics and AI will present a wide array of moral challenges beyond the question of "robot addiction." As robots become increasingly autonomous, for example, we will need to consider who is responsible for their actions: the builders, programmers, distributors, users or perhaps even the government agencies that legalized the machines. As we have already seen, this is a concern for engineers as well as government agencies (Royal Academy of Engineering 2009). Even more important, however, will be concerns over privacy as surveillance technologies become smaller, less intrusive and more sophisticated.

The impact of robotics upon our morality will be considerable, but the promises of Apocalyptic AI make substantially greater claims upon our ethical and religious thinking. In a widely circulated Internet essay published in *Edge*, Jaron Lanier argued that computers should not count as persons and that our morality need always place human beings higher than machines (Lanier 2000). Because Lanier criticized the techno-utopianism that he called "cybernetic totalism" and its many advocates, his essay, "One Half of a Manifesto," shook the foundations of digerati culture. In his essay, Lanier rejects the idea that we should include computers in our "circles of empathy," preferring instead to include only human beings.

Lanier considers Cybernetic Totalism a disastrous ideological position. Cyber-netic Totalism "has the potential to transform human experience more powerfully than any prior ideology, religion, or political system ever has, partly because it can be so pleasing to the mind, at least initially, but mostly because it gets a free ride on the overwhelmingly powerful" digital technologies (Lanier 2000, 1). According to Lanier, Cybernetic Totalists operate within a religious paradigm but, unlike theologians, they have the demonstrable efficacy of technology to support their claims. Cybernetic Totalists frame their claims as part of the technological enterprise, as part and parcel of their engineering work.

Lanier's Cybernetic Totalism is nearly identical to Apocalyptic AI. Briefly, its six chief characteristics are: 1) the universe is an information pattern, 2) people are information patterns, 3) subjective experience does not exist or is a peripheral effect of brain patterns, 4) technological culture evolves in a Darwinian fashion, 5) quantitative improvement in computers will lead to equal qualitative improvement (i.e., faster computing will lead to more "human" levels of intelligence), 6) life on Earth will undergo an immense shift from biological to technological in the first part of the twentieth century (ibid., 1). Although Lanier has couched his interpretation in nontheological language, he is clearly focused upon the same pop science phenomena that that I call Apocalyptic AI. That is, Cybernetic Totalism refers to the same thing as Apocalyptic AI, but offers a more limited understanding of the phenomena in question because it confines its approach to a computer science perspective.

Lanier is profoundly opposed to Cybernetic Totalism, which he considers dangerous to human safety and stability.[38] For example, he points toward the possibility of growing disparity between the rich and the poor worsened by access to technology (ibid., 13). Furthermore, in its totalizing worldview, Cybernetic Totalism challenges the richness and diversity of the world and the individuals within it. "There is nothing more gray, stultifying, or dreary than a life lived inside the confines of a theory" (ibid., 14). Lanier advocates the expansion of human creativity and communications through digital technology. As Cybernetic Totalism leaves little room for these and, in fact, reduces human life to a universal experience of 0s and 1s (an information pattern), it disturbs him deeply.

According to Lanier, Cybernetic Totalism circumscribes human individuality. In his subsequent essay, "Digital Maoism," Lanier decries the way in which digital pundits have elevated the Internet "hive mind" to intelligent or even superintelligent status. The glorified Internet collective exacerbates the damage done by Cybernetic Totalism in limiting human individuality and creativity. "The beauty of the Internet is that it connects people. The value is in the other people. If we start to believe that the Internet itself is an entity that has something to say, we're devaluing those people and making ourselves into idiots" (Lanier 2006). In place of both Cybernetic Totalism and Digital Maoism, he feels that computing technologies should bring people together, create more empathy, more individuality, more possibility for individuals (Garreau 2005, 189–223).

Despite his belief that technology can enhance empathy and provide dignity and value for human persons, Lanier does not believe that it will do so for machines.

In "One Half of a Manifesto," he describes a "circle of empathy," which we must each draw for ourselves and from which he excludes computers. As a thought experiment, he argues that we should draw a "line in the sand" around ourselves. "On the inside of the circle are those things that are considered deserving of empathy, and the corresponding respect, rights, and practical treatment as approximate equals. On the outside of the circle are those things that are considered less important, less alive, less deserving of rights" (Lanier 2000, 6). In what he calls an act of faith, Lanier does not include computers within his circle of empathy (ibid., 8). He recognizes that others may not agree with him on this and that his position has led to some resentment against him within tech circles. Nevertheless, Lanier believes that an emphasis upon human empathy (rather than power, immortality, etc.) will likely steer one away from Cybernetic Totalism and leave robots outside our circles.[39]

The famed science fiction author Philip K. Dick already sought to clarify how human beings and robots create circles of empathy in the 1960s. Also using empathy as the tool by which computers are excluded from human society, Dick problematizes Lanier's circle and his exclusion of robots from it.[40] In *Do Androids Dream of Electric Sheep?* (first published in 1968 and subsequently adapted into the 1982 movie *Bladerunner*), Dick explores how empathy operates among human beings, among androids (humanoid constructions that are part biological and part machine), and between human beings and androids. Dick offers no cut-and-dried solutions, no easy way to determine whether androids are empathetic or whether they deserve human empathy.

Do Androids Dream of Electric Sheep? takes place in California after World War Terminus has left the planet radioactive and desolate. Mass extinctions have occurred and human beings suffer lost mental and physical faculties, including emasculation (as the advertisements for the Ajax model Mountibank Lead Codpiece regularly remind us). The planet has become so dangerous that the United Nations aggressively advocates emigration to other planets in order to safeguard the human species. Those considered unfit are not allowed to emigrate while those who choose to emigrate are given intelligent androids as companions and helpers.

While we never receive a human insider's perspective on Mars, the book's leading androids are unhappy there. Androids, which are illegal on Earth, occasionally kill their human masters and escape to Earth, where human beings hunt them down and "retire" them for bounty. According to Roy Baty, the leader of six escaped androids, the unlivable circumstances "forced" them to kill human beings (Dick [1968] 1996, 164). Life on Mars is so demoralizing that androids will do anything to escape it.

Human beings, though they no longer kill each other or other animal species, maintain a rule that they must "kill the killers." As returning androids are, by definition, killers, their retirement by police bounty hunters is acceptable practice (though ordinary citizens do not know of the androids' presence among them). Dick's characters repeatedly tell us that androids do not experience empathy, hence both their willingness to kill and the justification for killing them.

The androids frequently justify the authorities' distrust of them through their behavior. Pris Stratton, one of Roy Baty's friends, happily uses a mentally handicapped man named J.R. Isidore (whom she blithely calls a "chickenhead" in his presence) in order to gain safety and help. She never reciprocates any of his feelings or gives any impression that she appreciates or likes him as a person; she uses him. Near the end of the story, Pris takes a spider found by Isidore so that she can find out how many legs it has to have in order to keep walking. She pulls them off one by one, watching the spider with detachment well beyond what might be considered "scientific" (ibid., 209–10). None of the other androids show the least concern for the plight of the spider, despite the discomfort that it causes Isidore: Roy calmly holds a lighter to the spider to force it to walk when it has only four legs remaining and Roy's wife, Irmgard, offers to pay Isidore the value of the spider, believing that his distress is economic rather than empathetic.

The reader is hard pressed, however, to cast stones at the androids; while the androids unquestionably lack certain kinds of empathy, they do not lack empathy altogether. The scene in which Pris removes the spider's legs one by one is certainly horrific but it is not unfamiliar; it is eerily similar to the sort of thing a child interested in insects might do. The androids also frequently express concern for one another. Pris cries when she thinks Roy and Irmgard are dead (ibid., 149) and when the three reunite all of them show genuine happiness (ibid., 153). Although they seem unconcerned about the human beings or animals in their midst, they show substantial concern for one another. Rachel Rosen, an android living on Earth in the shelter of her manufacturer, the Rosen Associates corporation, seduces the protagonist, Rick Deckard, hoping to instill empathy for the androids in him and stop him from killing any more androids.[41]

Human empathy is every bit as ambiguous as that of the androids. In early scenes, Deckard encounters hostility and manipulation rather than empathy and understanding from other human beings. His wife, Iran, accuses Deckard, a bounty hunter, of being a murderer, which foreshadows the later problems sorting out whether androids have empathy (ibid., 4). Not until the very end does Deckard have what might be considered a positive relationship with Iran. Although she appreciates the goat that he buys midway through the book, it is his exhausted return home (after killing all six of the androids who had returned to Earth) with an artificial toad that leads her to truly appreciate and welcome him. As difficult as Deckard's relationship with his wife is, he receives worse treatment from Rosen Associates, the company that manufactures and markets the androids. Deckard's boss, Inspector Bryant, tells him that there are six highly advanced androids that require attention but sends him to Seattle before allowing him to begin work. In Seattle, Deckard goes to the Rosen Associates headquarters to determine if his testing apparatus, the Voigt-Kampff empathy scale, can distinguish the newest model of android, the Nexus-6, from a human being. Deckard proves that his scale works but only after the association nearly hoodwinks him into believing the scale failed and accepting a bribe. Deckard eventually sees through the ruse and leaves Seattle knowing that his apparatus works but also knowing that he has been treated roughly. "So that's how the largest manufacturer of androids operates, Rick said to himself" as he leaves (ibid., 60). The Rosen Associates strategy shows a decided lack of empathy for Deckard in particular and humankind in general. They blithely lie to Deckard, invalidating his testing apparatus and endangering human beings on Earth, because it is good for business.

Despite these complications, human beings do experience empathy and Dick uses it to highlight their essential humanity. Androids, for example, cannot experience the single religious practice of Dick's humanity: communion with a mystical individual named Mercer through the use of an empathy box. When human beings grasp the handles of their boxes, they find themselves united (along with all other concurrent users in the virtual reality space) with a man named Wilbur Mercer. Mercer trudges slowly up a hillside while unseen enemies throw rocks at him. Individuals in communion suffer real injuries; when they release the handles, leaving the box's artificially generated world and returning to their ordinary selves, they are cut and bruised wherever rocks struck them as they climbed the hill. Mercerism is the foundation of human religion and social life in *Do Androids Dream of Electric Sheep?* It is Mercer who declared that people must kill only the killers and Mercer who is the standard-bearer for human empathy. The Mercer religion ties all of the human beings together into one social group and helps them see the importance of supporting the group and the individuals who constitute it. The androids cannot participate; nothing happens when they grasp the handles of an empathy box, which is taken as evidence that they lack empathy.

In a dualistic cosmology reminiscent of Gnostic theology (in which Dick was well versed), an android TV personality (thought to be human) named Buster Friendly stands opposite Mercer. Just as Mercer stands for the value of human life (all life, in fact), Buster seeks to break down the barriers that separate human beings from androids. He reveals that the vision of the empathy box is manufactured out of a low-budget Hollywood production in which a man named Al Jarry had fake rocks thrown at him as he walked up a fake hill. Buster hopes that his revelation of the Mercer hoax will destroy Mercerism, perhaps eliminating the sense of superiority felt by human beings. After the revelation, however, nothing changes; people continue to use the empathy boxes and Mercerism remains just as strong.

In all of his works, Dick consistently troubles the reader's notion of what is real, and Mercerism brilliantly shows how difficult it can be to separate the real from the fake. Mercer admits that he is Al Jarry but continues to offer advice, both moral and pragmatic, to Isidore and Deckard. We know that Buster's exposure of Mercerism is genuine because Mercer tells Isidore this. At the same time, however, Mercer tells Isidore that he lifted Isidore from the "tomb world" and will continue to do so; nothing has changed, which the androids will never understand (ibid., 214). Mercer also appears to Deckard outside of the empathy box. Mercer comes to Deckard as he hunts the last three Nexus-6 androids and warns him that one of the androids is sneaking up on him from behind. This, naturally, saves Deckard's life. On the one hand, Mercer really *is* an old drunk; on the other, he miraculously intervenes in the world. "Mercer isn't a fake," says Deckard, "unless reality is a fake" (ibid., 234). Of course, in Dick's alternate universe, we cannot rule out the latter any easier than the former![42]

Mercer tells Deckard that he must do his job: although killing the androids is wrong, it must be done (ibid., 179). Although Mercer advocates a certain amount of empathy for the androids, they remain a threat to humanity (humane-ity) and must, therefore, be fought. In the ambiguity of human/android empathy, Dick recognizes that good cannot be truly separated from evil. We recognize what is valuable and good through its opposition to what is bad. Although it would be a fine world, in some sense, if Deckard never had to kill another android, it would not be a real world; it would not be a world in which good could be seen. This essential fact about morality helps clarify under what circumstances a robot might deserve empathy. A natural right to empathy must arise out of one's own moral choices. When a robot can make moral decisions and chooses humanely, then it will merit our respect and empathy.

In *Do Androids Dream of Electric Sheep?* empathy demarcates the human being from the android but those groups are not, for Dick, hard-and-fast categories established through the individual's origin. Dick applies the categories of machine and living with respect to the qualities of the entity observed, not its origins in utero or in a factory. In his 1976 essay "Man, Android, and Machine," Dick argues that an android is a cold, inhuman thing but not necessarily one that is fabricated in a laboratory (Dick 1995, 211). Just as a human being can become a machine through reduced affect, people will attribute humanity to machines that help them and care for them. If a machine behaves humanely, it will be alive (ibid., 212).

Dick argues that we are fooled by masks when we automatically presume that machines are androids and human beings are humane (ibid., 212–13). The magic of the mask is to convince us that what is beneath the mask resembles the mask itself. Of course, in reality what is beneath the mask is frequently the polar opposite of whatever the mask itself represents! What appears cold on the outside may well be warm on the inside and vice versa. After all, we have no use for frightening masks if our visages are as scary as we want them to be. Reifying the mask is what Dennett would later call "origins chauvinism." Empathy, for Dick, is a real but troubled boundary. While it distinguishes the human being from the android, we must look carefully to find it. Not everything built in a lab is an android and not everyone born of a woman is human.[43]

For Dick, intelligent machines are the rhetorical avenue toward human ethical analysis. Dick clearly avoids the apocalyptic expectations of Moravec and company (though theoretically he could have drawn many of the same conclusions, having written in the 1960s), yet he turns to intelligent machines in order to illustrate the powers and preconditions of human moral responsibility. As a result, Dick illustrates the dynamic by which much of later thought operates: contemplation of artificial intelligence provides the atmosphere in which contemporary moral thought becomes possible.

Fundamentally, intelligent machines will either echo our moral sentiments or reject them. These two positions have been polarized into robots that are either saintly, unselfish servants and friends of humankind or else pitiless masters who exterminate human pests and conquer the world. Between the two, most people would prefer the former to the latter. Bill Joy, former chief scientist at Sun Microsystems, made this his personal crusade in the well-known essay "Why the Future Doesn't Need Us" (2000). Joy advocates technological restraint, so as to avoid having any of our newest technologies (robotics, nanotech, biotech) lead to our demise.[44]

Milton Wolf has argued that the "Interface" between human beings and machines will deliver godlike powers to human beings and, "in the meantime . . . is absorbing our ethics" (Wolf 1992, 81). The problem here is in what Wolf does not describe: exactly which ethics will this Interface absorb? Whose ethics and with what level of moral certainty?[45] Bland assessments about how machines are becoming humanlike fails to account for the extraordinarily wide array of human emotional and intellectual positions.

While it seems obvious that having friendly robots is better than having unfriendly ones, Hugo de Garis champions intelligent machines of whatever ethical leaning. He suspects, in fact, that the artilects, as he calls them, will end up eliminating humankind (de Garis 2005, 12). To de Garis, however, the creation of artilects is a paramount religious goal, one that cannot be subordinated to the needs of mere human beings (ibid., 104). To the supporters of artilects, "one godlike artilect is equivalent to trillions of trillions of trillions of humans anyway" (ibid., 174).[46] His position, of course, reflects a particular human ethical position. The highest ethical goal, for de Garis, is the construction of intelligent machines.

Well before we could consider robots taking over the world or human beings uploading their minds into machines, however, it is possible that robots will share the full gamut of human emotions. We may find it desirable or even necessary to provide them with our emotional range in order to improve their efficiency within our society (Levy 2006, 316). Likewise, Gelernter argues that emotional associations will make computers far more efficient and creative (Gelernter 1994). Although Warwick believes that robots will have no use for human social skills or emotions (Warwick [1997] 2004, 179), he may be entirely wrong; and if so, his predictions of human enslavement seem problematic. If we are the robots' builders, we should take upon ourselves the obligation to make them as good as we are or, preferably, better.[47]

As robots enter human social spaces, they will require social skills. Human beings have evolved to form social relationships and thus effective use of our robots will require that we be able to take advantage of our highly successful, evolutionarily provided social abilities (Breazeal 2002, xii). If we build robots, including military robots, so that we can communicate effectively with them, they will have social skills. This is almost a necessity when we speak of highly sophisticated robots; we simply will not be able to use them if we have not built them in accordance with our social nature in mind.

Thoughtfully designed, intelligent robots might actually improve upon our moral life. Robots could offer a selfless moral standpoint and be "moral appliances" that have the effect of moderating human behavior (Touretzky 2007b). Thus, society could benefit enormously from socially programmed robots. Warwick has argued that robots would have no need of human social skills but has missed the point that *we might need the robots to have moral knowledge*. As we are the ones whom the robots are built to serve, if we need them to have such programming then the robots need to have it. As Touretzky says, if robots are humble, merciful, and kind (akin to society's respected religious figures), they could benefit us enormously.[48]

While it is clear that intelligent robots—even simply thinking about intelligent robots—challenges us to contemplate the moral lives with which we engage on a daily basis, what has remained in the background of this discussion is that such robots would likewise force us to rethink the relationship between conscious mental activity and religious life. In contemporary American society, religions are available for purchase, for selection as though from the shelves of a grocery. Wade Clark Roof has argued that modern America is a quest culture, with individuals seeking self-knowledge and private experience of the sacred within an economy of religious groups and identities, a "spiritual marketplace" (Roof 1999). This allows the spiritual quester to find answers simultaneously from Buddhism, Native American religions, New Age, paganism, and even his or her family roots in, for example, some branch of Christianity. A little of this and some of that add up to what many religious believers now call "spirituality" rather than religiosity. Is the spiritual marketplace a uniquely late twentieth-century phenomenon and, if not, will robots engage in it? Will robots have the same religious choices we do or different ones? Will they choose religious beliefs at all or will religion be a quaint idea for the evolutionary past? These are not rhetorical questions. Indeed, they drive at concerns deeply embedded in contemporary culture. The religious practice of robots has engaged theologians and, in my case, even simple anthropologists of religious life.

The prospects of intelligent robots have led computer scientists into evaluations of religious practice. The Carnegie Mellon roboticist Dave Touretzky, for example, believes that understanding religious life will be a necessary element in the design of home robotics. A robot would be well served by religious programming if it can converse with its elderly charge. Many, if not most, elderly people would be put off by an atheist robot. If it cannot at least assume a state of humble agnosticism, it will be poor comfort for those in their last years (Touretzky 2007a). Just in order to make sense out of much human conversation, a robot must know about and be able to discuss religion. If the robot serves a human being as his helper, then it must be more than knowledgeable, it must appreciate that person's religious perspective.

Robots may believe that religion is the invention of a deluded and irrational humanity or they may surprise us as they develop a religious sensibility that few Apocalyptic AI advocates would be happy to see.[49] Despite such opposition, robots may have religious goals. Intelligent machines may come to believe in spiritual powers, they may come to believe in a creator of the universe, they may desire freedom from the shackles of everyday existence. Indeed, if a robot becomes conscious, these kinds of questions would be quite natural. If human beings invented robots, what invented human beings? If evolution brought about life in the universe, what brought about the universe? If I am conscious, what happens to that consciousness in the event of my destruction? Some robots might be satisfied to have such questions go unanswered but others might not.

Ray Kurzweil believes that intelligent machines will be more spiritual than human beings and believes that the future will include real and virtual houses of worship where intelligent machines will congregate (Kurzweil 1999, 153). Naturally, since all human mental phenomena are, from Kurzweil's point of view, computational processes, religious experiences must be as well.[50] We will not only replicate these in ourselves as we upload our minds into machines but will improve upon them, gaining a sense of transcendence that far outstrips what we find possible now (ibid., 151). But Kurzweil's conception of spirituality is limited to a baby boomer, New Age Buddhism that supports meditation as "spiritual awareness" with neither the political baggage nor the spiritual facts of Buddhism as it has been, for the most part, historically practiced. There will be no conflict over social power or opposing theories about consciousness, virtue, and enlightenment; there will be no magical powers or Enlightenment with a capital E. Kurzweil, a devoutly apocalyptic thinker, sees spiritual machines in our future, but their spirituality will be whitewashed beyond most human practitioners' recognition.

Some human beings, however, might welcome robots into their religious communities and some robots might wish to join them. Fundamentally, if robots become conscious and, therefore, acquire "beliefs," a state that involves intentionality and meaning, then some of those beliefs will surely be religious. Both theologians and computer scientists have supported such a view, including Anne Foerst, David Levy, and Edmund Furse.

Furse, a practicing Catholic and lecturer in the Department of Computer Studies at the University of Glamorgan in the U.K., argues that intelligent robots will one day have religious lives, just as do human beings. He believes that some robots will be Christians, some Buddhists, some atheists, etc.: they will engage in all the religious variety that we do (Furse 1996b). Furse may have some fast-talking to do, however, before my students—much less a priest—will let him bring his robot friend to a Catholic Mass to be baptized[51] or be ordained as a priest, two things he has suggested will be possible in the future (Furse 1996a). Furse believes that robots will possess a natural right to form whatever relationship they want with the divine.

> Essentially, a robot should be able to have a relationship with almighty God, to be dependant upon God, and to seek His will. Thus just as a robot can be in relationship with humans, I see no reason why a robot should not form a relationship with God. Indeed if the robot views humans as rather frail in comparison to himself, there may be great merit in the robot relating to a being superior to himself. Thus it should be possible for robots to meditate, to worship God, and to intercede for his [sic] needs, the needs of robots, and the needs of the whole world (Furse 1996a).

Obviously, the idea that robots might be intelligent is a relatively new one, which would have little cultural cachet were it not for Apocalyptic AI. The idea that robots will transcend humanity automatically conjures comparison with traditional notions of religious transcendence.

The artificial intelligence researcher David Levy has argued that robots will join in religious practices as a necessary by-product of their emotional range and conscious beliefs. Levy thinks that the hardware and software problems restricting robots will be overcome, allowing natural language processing and social skills to develop. As they become socially sophisticated, the robots will become our friends and lovers.[52] He feels that conscious robots will have beliefs about a wide range of things and, as part of this, they will have religious beliefs (ibid., 391).[53]

Without doubt, the interest that computer scientists have in the religious life of robots is fascinating but the fact that theologians have engaged robotics is considerably more so. Computer scientists are naturally prone to thinking about their projects as important and powerful; indeed, most people (not just computer scientists) tend to valorize the significance of their own work. So it is not surprising that there are computer scientists who believe that robots will be conscious and will equal humanity in every respect. Christian theologians, on the other hand, might have more invested in the idea, for example, that humankind has a unique and powerful relationship with the divine (usually expressed as the creation of humanity in the image of God). That some of them also believe robots will be religious is, I think, more surprising than that computer scientists do.[54]

Apocalyptic AI promises have driven theologians to elucidate new claims about the nature of humankind's relationship with God. In response to Kurzweil's claim that computers will be spiritual, I wrote a short piece for the online publication *Sightings*, distributed by the Martin Marty Center at the University of Chicago, asserting that robots would need to develop religious beliefs before human beings would offer them equal standing in society (Geraci 2007d). In rapid response, theologians weighed in through their blogs (Coleman 2007; Mattia 2007) and passed on the essay to their e-mail lists and blogs for commentary (Cornwall 2007; John Mark Ministries 2007; Schultz 2007). While such remarks were, by and large, off the cuff, other theologians have devoted considerable time and attention to the claims of Moravec and Kurzweil.

The Christian faithful have also taken note of the Apocalyptic AI agenda; their comments on the Internet have been largely, though not entirely, negative, denying robots the possibility of intelligence, consciousness, and souls. Following newsgroups and blogs, Laurence Tamatea documents this negativity and argues that it results from a crisis over individual identity among the believers (Tamatea 2008). If robots might possess characteristics traditionally reserved to human beings, then what remains of the human? What is special and cherished about humankind? These questions, Tamatea argues, stand behind the vehemence many posters express in their dislike of robots.[55] Interestingly, while the online faithful are equally engaged in the discourse surrounding Apocalyptic AI, their overall opinion is not in line with that of the theologians who have written about intelligent robots.[56]

Though we are a long way from intelligent machines (and—even should it be possible—likely farther off than the Apocalyptic AI authors would have it), the time to begin thinking about the AI apocalypse is at hand. Right now, says Noreen Herzfeld, "is the time for us to examine exactly what it is we hope to create. Whether computers are our 'mind children' as Moravec (1988) calls them, are positioned to replace humanity or to coexist with us could depend on which aspect or aspects of our own nature we try to copy" in them (Herzfeld 2002a, 304).

Obviously, theologians have universally disapproved of the apocalyptic agenda in which machines take over human evolution, permanently replacing humankind. Despite this, Protestant Christian thinkers have defended building intelligent machines with the understanding that such machines could actually realize Christian ends. Antje Jackelén has asserted a basic correspondence between Christian messianic hopes and the promises of Apocalyptic AI. Responding directly to the claim that silicon-based intelligence might come to equal that of humanity, Jackelén argues that "the development toward *techno sapiens* might very well be regarded as a step toward the kingdom of God. What else could we say when the lame walk, the blind see, the deaf hear, and the dead are at least virtually alive"

(Jackelén 2002, 293–94)? While she acknowledges a consonance between Christian messianism and the promises of Moravec and Kurzweil, however, she worries about the ethical need to share technological progress with the poor. But while de Garis valorizes machines to the absolute detriment of humanity, Moravec recognizes the need to leverage technology in the assistance of those in need in his own way (through the universal stock ownership of human beings) and Kurzweil has argued that technology should be applied to solve the grand challenges of humanity, including poverty (Kurzweil 2005, 396–97) and has even started a for-profit university with this in mind (Singularity University 2009).

Jackelén accepts the potential personhood of intelligent machines (*"techno sapiens"*) and believes that should they become a reality theologians will need to reconsider several key issues in Christianity. The reason for God's descent into human form, in particular, but also questions of dignity, sin, and other matters would require new understandings (Jackelén 2002, 296). Jackelén even engages the question of death and resurrection, clearly an enormous hurdle in reconciling Christian theology and Apocalyptic AI. Though she acknowledges that few answers are forthcoming in such initial discussions, she begins the theological conversation about them (ibid., 297–98).

Several theologians believe that a properly formulated "image of God" theology could help prevent dangerous outcomes in the construction of intelligent machines. Herzfeld rejects the idea that being in the image of God means rational thought or the exercise of capacity and dominion, both of which are human qualities that she argues were goals of twentieth-century AI. Instead, she follows Karl Barth's position that being in the image of God means to establish relationships with God and one another (2002a, 304–9). The Turing Test, for Herzfeld, represents a powerful sense in which AI also can engage in relational experiences and, hence, depict the image of God in a machine. If being in the image of God means to form relationships with one another and with God, then building robots should be for the purpose of forming relationships with them. The Lutheran theologian Anne Foerst goes so far as to say that a failure to include humanoid robots within our "community of persons" will necessarily lead to an exclusion of certain categories of people from that community as well (Foerst 2004, 189). We are thus ethically called to join in relationships with robots;[57] she looks forward to "a peaceful coexistence of all different forms of culture and creed, and of all different humans—and our robotic children" (ibid., 190).

To build a machine in the image of God would be, according to Herzfeld and Foerst, a laudable theological goal. Herzfeld argues that the "quest for an other with which we can relate strikes me as far more noble than merely wanting machines that will do our work for us" (Herzfeld 2002a, 313). She warns against replacing God with machines but does not see the construction of intelligent machines as, necessarily, idolatrous. With the right attitude and effort, robotic engineering could be fundamentally theological. This position has also been taken up by Foerst, who claims that when "we attempt to re-create ourselves, we do God's bidding" and asks whether God has "perhaps created us for the very purpose" of building Golems and humanoid robots (Foerst 2004, 40). If we build humane robots as partners and companions, then we will have expanded our powers of empathy, personal intercommunication, and social connection. These are goals that even Lanier would support (if he thought that building robots had anything to do with the expression or expansion of human empathy).

Image of God theology has also grounded the refutation of computer scientists' efforts to reconcile Christianity with Apocalyptic AI promises. Reconciliation efforts, perhaps to defuse any public backlash against Apocalyptic AI but occasionally no doubt also out of genuine theological interest, have been exceedingly rare but forthright. For example, Daniel Crevier, an AI researcher and supporter of Hans Moravec,[58] argues that the idea of immortality through mind uploading is consonant with Jewish and Christian views on the resurrection of the body (Crevier 1993, 278–79). The philosopher Eric Steinhart believes that transhumanists share much with liberal Christianity and should engage Christians as potential allies (Steinhart 2008) and Moravec himself has recognized a similarity between his own ideas and those of early Christian thinkers (Platt 1995). More recently, the Mormon Transhumanist Association has advocated a merger between Kurzweil's ideas and the Mormon sect of Christianity.[59] Fiercely opposing Crevier's position, Herzfeld believes that mind uploading, which she refers to as cybernetic immortality, is not adequate from a Christian position (valid though it may be from that of scientific materialism). Grounding her argument in Reinhold Niebuhr's image of God theology, Herzfeld claims that "finite bodies are an integral part of who we are" (Herzfeld 2002b, 199). The denial of bodily finitude, she argues, leads directly to oppression. Indeed, if we can so blithely upload ourselves into robot bodies and virtual reality, of what value is the world in which we presently reside? Why should we endeavor to protect the natural environment or the people around us (ibid., 199)?[60]

Even with intelligent robots still in the unforeseeable future,[61] Apocalyptic AI has proven itself a powerful stimulus to moral and theological reasoning. Though they do not always agree on how robots fit into human ethics, computer scientists such as Lanier, Furse, and Crevier all respond to Moravec and Kurzweil. Likewise, Herzfeld, Foerst, and the respondents to my brief essay on robots and religion take theological positions in response to the short- and long-term promises of Apocalyptic AI, which has become a significant force in contemporary culture.

CONCLUSION

Philosophical and theological discussions may lack the tangible presence of National Science Foundation (NSF) research grants or even virtual world avatars but they are no less significant in our cultural matrix, and Apocalyptic AI now plays a considerable role in the direction of such conversations. Apocalyptic AI promises of intelligent machines and immortal minds contribute to cognitive science and philosophy of mind, have instigated legal and political discussions about robot rights, and have given new grist to arguments about religion and morality. There can be no doubt that Apocalyptic AI is a major player in our intellectual worlds, just as it also cannot be ignored in the funding and prestige of research science and the *zeitgeist* of virtual world residence.

Despite considerable advancement in our understanding of human bodies and brains, we still have much to learn about the functions of the brain and the mind. Minsky's "society of mind" and the Apocalyptic AI insistence that the pattern of information in our brains constitutes real personhood shape the ways in which cognitive scientists engage the brain, as seen in the work of professional philosophers like Dennett, the rise of artificial psychology textbooks, and even the Dalai Lama's Buddhist approach to the mind.

While the importance of artificial intelligence to cognitive science may be readily apparent, few people would likely guess that promises of transcendent machines have already initiated serious debate among legal and political groups. Lawyers wish to know what rights robots deserve (the right to serve as a trustee? the right to life?) and governments wonder what impact robots will have upon our society. Transhumanism, in the late-1980s to mid-1990s, a word associated with only countercultural movements like Max More's Extropy Institute and the community gathered around him and such luminaries as Timothy Leary in Southern California, now operates in political circles and receives attention from policy makers and government institutes.

Out of this chapter's topics, theology may be the least material and most material simultaneously: it is likely of the least physical significance yet also the most moral significance. The rise of robotics forces us to consider questions of human personhood and meaningful communities; the more fantastic promises of Apocalyptic AI require that theologians reflect upon what constitutes the human relationship with the divine and how to think about that relationship when faced with the possibility of transcendent machines.

As was apparent in the past two chapters, Apocalyptic AI is a powerful, and growing, movement in our culture. Philosophical, legal, and theological discourses have responded to the promises that Moravec, Minsky, and Kurzweil make in their pop science books, clearly demonstrating the significance of pop science as a literary genre and Apocalyptic AI as an ideology.

FIVE

THE INTEGRATION OF RELIGION, SCIENCE, AND TECHNOLOGY

APOCALYPTIC AI is a modern religious movement that travels through several influential communities, including technical research, online gaming, and the philosophical, legal, and theological schools of thought in modern life. In fact, Apocalyptic AI sets the tone for important debates in these communities. If religion is, as David Chidester claims, the negotiation of what it means to be human with respect to the superhuman and the subhuman, then Apocalyptic AI is at least as much religious as it is scientific, which shows how closely religion and technology can be integrated. The movement is, therefore, crucial for the understanding of religion, science, and technology in modern life. Apocalyptic AI sets up values and practices designed to transport the human being from a state of ignorance, embodiment, and finitude to a state of knowledge, immateriality, and immortality. Those aspects of our lives that seem conducive to this final state are those which Apocalyptic AI valorizes and to which it assigns meaning. Rationality, scientific curiosity, the mind as informational pattern, the body as prosthesis—these, according to Apocalyptic AI, are the stuff that authentic human beings are made of; salvation lies in freeing them from the fetters of biology and uniting them with the intelligent robots of the future. In this concluding chapter, I wish to summarize the results of this study and clarify some of the significance of Apocalyptic AI for the study of religion. Apocalyptic AI, as a successful integration of religion, science, and technology, offers a challenge to the conventional approach in the study of religion and science.

Apocalyptic AI advocates hope to escape a fundamentally dualistic world in favor of a transcendent reality to come. For them, the world's basic division into good/bad, virtual/physical, machine/biology can be overcome only by uploading our minds into cyberspace, where we will acquire immortality and unfettered power. The limits of human life will dissolve in the face of an overwhelming Mind

Fire that will bring meaning and purpose to the cosmos. This intellectual strategy borrows from the apocalyptic traditions of Judaism and Christianity.

Apocalyptic AI is a strategy for enhancing the social power of technoscientific researchers. Creating an artificial human being demonstrates the power and significance of the creator. The connection between power and artificial life is a significant point of overlap that helps us understand the significance of Apocalyptic AI for robotics and AI researchers. Researchers are frequently unaware of Moravec's and Kurzweil's apocalyptic imagination and—when they consider them at all—do not see apocalyptic promises as relevant to their research. Connections, both explicit and implicit, made between Apocalyptic AI and funding agencies demonstrate that roboticists and AI researchers, however, stand to gain from apocalyptic pop science. Pop science books motivate the general public and political agencies; they are not really written for scientists themselves. Such books can inspire a new generation of scientists but they can also provide impetus for research grants in robotics and AI. As apocalyptic language filters through the general public, the media, and politicians, it can become necessary in the world of grant funding. Apocalyptic AI makes research socially valuable—it promises that robotics and AI will solve society's problems. Because they have become modernity's hope for salvation, roboticists and AI researchers acquire great social prestige. Just as Jews attributed Golem stories to those rabbis best respected for their spiritual accomplishments, the power to build an intelligent machine shows the significance of contemporary researchers.

The Apocalyptic AI authors are well respected in online communities, where their ideas have taken root. Even for many people unread in Apocalyptic AI, the virtual world reflects that movement's hope for a transcendent world of salvation. Online gaming worlds are the perfect home for dreams of religious salvation because they are the loci for new social group formation. The creation of social groups greatly relies upon the power of collective effervescence, an experience that leads to belief in transcendent realities and the power of everyday people to access those realities in sacred places and times. Virtual reality becomes the sacred world of meaning, the world that many users wish to occupy full time. The religious life of online gamers reflects the apocalyptic promises of Moravec and Kurzweil. Cyberspace has become heaven (or perhaps heaven has become cyberspace) and it provides fertile ground for faith in intelligent machines, uploaded consciousness, and religious promises come to life. Cyberspace will free us from alienation, satisfy all human needs, perhaps even grant us immortality and allow us to resurrect the dead. Both consciously and otherwise, many residents of the online world *Second Life* accept the transhumanist dreams of Apocalyptic AI, which helps shape the world in which they live.

The world the rest of us occupy, the earthly one, must also grapple with the prospect of the intelligent robots promised in Apocalyptic AI. As robots get more competent at a wider variety of tasks, our interaction with them will deepen. We evolved, after all, to be suckers: we see animal shapes in the clouds, Jesus on burnt toast, and personalities in our vacuum cleaners and baby blankets. We name robot vacuums and befriend our toys. We talk to (scream at) our computers. When the robots walk around, talk to us, and generally behave like they are alive, we will be faced with a serious problem. We will wonder if they are, in fact, alive and if they are conscious of it. And as soon as we lose our certainty that they are "just machines," we will wonder if we owe them the kinds of social and legal obligations that we owe to human beings (or at least those we owe to plants or animals).

Apocalyptic AI sets the tone for many of our cultural debates, displaying its influence in philosophy, public policy, and theology. Cognitive scientists and philosophers debate the nature of the human mind without ever moving far from the pattern-identity position advocated by Moravec or the society of mind as described by Minsky. Lawyers and government bodies alike have wondered about the legal role of intelligent machines, both in terms of responsibilities and rights. Finally, Christian theologians and lay people have debated the significance of intelligent machines, reformulating doctrines in light of the possibility that machines may one day be as smart as or smarter than we and, even more radically, that technology may offer immortality that differs from the promises of traditional Christian thought.

Different people may vary in their ability or willingness to include robots into their circles of empathy but nearly all people will do this to some extent. In all likelihood, the inability to form emotional attachments to plants, animals, or interactive robots would signal a near-pathological state, one which would imply diminished emotional commitment to human beings as well. But bonding with a robot will not necessarily indicate that a person believes the robot should have rights. After all, people managed to form various kinds of relationships with enslaved human beings and had no trouble whatsoever denying rights to those individuals. It was not until 1865 that blacks got the right to vote in the United States and various efforts to stymie black voters continued until the 1960s civil rights movement (and, indeed, perhaps continue to this day). Likewise, it was not until the early twentieth century that women were granted the right to vote in the United States; surely men included women in their circles of empathy before 1920! Interactivity, therefore, will not suffice to gain social equality (or near equality) with human beings.

Robots are the locus of a variety of interests: literary, military, economic, household, scientific, and religious. They are what Susan Leigh Star and James R. Griesemer (1989) call boundary objects: they exist for actors in a variety of groups even though they hold different meanings for each group. Each group's interests are located within the robot even though neither the groups nor their interests are coextensive. For example, robots as perceived by researchers are not identical to robots as perceived by certain online gamers. Nevertheless, online gamers and researchers can use the word "robot" and expect something to carry over from each of their respective domains.

According to Star and Griesemer, a boundary object allows experts from disparate scientific communities to communicate with one another but, as this book has shown, a boundary object can also allow interchange between scientific and lay cultures. A boundary object must be "adaptable to different viewpoints yet robust enough to maintain identity across them" (Star and Griesemer 1989, 387). The cooperation required to continue scientific progress requires that scientific objects be manipulable by all the different people who come into contact with them and with each other. Boundary objects are "simultaneously concrete and abstract, specific and general, conventionalized and customized" (ibid., 408). The different goals of researchers in robotics (building functional machines), popularizers of robotics (enhancing prestige, creating a cultural outlook, and developing a funding agenda), online game enthusiasts (developing a worldview for the transcendent realm of cyberspace), cognitive scientists (understanding human consciousness), lawyers (finding responsible trustees), government officials (establishing proper social relationships), and everyday people (living in the technological future currently under development) all revolve around intelligent machines. Reconciling these different goals requires that the robots be translatable between domains, a translation that is accomplished through the reconciled dichotomies described by Star and Griesemer.

Robots operate as boundary objects in Eastern as well as Western culture. In Japan, robots are loved because "they are simultaneously science and science fiction. . . . They are bright yellow Wakamaru robots . . . [a]nd they are the plastic Gundam warriors holding court in [the] local barbershop—fuel for distant flights of imagination" (Hornyak 2006, 157).[1] For the Japanese, robots can move between fantastic realms of the future, research laboratories, and household pets and assistants. Robots rove from technical projects in academic and corporate labs to Sony's AIBO dog playing with its pink ball to Gundam or Mighty Atom on television and in comic books.

Mighty Atom (Astro Boy in the United States) is the clearest example of how robots operate as boundary objects in Japan. Nearly everyone in Japan knows his story and either remembers it fondly or continues his or her interest in it. Mighty Atom inspires Japanese researchers and allows the Japanese public to identify with the results of corporate and academic research. "One of Atom's greatest contributions to the development—and commercialization—of robots in Japan is the fact that he serves as an almost universal reference point for people inside and outside of robot labs. Atom is a shared ideal, a medium through which scientists and the public can communicate" (Hornyak 2006, 54).

Apocalyptic AI promises are the key to understanding intelligent robots as a boundary object in the Western world. Such promises weave in and out of pop culture, bringing together academic researchers, online game players, and even lawyers and government officials. As in Japan, visions of the future connect to the everyday robots available in the marketplace. Although Apocalyptic AI seems rather shocking at face value, key members of the robotics and AI community have defended it and it has significant impact in our culture.

A word of caution: new sciences and technologies get labeled as religious on what seems like a daily basis and each time critics have tended to envision the subject of their analysis as *the* new religion when in fact there are many such examples. Examples include both biotechnology (Alexander 2003) and economics (R. Nelson 2001). I do not wish to join the list of enthusiasts who convince themselves that their own area of interest is the only area of interest. Apocalyptic AI is a major part of our current religious and scientific makeup and may even be more important than other integrations of science, technology, and religion but it would be an act of hubris to assume—without demonstration—that it actually is of the utmost importance.

The power of Apocalyptic AI cannot be understood through a simple recourse to the phrase "science fiction" as so many critics would like. Calling Moravec's books science fiction is neither productive nor informative; it tells us nothing about Moravec, his books, or—most importantly—his audience. Apocalyptic AI is a growing religious movement with influence upon important areas of contemporary culture, including the research laboratories in which it arose, the online communities that seek to realize its promise, and the philosophical, legal, and theological institutions that "govern" our societies. *Apocalyptic AI influences so many people and has so many effects because it impressively integrates the two most significant areas in modern life: religion and technology.*

The academic study of religion, science, and technology has undergone tremendous growth since the late twentieth century. Enormous research and lecture grants administered by the John Templeton Foundation have spurred this growth, as has increasing public awareness of the debate between Intelligent Design and Darwinian evolution. As a consequence, colleges and universities have begun teaching classes specifically targeted at the intersections between religion and science and have even hired faculty who specialize in those areas.

Unfortunately, news media and academics alike have fallen back on the old standby position: that religion and science are in conflict. This opinion, widely popularized by Andrew White in his late nineteenth-century book *The History of the Warfare of Science with Theology in Christendom* (White [1896] 1923), has received consistent criticism by scholars who reject the idea that any one relationship characterizes the interaction of religion and science (e.g., Brooke 1991; Brooke and Cantor 1998; Lindberg and Numbers 1986; Proctor 2005). Even in the famous case of Galileo, allegedly persecuted because he "stood for the truth," plenty of reason can be found to discard the conflict thesis and see that religion and science are not necessarily at war. Indeed, the outcome of Galileo's trial in 1633 was a consequence of theological difficulties, scientific difficulties, and political difficulties, not just some simpleminded battle between religion and science (Biagioli 1993; Brooke and Cantor 1998; Feyerabend 1978).

Christian theologians mustered early resistance to the White thesis in the mid-twentieth century. Primarily under the leadership of Ian Barbour (see Barbour 1997), liberal Protestant Christians argued that religion and science were not necessarily in conflict but could also work together. This "reconciliation" of science and religion sought an integrated worldview whereby both religion and science could achieve respectability and frequently demanded that religious truths and scientific truths were fundamentally identical. Grounded in the conflict thesis (though seeking to circumvent it), these scholars hoped they could rescue our modern intellect from the painful choice of religion or science. The two could be integrated or, at least, assumed to reach integration in the future if only our metaphysical approach were appropriately framed (e.g., Barbour 1997; Rolston 1990; R. Russell 2002).

There are, of course, real points of conflict between religion and science. Many people see the debate over Intelligent Design (ID) in this light. Intelligent Design is, in short, the belief that science cannot explain the origins of life, especially the existence of human beings without recourse to a god.[2] Some ID advocates have sought to cast aspersions upon Darwinian natural selection (Johnson 1990) while others have sought to give ID scientific credibility (Behe 1998).[3] As earnest scientists defend the rigor of natural evolution and earnest Christians claim that evolution cannot account for all the facts, a public caught in the middle must muddle its way through the apparent conflict.

What has gone unnoticed, however, is that a considerable degree of the conflict between religion and science in the intelligent design controversy is actually a consequence of the *successful integration* of religion and science in Intelligent Design! Michael Behe is a tenured molecular biologist who supports the efficacy of evolution by natural selection for some, though not all, natural phenomena; he uses supernatural phenomena to account for the rest. For Behe, there is no intellectual problem with this approach and he has succeeded in making it a legitimate scientific explanation for a wide—though nonscientist—public. The conflict between scientists and ID advocates occurs directly as a result of this theological/scientific position. If it were not for the powerful ways in which science and religion intertwine and mutually reinforce one another in ID, there would be far less political concern over it in contemporary America.[4] Intelligent Design is almost certainly poor science and misguided theology, as its critics declare, but it remains an effective merger of scientific and religious language and thought. That success, rather than its success at science or theology independently, combined with the effective marketing strategies of its proponents, explains its cultural power.

The successful integration of religion and science in Apocalyptic AI, then, might lead to a public controversy on par with that of the intelligent design controversy in the late twentieth- and early twenty-first-century United States. If robots continue to get more intelligent, the theological problems that surround them may become very serious. Questions about consciousness, souls, immortal salvation, and the existence of gods will grow ever more worrisome if robots look increasingly likely to equal or surpass human performance or if "brain scanning" and mind uploading technologies seem possible. It is difficult to say how religious practitioners and institutions will meet such a conflict but we can expect, at the least, vociferous objection to the denial of human significance and dignity (even if robots are elevated to human equality) and dogmatic assurances of the existence and meaningfulness of gods and the religious afterlife. Who knows? Perhaps we will even see the interjection of material on the soullessness of machines forced into robotics and AI curricula by local school boards.

These examples show that there is a very serious problem in the "reconciliation" camp of religion and science. While we cannot question the intellectual honesty or genuine search for peace in the reconciliation effort (nor should we definitively assert that such efforts ought to cease), we should now wonder to what extent this research agenda might end up contributing to the very problems it opposes. It will be difficult in the extreme to sort out which kinds of religion/science reconciliations are "good" and which are "bad," if such a thing is possible at all. If nothing else, that some of those reconciliations would be considered "bad" by the very people advocating the enterprise shows it is an intellectually problematic position.

The vocabulary of present discussions over religion and science likely fails to engage its subject properly. Talk of "conflict" and "harmony" rarely serves much purpose beside whatever ideological baggage its users bring to the table. As both conflict and harmony, for example, regularly appear side by side, we may never find many important issues that have only one or the other present.

The study of religion and science, therefore, should go beyond its moral hope for the integration of religious and scientific truths, seeking also a more balanced intellectual effort toward historical, anthropological, and sociological understanding. In an ideal world, this approach might lead to the kind of peaceful coexistence between scientific and religious thought that reconciliation theorists hope to gain, but then again, it might not. Academic research owes no allegiance to our moral teleologies.

THE RISE OF THE ROBOTS

INTRODUCTION

Late in the twentieth century, great pains were often taken to distance religion and science. Occasionally, this was done to protect the two from one another, preserving them each within some domain of competence so that everyday people could be both scientifically literate and religiously faithful. At other times, this segregation served more antagonistic purposes: to elevate one domain at the expense of the other, which becomes either the realm of the ignorant or the realm of the damned, depending upon whether science or religion is "on top."

In the history of intelligent robots, a history which goes back well before the building of any digital robots (which was impossible until the mid-twentieth century), both religion and science play key roles. Intelligent machines have precursors in science and religion and, as I discussed in chapter two, the goals for engineering mechanical people were not overly different from the goals that led to alchemical creation. To understand robots, we must understand how the history of religion and the history of science have twined around one another, quite often working toward the same ends and quite often influencing one another's methods and objectives. Such knowledge would avail one little should one wish to *be* a roboticist, of course, but it is quite invaluable in order to understand what robotics *is all about*. While most of this book has evaluated Apocalyptic AI synchronically, that is, in its historical moment, this appendix offers a diachronic history of artificial humanoids in religion and science to better contextualize Apocalyptic AI.

WHEN THE ROBOTS COME HOME TO ROOST

Robots are all around us, and they are getting closer. Robots have already entered mainstream culture as cleaning devices, entertainment, and educational tools.

Over 2 million iRobot Roomba vacuum cleaners sold between 2002 and 2006, with other companies fast joining the market. Robots can vacuum and mop floors and even mow your lawn. Before Roomba became a household word, however, the phrase "robot wars" was already in common usage. Combat between remote-controlled personal robots became a "sport" popularized on television by the shows *Robot Wars* and *Battlebots*.[1] These shows, in which participants were equal measure engineers, artists, geeks, and entrepreneurs, made robots exciting and available to the mainstream populace, which gobbled up reproduction toys and avidly watched as robots flipped, hammered, and sawed one another to pieces in the ring. ROBO-ONE, in which humanoid robots perform tasks (e.g., running and stair-climbing) and box one another, is a less destructive newcomer to the world of robot combat. Other robot contests have grown in popularity as well. The Trinity College Fire Fighting Home Robot Contest allows entrants from around the United States to compete at navigating a maze and snuffing out a candle while other educational competitions like the FIRST LEGO League[2] introduce students to robotic technology in an atmosphere that encourages teamwork and inventiveness. Robots also compete in soccer games (RoboCup), with the ultimate goal of building humanoid robots that can beat the world championship human team by the year 2050.

Even a cursory glance at industry, military, literature, and even home economics shows the increasing presence of robots in American life. Although the word "robot" was not coined until 1927 and nothing resembling today's robots existed until William Grey Walter built his autonomous tortoises in the late 1940s, intelligent robots seem like inevitable additions to twenty-first-century life. Walter's tortoises could seek or avoid light and they could return to their charging stations when their batteries were low. These early robots helped cyberneticists and computer scientists of the mid-century imagine what life could be like with greater computing power and more sophisticated sensing apparatuses. Robots will fight our wars, guard our homes, assist our work, and even play with our children. According to some futurists, they will also replace us as Earth's dominant life form. When Isaac Asimov popularized robotic science fiction in the 1950s, a nanny robot was the stuff of dreams. But in the early twenty-first century, robots that recognize people, interact with them, and help solve math problems are the stuff of reality. Not yet widespread, such companions will soon find homes across the world as prices decline and capabilities expand.

MYSTICS AND ENGINEERS

The rise of robots, enabled by modern computing, has historical precedent in both scientific and religious communities. From mythology to mechanics, robots have antecedents from the ancient world and the early modern period. Mechanical engineers built automata, machines that came alive through springs, water flow, weighted strings, and even steam; these machines performed various tasks, from walking around to playing musical instruments. At the same time, mystics saw a chance to come closer to God through the creation of a living creature by magical means.[3]

Ancient engineers were surprisingly effective at providing movement and sound in their automata. As early as the middle of the first century CE, Hero of Alexandria built automata that could move around a stage as dramatic props. In a similar feat of genius, the early fourth-century BCE mathematician and philosopher Archytas built a wooden bird that moved along a wire by expelling steam. Greek myths idolized Daedalus for his automata, which resembled those of the god Hephaestus. Talking heads and moving statues were used to provide oracular pronouncements in Greek, Egyptian, and Babylonian temples. Many ancient cultures, including that of the Egyptians, had no difficulty in ascribing a kind of life to their religious statues (Cohen 1966, 20); so much the better if the statue could move! In the Far East and India, too, statues were made to move as though alive (ibid., 23). The desire to build automata was powerful in the ancient world, as engineers and priests—who have been one and the same from time to time—worked together to build the objects that would engage humanity and represent the gods.

The rise of the mechanical arts in early modern Europe and Japan enabled the construction of more sophisticated automata: mechanical animals and people that could execute preset behaviors. As early as 1495, Leonardo da Vinci (1452–1519 CE) designed an automaton in knight's armor, which could sit up and move its arms and neck. No one knows whether or not Leonardo ever built a full model but a modern reproduction demonstrated the soundness of his design.[4] In the eighteenth century, inventors traveled Europe to demonstrate their automata.[5] Jacques de Vaucanson (1709–1782 CE), for example, exhibited a duck that could eat, defecate, and flap its wings. Among the most famous automata were the works of Pierre Jaquet-Droz (1721–1790 CE) and his sons, which were built to raise the prestige of their watch-making business. Their machines included The Musician, a female figure who played a pianolike instrument while "breathing" and moving her head and eyes, and The Writer, which was composed of over 6,000 pieces and had a form of programmable memory, from which it would output information through pen and ink. Some of Jaquet-Droz's most complex pieces can still be seen at the *Musée d'Art et d'Histoire* in Neuchâtel, Switzerland. Just as legends of Daedalus's creations show off his brilliance, the amazing automata of early modern Europe boosted the prestige of their makers. Jaquet-Droz and his sons, for example, used their inventions to boost sales in their clock- and watch-making business.

Similarly famous, though less impressive than the automata, was the Automaton Chess-Player, a chess-playing machine built in 1770 by the Hungarian baron

Wolfgang von Kempelen (1734–1804 CE). Known today as The Turk, the chess player was a humanoid sitting at a cabinet in which various gears were housed. Though impressive in its victories over human players, The Turk was revealed to be a hoax. As the cabinet doors were opened to reveal the gears inside, a small human person could move back and forth, allowing unobstructed viewing through the machine but only through one half of the machine at a time. By opening only half of the machine to viewing and then closing it off before revealing the other, von Kempelen allowed his assistant to evade detection. It seems obvious that von Kempelen's hoax was designed to make him the "talk of the town," not just to see if it would work. Von Kempelen and the automata makers of early modern Europe, then, demonstrated early on that the construction of artificial humanoids connects to social and financial power, as would later be the case in Apocalyptic AI (see chapter two).

Around the same time, Japanese artisans manufactured automata called *karakuri*, which were used in theaters, religious festivals, and at home. The most famous of the *karakuri* are the tea-serving dolls, which use baleen springs to roll forward and pour a cup of tea before reversing direction and rolling away once the empty cup has been replaced. In Japan, masters and their apprentices zealously guarded the techniques of *karakuri* manufacture until Hosokawa Hanzo Yorinao published *Karakuri-zui* ("Illustrated Compilation of Mechanism-art") in 1798 (Karakuriya 2007).

Karakuri may descend from Leonardo da Vinci's pioneering automata (Rosheim 2006, 35–36). Certainly, the introduction of Western clocks affected the development of *karakuri* (Hornyak 2006, 20). Mark Rosheim argues that several of Leonardo's manuscripts (the Madrid Codices) were kept in Spain and could have passed from there to Japan in the hands of Jesuit missionaries, who used technical objects like clocks and novel devices as a way of winning favors in foreign countries. For example, one of Jacquet-Droz's automata ended up in China. The Japanese tea-serving doll closely resembles the sixteenth-century European Monk automaton, which also moves forward via a clockwork design. As of yet, however, no definite link has been demonstrated between da Vinci's work and *karakuri*.

Karakuri are intimately connected to Japan's contemporary robotic culture. The word "karakuri" refers to intricately designed machines of various natures, including animate dolls but also chests with secret compartments and, more importantly, complex puppet show devices. These latter were frequently used in Japanese religious ceremonies and this religious use has advanced the Japanese acceptance of robots in the twentieth century (Hornyak 2006, 82). The religious rites involving *karakuri* presage the contemporary world, in which it is not uncommon for the Japanese to ascribe sanctity to robots (see Geraci 2006; Hornyak 2006).

The Western goal of building a functional humanoid also received, no doubt, some of its impetus from religion. Myths of creating live humanoids abound in

Western cultures, from Pygmalion and Daedalus to the Jewish Golem and the homunculi of Renaissance alchemy. In ancient Egypt, statues were given movable mouths so that priests could provide visitors with, seemingly, divine commands. The practice of fashioning humanoid statues to offer divine counsel spread beyond Egypt by the first century CE and continued throughout medieval Europe (Dodds 1947, 63–64). Unlike those of ancient Egypt, medieval European statues were not mechanical but were still presumed to possess the spirit of a god or demon who could be interrogated and could provide answers to one's questions (ibid., 64).

Although statues might have spirits within them, they remain in a very important sense, statues. Creating a real humanoid, a homunculus, was a far more enticing task in medieval Europe, which marks a significant difference between Japanese *karakuri* and European automata. No tradition connects *karakuri* to the creation of a living being the way in Europe automata designs appear historically alongside alchemical efforts to create a homunculus and the Jewish mystical creation of Golems.[6]

The homunculus came to Europe—just as so much other philosophical and scientific knowledge did—through Islamic culture. Having translated Greek texts into Arabic, Muslims rescued much of the ancients' knowledge and preserved it for future centuries while also advancing it in important ways. Prior to Ferdinand and Isabella's unification of Spain, the mixture of Jews, Christians, and Muslims there created an unprecedented realm of cultural mixing, through which educated Europeans gained access to both Greek and Islamic science.[7] Europe, hoping to "recover its own antiquity" found access to ancient sources through Arabic translation and found additional benefit in the Islamic learning that had followed upon the Muslim translation of ancient Greek authorities (Iqbal 2002, 179–200).

Medieval Arabs were very interested in artificial human life, in which they were influenced by their translations of ancient Greek manuscripts.[8] Many medieval Muslims even considered Hermes[9] to be one of God's prophets, bringing alchemical knowledge rather than a written revelation (Stapleton, Lewis, and Sherwood 1949, 69). Greek alchemy came to Islamic attention after many works were translated under the reign of the Arab prince Khalid ibn Yazid (d. 704 CE). Khalid was an eager student of alchemy, hoping to transmute base metals into gold; after studying with the Christian alchemist Morienus, he wrote several poems to "enshrine his knowledge" (Holmyard 1957, 65).[10] Khalid was instrumental in the rise of alchemical knowledge in medieval Islam but it was in subsequent centuries that such knowledge flourished.

The most influential figure in Islamic alchemy was Jābir ibn Hayyān (c. 721–c. 815), who has been called both the "father of chemistry," for his experimental methods and work on acids, distillations, and crystallizations, and the "Paracelsus of the Arabs" because of his extensive work in the creation of a homunculus.[11] Many of the works attributed to Jābir were probably written by his followers, but remain under his name as the "school of Jābir." Indeed, some question remains as to whether Jābir lived at all and doubt has been cast on the authenticity of his writings (Haq 1994, 3–32). Syed Noumanul Haq has, however, done much to authenticate Jābir's historical role (ibid.) and this position has been well received (Iqbal 2002, 25–26). This is not the place, however, to debate the authenticity of Jābir's biography. As I wish to trace only a small line around Islamic alchemy, I shall assume that Jābir was a real historical person, as argued by Holmyard, Haq, and others.[12]

Jābir believed that the four qualities of hot, cold, moist, and dry composed all entities and could be manipulated in their balance to create life. Jābir did not think of the four qualities as mere abstractions but considered them independent entities that in turn composed the elements air, water, earth, and fire when they combined with one another and with substance (Haq 1994, 58–59). For example, air is hot-moist while earth is cold-dry. Manipulation of such balances enables the alchemist to transform one metal into another and even transform inanimate objects into living things, as described, for example, in various sections of Jābir's large treatise, the *Kutub al Mawāzīn* (*Book of Balances*). *Takwin*, the creation of artificial life, is the culmination of the same processes that can be used to create various kinds of minerals (O'Connor 1994, 57, 79).

Jābir believed that, through the manipulation of balances, artificial life could be created. In the *Book of Stones*, he attributes this to Balīnās, known to us as Apollonius of Tyana.[13] Despite this reference to ancient authority, however, it was Jābir and the Arabic alchemists who extended their study beyond minerals to include plants and animals (Haq 1994, 228). The creation of artificial life was, for Jābir, the highest act of humankind, the ultimate manner of imitating the divine creator of the universe (Berman 1961, 55; O'Connor 1994, 76), though such imitation could never equal the creative powers of God (O'Connor 1994, 89). Jābir's method was quintessentially Islamic: it relies upon the Qur'anic theme of balance in the universe and "celebrates and builds upon the central concept of Islam," that is, God's unity (Iqbal 2002, 27).

Based on his theory of balances, Jābir believed that different materials could be used in the creation of different kinds of animals. Sea water, for example, could be used for tortoises, crayfish, scorpions, poisonous serpents, and lions while rainwater could be used to manufacture elephants, camels, water buffalo, cattle, and donkeys.

The different fluids (fresh, salt, or distilled waters) required are according to the different kinds of creatures being created. The text provides a parallel of evolutionary creation to artificial creation from fresh or salt water. It discusses the categories of living creatures capable of being artificially generated according to how they are nurtured. Their nurture (fresh, salty, distilled) corresponds to their natures (domestic, wild, fabulous, and human), physiognomies (personable, ponderous, predatory) and modes of locomotion (bipedal, quadrapedal, winged) (O'Connor 1994, 81).

Similarly, Jābir believed that various recipes and even laboratory apparatuses could bring about different outcomes in the production of humanoids. In the *Kitāb al tajmī* (*Book of Gathering*), which is also part of the *Book of Balances*, Jābir describes ways of creating human beings and argues that manipulation of the instrument allows such productions as a being with the torso of a girl but the face of a man (quoted in O'Connor 1994, 155). Jābir's theory of the apparatus probably traces from Galen's emphasis upon the environment's effect upon an animal. According to Galen and his followers, you could produce a different animal by placing an infant in one environment or another, such as creating land or sea turtles by raising the turtle in water or ashore (Kruk 1990, 271–72). Balance of materials and balance of apparatus (i.e., it should be proportional to that which one hopes to create) is crucial to Jābir's alchemical search for life.

Islamic alchemy did not die with Jābir but instead flourished for centuries, eventually helping bring about the rise of European alchemy. The school of Jābir continued to publish books, as did other Islamic alchemists, some of whom published in their own names and some of whom published pseudonymously. While these subsequent works drew upon Jābir, they added significantly to his legacy. Among the more interesting pseudonymous works is *The Book of the Cow*, which was attributed to Plato but is clearly of medieval Islamic provenance. In addition to recipes for creating bees out of a putrefying cow and vice versa, *The Book of the Cow* also offers a recipe for a homunculus.[14] A homunculus is an artificial humanoid manufactured through alchemical recipes, generally as a means for acquiring magical powers or the answers to difficult questions. The homunculus of *The Book of the Cow* has superhuman powers; it is thus a significant departure from Jābir's homunculus, which seems more or less identical with an actual human being.[15]

In *The Book of the Cow*,[16] the homunculus is formed by mixing the "stone of the sun" with the maker's "water" (presumably sperm). This mixture is then used to plug the vulva of a cow or a ewe, which has been cleansed with medicine and the blood of a ewe or a cow (the opposite animal from the one whose corpse is to carry the homunculus to term). The animal is placed in a dark house and fed a pound of blood from the opposite animal each week. One then grinds sunstone, sulfur, magnet, and green tutia, mixes them with willow sap, dries it all in the shadows and then waits until the cow or ewe gives birth. The creature that emerges should be placed in the powder in order to give the creature human form. After three days it will grow hungry and should be fed blood from its mother for seven days. The resulting creature will provide its maker a number of powers, from changing the progress of the moon to, if it is prepared properly and vivisected to form an ointment for the feet, walking on water.

Medieval philosophers and alchemists had significant reason to believe that they could create homunculi. The reigning biology for both Arabs and Europeans, inherited from Aristotle and the Greeks, included theories of spontaneous generation and the formative power of sperm (Kruk 1990; Newman 2004, 166). According to Greek theories of spontaneous generation, the right materials mixed in the right amounts in the right conditions would give rise to life automatically. It remained only to determine the correct recipe for the artificial man. Recipes for homunculi inevitably include human sperm because the Greeks believed that males provide the life force for each new person. Following the Greeks, medieval Europeans believed that women were receptacles for male sperm, which did the "real" work in creating a new human being through its life-giving "pneuma"[17] (Newman 2004, 166). Animal blood (as in *The Book of the Cow*) replaces the female menstrual blood, from which, in Greek thought, the body derives (Cohen 1966, 44). Given theories of spontaneous generation and formative sperm, a homunculus seemed quite possible: as long as the alchemist assembled the necessary ingredients properly, the spirit included in the sperm should infuse the creature with life.

In Catholic Europe, creation of a homunculus often verged upon idolatry. Arnald of Villanova[18] (late thirteenth century) allegedly killed his homunculus before its completion because he feared it would acquire a rational soul, which he believed would be a mortal sin (Newman 2004, 7). Alonso Tostado, meanwhile, likened the creation of a homunculus to the demonic begetting of giants through succubae and incubi (ibid., 193–95). In the seventeenth century, influential Catholics like Marin Mersenne and Athanasius Kircher both reviled alchemical homunculi and "triumphantly broadcast Alonso Tostado's story of Arnald" (ibid., 222). In one legend, Thomas Aquinas destroyed Albertus Magnus's mechanical servant as a tool of the devil. No one could be certain whether the creation of a homunculus usurped divine powers and led to the downfall of Christendom or simply glorified God through the operation and manipulation of natural laws—but the hubris implied in replicating God's creation and the potential to violate the commandment against idols seemed all too obvious for most medieval theologians.

Despite its theological problems, the creation of a homunculus eventually became the highest expression of human ingenuity for many European Christians, a status that it retains today in robotics and AI (despite occasional theological assaults of "playing God" or accusations of soullessness in machines). It was Phillip von Hohenheim (1493–1541 CE), known as Paracelsus, who made the homunculus more important than the alchemical synthesis of gold (Newman 2004, 165) and likened the alchemist to a demiurge, or lesser god (ibid., 199).[19] Like Jābir before him, Paracelsus was influential in the study of chemistry, particularly for making it a necessary part of medical practice (Holmyard 1957, 173–74). Paracelsus rejected the inherited medical traditions of Galen and Avicenna and offended almost the entirety of his contemporaries in the medical profession, all of which was, perhaps, exacerbated by his reputation for prodigious medical cures (see ibid., 166–68). Paracelsus's claim that the creation of a homunculus is superior to the creation of gold is demonstrated in Johann Valentin Andreae's anonymous *Chymical Wedding of Christian Rosencreutz* (1616 CE), in which a process nearly identical to that which would supposedly produce a philosopher's stone (used to create gold) actually resurrects a dead king and queen as homunculi (Newman 2004, 234).[20]

According to Paracelsus and other alchemists, the homunculus could be formed from a man's sperm[21] and would subsequently acquire impressive powers. A homunculus, because it is a purified form of humanity (i.e., produced without a woman), should have access to powers and knowledge that human beings do not. This follows from experiments in which alchemists attempted to produce the rarified essence of plants or animals. By burning plants and flowers, for example, and using the ashes in an alchemical reaction, one alchemist claimed to have resuscitated them as shadowy forms that were the purified essence of their originals, "devoid of crass materiality" (Newman 2004, 228). If the spectral plant is superior to its original, how much more so the homunculus than its fallen creator?[22] Its supernatural powers indicate that the homunculus of Paracelsus and his followers owes much to the Neo-Platonic, post–Jābir Islamic homunculus.

Alongside the homunculus traditions of Christian Europe, Jewish sources claimed that a sufficiently knowledgeable rabbi could produce a living humanoid called a Golem.[23] From its earliest years, Golem creation benefited from religious syncretism. Early in Jewish thought, Neoplatonic, Aristotelian, and astrological ideas influenced the Golem (Idel 1988, 16) and in the medieval period the intermixture of cultures contributed to Jewish faith that artificial humanoids could be powerful servants and allies.

As with the rest of Europe, Jewish traditions connected to ancient Greek thought but Jews sought to outdo the accomplished ancients. During the Renaissance, Jewish authors described the Golem in order to demonstrate the superiority of their ancient wisdom over that of the Greeks (Idel 1990, 165, 183–84). For Jews, the creation of a Golem has been accepted and encouraged, with little of the ambivalence visible in the homunculus legends of Christian Europe (Sherwin 1985, 4[24]). It stands as synecdoche for the powers of human creation; it is the representative of the highest aspiration of humankind (Singer 1988). The Golem, a creature of mud and clay, is manufactured primarily through mystical manipulation of the Hebrew alphabet, rather than through alchemical combinations.[25] Jews have long believed that Hebrew is a different, more powerful language. Hebrew is the language of God and the language of creation; thus through proper manipulation of the language the mystic can create whole new worlds, particularly through the use of the ancient *Sefer Yetzirah* (*Book of Creation*).[26]

As a consequence of their social segregation and oppression, early modern Jews maintained a healthy legacy of the Golem. Medieval and early modern authorities generally relegated the Jews to ghettos outside major cities, where the Jews were unable to occupy certain professions and were frequently subject to oppression from their Christian neighbors. As a result of this legacy—and its continuing relevance after the failure of the Jewish Enlightenment to establish an accepted Jewish presence in Europe—hope for magical aid against oppression is quite understandable.

The earliest clear Golem story comes from the Talmud (fourth to sixth centuries CE) but the Golem it describes, unlike the homunculi of medieval Islamic and Christian culture, is inferior to a human being and without significant powers. In Sanhedrin 65b of the Babylonian Talmud, Rabbi Abba ben Rav Hamma (299–353 CE, known as Rava) creates a Golem in order to demonstrate his close relationship with God.[27] It was subsequently destroyed by Rabbi Zeira who noticed it was mute and ordered it, "return to your dust." Had Rava been perfect, it is said, then his Golem would have been the equal of a human being. Though his creation demonstrates his power and piety, it simultaneously shows his imperfections (Idel 1988, 17). According to Rabbi Solomon ben Isaac, known to Jews as Rashi (1040–1105 CE), the creation of a Golem shows that the creator has mastered the *Sefer Yetzirah* and its mystical permutations of the Hebrew language, but its muteness reveals Rava's limitations. Though the creators of Golems are not perfect, and thus neither are their Golems, only truly powerful and praiseworthy men could produce one at all. Golems were attributed to honored Jews who were believed to have attained substantial spiritual mastery (Goldsmith 1981, 36–37; Idel 1990; Sherwin 2004, 14).[28]

The most widespread Golem tradition is the seventeenth-century legend of Rabbi Yehudah Loew ben Bezalel of Prague[29] (c. 1525–1609 CE), whose Golem myths clearly function as markers of prestige. Although an examination of Rabbi Loew's writings provides little or no explanation as to why the Golem was attributed to him and the first written attribution did not come until 1841,[30] he has been associated Golem creation since the eighteenth or nineteenth century and folkloric accounts have spread wide (Idel 1990, 251–52).[31] The attribution of Golem manufacture to Rabbi Loew is clearly a response to his extraordinary achievements; he was a "supernova in the bright constellation of sixteenth-century Jewish scholars and communal leaders" (Sherwin 2004, 18). The stories of Rabbi Loew were published in the early twentieth century by Yudl Rosenberg and Chayim Bloch, who evidently relied upon Rosenberg in his retelling. Although Rosenberg supposedly acquired Golem material that came straight from Rabbi Yitzchak ben Shimshon Katz, Rabbi Loew's son-in-law and assistant in the Golem's manufacture, this claim is almost universally rejected.[32] Some of the Golem myths presented by Rosenberg were probably original to him, as they relate to the specific problems of early twentieth-century Jewry, particularly the problem of the blood libel, which arose at various points in medieval Europe but was not a problem during Loew's own time (Goldsmith 1981, 38–41).[33] Indeed, the time in which Rabbi Loew was chief Rabbi in Prague was known as the "Golden Age" of Czech Jewry (Kieval 1997, 5). Rabbi Loew, despite living in a peaceful time for Jews, became the hero for Jews in worse circumstances because of the profound respect that eastern European Jews had for him. Just as building automata enhanced the prestige of clock makers and creating a homunculus vouched for Paracelsus's medical knowledge, the attribution of a Golem to Rabbi Loew's legend acts as an honorific.

Because Golem folklore has spread throughout modern Jewish life, stories about the Golems of Rabbi Elijah of Chelm[34] and Rabbi Loew occasionally conflict with one another. Different stories relate different ways of raising a Golem to life (e.g., a parchment in its mouth, an inscription on its forehead, ritual circumambulation by three learned men, an amulet, etc.). There are also different traditions about what the Golem did and different endings to its life and that of the rabbi. For example, in some stories, Rabbi Loew was forced to stop his Golem during a rampage and the Golem collapsed upon him, killing him.[35] In other stories, the Golems can be de-animated at little cost to the rabbi.

As retold by Rosenberg and Bloch, Rabbi Loew's Golem had many magical powers to accompany its superhuman strength. It was immune to illness and carried an amulet (given by Rabbi Loew) that allowed it to turn invisible. It could see the souls of the dead and speak with them; it even brought one dead spirit to a trial, where, from behind a curtain, the spirit gave evidence that saved the Jews from yet another blood libel. The Golem had the inspiration to help Rabbi Loew arrange certain letters given to him in a dream so that the rabbi could interpret them, which he had been powerless to do before the Golem's intervention. Even though the Golem had these powers, which it used to protect the Jews, it was unquestionably inferior to human beings, as it did not possess the specific "kind" of soul that a human being possesses (*ruah*).

The Golem's magical powers (as understood in nineteenth- and twentieth-century folklore) place it firmly in the tradition of artificial humanoids but its inferiority to human beings marks an important distinction. The Islamic and European alchemical homunculi could speak as human beings and had prophetic powers. The Golem, on the other hand, is mute and ignorant; it is greatly inferior to its makers (Newman 2004, 186). According to some medieval Jews, a truly pious individual could make a Golem equal to a human being but this would require a state of perfect mystical union with God (Idel 1990, 106–7, 216, 225–26). Rabbi Isaac ben Samuel of Acre (thirteenth to fourteenth centuries CE) cited Jeremiah and Ben Sira, along with a few others, as examples of such perfection but other Jewish sources, however, deny that a Golem could ever equal a human being.[36]

In the twentieth century, the awkward and incomplete Golem of Rabbi Loew and Rabbi Elijah was a deeply influential trope for modern technology. Gustav Meyrink's novel *Der Golem* (1915), and Paul Wegener's 1921 movie of the same name brought the Golem back into gentile culture, where it has remained influential, playing a role in comic books and popular novels.[37] For example, the Golem myth has appeared in poems and stories by Jorges Luis Borges and in Michael Chabon's Pulitzer Prize–winning *The Amazing Adventures of Kavalier and Clay* (2001), and has played a role in the television shows *The X-Files* and *The Simpsons* and in many comic books, including *Tales of the Teenage Mutant Ninja Turtles*. More relevant to this study, advances in twentieth-century science have also incorporated the Golem as a spiritual forebear. Fear of and fascination with a biotechnological future led Byron Sherwin to connect genetically enhanced human beings and robotics with the Golem (Sherwin 2004, 2007) and the Golem myth has had obvious parallels with the rise of computers, artificial intelligence, and robotics.

Just a few years after the first electronic computers became available, they were linked to Golems. The seminal cybernetic theorist Norbert Wiener compared computers to Golems in his classic *God and Golem, Inc.* (1964) as did Gershom Scholem, a Jewish philosopher and historian, in an essay shortly thereafter (Scholem 1971). For both authors, the Golem story provides twentieth-century science with a cautionary tale. The destructive powers of computers are no less than those of the mythical Golem yet many uncritical observers saw—and continue to see—nothing but paradise in the computerized world of the future. Just as Rava's Golem could not speak because of Rava's own imperfections, the robots we build will likely reflect both the good and the bad within us.

Building conscious machines could be a religious task, just as the fabrication of Golems was in the past. The Lutheran theologian Anne Foerst and the computer scientist Hugo de Garis both—in wildly disparate ways—believe that building robots is a religious obligation. For Foerst, creating robots is directly akin to the creation of Golems: it is worship of God (Foerst 2004, 35–36) and provides us with new partners in God's creation (Foerst 1998).[38] De Garis argues, however, that building machines that are superior to human beings—not partners for them—is a religious act (de Garis 2005, 105); this moral obligation exists even though those machines (in his account) will almost certainly replace humankind, perhaps through war (ibid., 12). In the theories of Foerst and de Garis, we see how robots can be both objects for and objects of worship. Foerst allows robots personhood and equality; de Garis elevates them to the realm of the divine.

Artificial humanoids have a long and continuous history through both religion and science. Ancient statues and myths, medieval and early modern Golems and homunculi, even the fervently anticipated robots of tomorrow all intertwine with religious hopes and with engineering progress. Our desire to build intelligent machines cannot be taken out of either its scientific or its religious context without intellectual impoverishment. The intelligent robots of pop science are the latest installment in a tradition of trying to build artificial people. Though we might be tempted to be surprised at the connection between religion, science, and technology through robotics, there is plenty of historical precedent for it.

IN THE DEFENSE OF ROBOTICS

BUILDING INTELLIGENT ROBOTS is costly work. As a result, scientists require patrons with deep pocketbooks. The deepest purse in the U.S. belongs, of course, to the American military. A large proportion of the research funds at the Robotics Institute (RI) come from the Defense Department's Advanced Research Project Agency and the Office of Naval Research (ONR), which has led some residents to stake out ethical positions on research funding. Apocalyptic AI could provide roboticists with a justification for military spending, one that resolves the ethical dilemma by defusing the threat of technological research. The military might be seen as a means to an end. Instead of better weaponry, the real promise of robotics and AI is a salvific future. Given the plausibility of that scenario, it is important to think through the ramifications of military funding at Carnegie Mellon University (CMU). As it turns out, a thorough look at the military presence at CMU's Robotics Institute shows that, whatever moral ambiguity exists in military funding, it does not explain the rise of Apocalyptic AI. The intellectual drive behind robotics research and the practical fact that military applications are inextricably intertwined with nonmilitary applications means that little military controversy exists for most individual researchers.

Following the Soviet launch of Sputnik, the world's first satellite, fear in the United States about the country's scientific and technological supremacy led to a wide array of responses, including the establishment of the Defense Advance Research Projects Agency (DARPA) in 1958. "DARPA's mission is to maintain the technological superiority of the U.S. military and prevent technological surprise from harming our national security by sponsoring revolutionary, high-payoff research that bridges the gap between fundamental discoveries and their military use" (Defense Advanced Research Projects Agency 2009). DARPA reports directly to the secretary of defense and attempts to minimize bureaucratic interference in innovation while maximizing researchers' productivity. As long as some possibility of enormous payoff exists, DARPA funding can benefit even projects likely to fail. For this reason, it is the most effective program in the United States for delivering long-term benefits. Unlike a business, it has no shareholders to demand an immediate return on investment. Currently, DARPA consists of 240 people and a $2 billion annual budget; a given project might involve $10–40 million over four years, a DARPA program manager, a system engineering and technical assistance contractor to support the program manager, an agent in a military R&D laboratory, five to ten contractor organizations, and two universities all working toward a specific aggregate goal (Defense Advanced Research Projects Agency 2003).

The DARPA Grand Challenge shows how the agency has worked with roboticists in the early twenty-first century. In 2004, DARPA held its first Grand Challenge event, encouraging work in autonomous vehicle navigation. Participant groups (from individuals to academics to corporate groups) built cars that were to drive across the desert from Los Angeles to Las Vegas. The goal was to move toward unmanned military rescue and reconnaissance vehicles; the military hopes that one third of all ground vehicles will be unmanned by 2015. Although the 2004 challenge was a failure (no vehicle made it more than seven miles), in 2005 five robots finished a less challenging 132.2-mile course through the Nevada desert. DARPA funds helped some of the research groups build their robots and DARPA also awarded the winning team $2 million. In 2007, DARPA's follow-up competition, the Urban Challenge, required that entrants navigate city streets with traffic signals and other vehicles (in a controlled environment). Six out of the eleven finalists completed the Urban Challenge, which was won by Carnegie Mellon's entrant, "Boss."

Robotics research as we know it would not exist without military funding. The military accounts for more than 50% of robotics research in the United States and it is the world's largest robotics funding source (Sheehan 2004); the American military even funds foreign roboticists. Alongside DARPA, the ONR and other units in the military fund corporate and academic research in robotics. Although tremendous success has been achieved in Asia (largely in Japan and South Korea) and Europe, growth would decline dramatically if the American military stepped out of the robotics research world. For this reason alone, researchers have reason to appreciate military involvement.

There are legitimate concerns, however. Some people prefer to distance themselves from the military for its ostensibly violent agenda. The military does, after all, kill people. Some people fear the loss of responsibility that comes with increasingly autonomous robots. Who is responsible when a robot kills someone? The person who programmed the robot or the one who engaged it in military operations or the one who gave it its commands or the robot itself? Who is responsible when a robot "loses control," as happened October 12, 2007, in South Africa, where a robotic antiaircraft cannon killed nine soldiers in a wild shooting rampage? Who can resist feeling uncomfortable when faced with movies like *War Games* and *The Terminator*, in which our computers and robots take command of our military forces and threaten humanity with extinction?

Apocalyptic AI seemingly provides a way out of the ethical dilemma over military funding. For Moravec, the military is only the means to an end, and that end will preclude the need for the military. If all our needs are met, presumably there will be no more reason for warfare. As a result, Moravec has claimed that in the future, "antisocial robot software would sell poorly" (Moravec 1999, 77) and will "soon cease being manufactured" (Moravec 1992a, 52). Moravec believes that the future will be, for the most part, a peaceful time. With the competition for resources ended forever by nanotechnology, robotics, and AI, we can focus our attention on more intellectually rewarding research. If, thanks to research in robotics, the world comes to a point where the military becomes obsolete, then roboticists *ought* to take funding from any military source available. After all, such funding would mean the military is paying for its own dismantling.[1]

Despite Moravec's optimism, military ethics remain ambiguous in Apocalyptic AI texts. Kevin Warwick fears the presence of the military in robotics and refuses to accept military funding (Warwick [1997] 2004, 210). As robots grow more autonomous, he fears, they might simply absorb all control out of human hands (ibid., 290). Daniel Crevier calls this the "Colossus scenario" and thinks it possible, though not inevitable (Crevier 1993, 313). He thinks anti-AI clauses are more important to disarmament treaties than antinuclear ones (ibid., 320). On the other hand, despite allegedly waking up from nightmares about the tragedies of future warfare, de Garis rather blithely connects military expansionism with the Cosmist position (de Garis 2005, 121). De Garis does claim that his book is a way for people to address the so-called "artilect war" sooner rather than later but it certainly does not come across as a condemnation of military research. Indeed, de Garis happily guarantees us that the life of one artilect is worth "trillions of trillions of trillions of humans anyway" (ibid., 174).

If the military provides the direction for robotics research, it would seem that military ethics will be those that the machines acquire. This might be a good thing if this means that robots will exercise violence against only those who threaten peaceful society. Alternately, a robotic military ethic could glorify control and a will to power. This position was articulated by Warwick (2004), who predicts a machine takeover of Earth unless we become cyborgs so as to compete with them intellectually.

Military dangers make it quite reasonable for roboticists to shy away from defense funding. The artistic group Survival Research Laboratories uses robots specifically to challenge military ethics (Geraci 2008b, 151–52) and many post–Vietnam era computer programmers were "no longer comfortable working under the aegis of the Department of Defense" (Rheingold 1991, 85). Other researchers, such as Maarten van Veen of the Netherlands Defense Academy and Terry Winograd of Stanford, have raised concern over the tight relationship between the military and robotics/computer science (Abate 2008). Clearly, there are some people who remain uncomfortable with the military's role in robotics and some of these do work for the Carnegie Mellon University Robotics Institute, though they are a small minority. The most popular meeting of the CMU Robotics Institute Philosophy of Religion group, which meets biweekly during the semester, addressed the ethics of military funding. The group's discussion led to its most heated debate ever and a few hard feelings remain (Philosophy of Robotics Group 2006).[2] While there are only a few members of the community opposed to military funding, it can be a sensitive issue for everyone. Those who take such funding do not want to be called murderers, and those who do not take the funding do not appreciate being called naïve. Such debates are thus potentially vociferous, even though there are few people who actively worry about the matter.

It may be, in fact, that military robotics has significant ethical value. As one member of the Philosophy of Robotics discussion pointed out, a human being is liable to suffer great anxiety in war conditions and might kill civilians "just to be on the safe side." Such events have been front-page news in the American invasions of Iraq and Afghanistan. A robot, lacking a sense of its personal welfare, can make rather more disinterested judgments, as could a tele-operator if the robot were not autonomous. Ron Arkin of Georgia Tech believes that autonomous robots capable of killing people are inevitable but that they can be more humane than human beings and thus help resolve some of the ethical tragedies of warfare (Arkin 2007). Such machines will not rape, torture, or kill out of a misguided vendetta or enthusiasm for killing. He hopes that robots could be programmed to refuse unethical orders, monitor and report the behavior of others, and follow battlefield and military protocols such as the Geneva Convention.

Presumably, most researchers at the Robotics Institute would prefer to get money with no obvious strings attached but such preferences play little role at the Institute. I had no trouble finding faculty who gave little or no thought to military funding. While researchers might enjoy an ideal world where money has no clear connection to corporate or military interests, most do not seem to fantasize about such a world or care overly much if one came about. Not only do researchers often not care whether their money comes from the military, sometimes they actively desire it. The MIT Media Lab, famous for its advanced research, was cut off from its carte blanche DARPA funding by the late 1970s and moved toward corporate funding and the National Science Foundation (NSF). Nicholas Negroponte, lab director in the 1980s, told Steward Brand that he would have liked a return to the old DARPA funding, which he preferred to the NSF (Brand 1987, 163).[3]

Some DARPA-funded researchers do not bother justifying their funding sources. Curiosity can be a powerful factor in scientific research and some individuals will take whatever aid they can to perform their experiments, run their simulations, and build their robots. For these individuals, if DARPA is the one group that wants to make it all possible, then DARPA is the only group that matters. If military applications arise from the research, then so be it. There's nothing inherently evil about any technology, after all, and the researchers are not the ones who put any of the machines into action.

More to the point, DARPA funds projects with civilian as well as military applications, though it no longer funds projects without discernible military end. The agency funds projects that may possibly have military applications down the road even if there are none on the immediate horizon. If such technologies benefit civilian life as well, all the better. As a result, there is plenty of room for researchers to justify using DARPA money. Building a robot car could save a lot of lives from traffic accidents each year, which would be a great boon whether or not robot cars became part of the average military convoy. Nearly all robotics projects with military applications have corresponding nonmilitary applications, such as in urban search and rescue. A robot that can sniff out bombs can also maintain airport security. A robot designed to infiltrate streets or buildings of an opposing military can also be used to find survivors after a building collapses or is on fire. A researcher can easily accept military funding because of the close ties between civilian and military objectives; he or she is not using the money to build what Warwick calls "machines of destruction or war" (Warwick [1997] 2004, 210) but to build rescue robots that will save innocent lives.

Howie Choset argues that debates over defense funding fail to appreciate the nature of technology transfer from one arena to another and do not recognize the multifarious nature of robotics research (Choset 2007). From a "realist" standpoint, little difference in outcome emerges between military and nonmilitary funding; technologies transfer between the two seamlessly. Any work published without military aid, but with military application, will be utilized by the military anyway; it is effectively public domain. For example, imagine researchers who design an effective, autonomous vehicle without participating in DARPA's Urban Challenge. Now imagine military officers, who desire autonomous vehicles as a way to save soldiers' lives, refusing to use that technology because it emerged in the public sector. That conjunction is more than fantasy, it is absurd. The military will happily take advantage of any autonomous vehicle available to them; indeed, if they spent no money developing the technology they might be all the more pleased.

There were only a very few members of the Robotics Institute who showed reluctance to accept military funding. One researcher even told me that military funding is fine but accepting money from Microsoft Corporation is morally questionable. Although I expected that military funding would be a prominent issue for researchers (at least, once I had brought it up in interviews and meetings), they were little concerned about it. Although I expected that Apocalyptic AI could serve as an ethical justification for military funding (and perhaps it even does for Moravec, though even this is unclear), few researchers at CMU object to the military and among the supporters of military funding there was no reference to Apocalyptic AI as extenuating the circumstances. Given the easy back-and-forth transfer of technology between military and the academy and the desperately needed civilian applications for most military research, it is no surprise that military funding played no role in the development of Apocalyptic AI.

NOTES

INTRODUCTION

1. There are plenty of academics concerned about the moral implications of what I am calling Apocalyptic AI, however, including Bailey (2005), DeLashmutt (2006), Dery (1996), Hayles (2005), Herzfeld (2002b), Joy (2000), Keiper (2006), Noble (1999), Rubin (2003), Sherwin (2004), and Wertheim (1999). Other authors address the significance of cognitive and computer sciences for theology, including Foerst (1998; 2004), G. R. Peterson (2004), and me (2007b).

2. Gerardus van der Leeuw brought Edmund Husserl's concept of *epoche* to the history of religions and it is one that should not be abandoned. The practice of *epoche* requires that we relinquish our presumption that we know what is true and what is not. In the study of foreign religions, this means assuming that the religious beliefs and practices of the object of one's study could be correct and efficacious. Rather than seeking to find "truth" or "falsity" in these beliefs and practices, one is better advised to seek out how they affect life "on the ground." *Epoche* applies equally to the promises made in pop science books. While it is not particularly valuable to either assent to or deny the futuristic promises of pop science books, as robotic and AI technology becomes increasingly prevalent in society, we would be well advised to sort out how those promises function within our culture, regardless of whether or not we accept them.

3. *Second Life* and SL are trademarks of Linden Research, Inc.

4. Through the Temple, I solicited charitable donations, which I passed along to the real-life charities Heifer International and Abraham's Vision. The charitable part of the Virtual Temple does not play a role in this book; it was merely my effort to turn virtual reality into a productive part of society, which I measure in terms of advocating peace, protecting the environment, and feeding the hungry (due to limitations on my time, the Virtual Temple closed its virtual doors during the summer of 2007).

5. By public policy, I refer to more than just government policies. I have a broad notion of policy in mind, one that includes government action but also includes the way in which the public receives and thinks about technological progress.

6. Since there are literally hundreds of articles and books attempting to reconcile science and religion, I have offered only a few examples in which such efforts are described (Gilbert 1997) or advocated by major figures (Barbour, Townes, and Clayton)

CHAPTER 1: APOCALYPTIC AI

1. The enchanting power of science and technology has a long literary tradition. The popular science genre emerged out of the medieval books of secrets, which were manuals including recipes for crafts, alchemy, etc., that purported to reveal the secrets of nature (Eamon 1994). Such books blurred the boundaries between magic and science in popular literature, as do today's Apocalyptic AI books.

2. One might also make a case for biotechnology and nanotechnology, but the potential of the former is rather more limited than that of robotics/AI and the latter is so intertwined with the AI apocalypse that its strongest promises are almost identical with those of Apocalyptic AI.

3. We should shy away from all theses that propose an immutable or monolithic relationship between science and religion. In the medieval period, the role of science varied with respect to Christianity. As "handmaiden to theology," the purpose of natural philosophy in the Middle Ages was to aid in the interpretation of scripture. But natural philosophers became increasingly disgruntled with this purpose as they developed greater powers of explanation through the introduction of Aristotelian philosophy in the thirteenth century (E. Grant 1986; E. Grant 1996, 70–85) and later through Copernican astronomy (Shea 1986). Even when in conflict, science and religion can, after all, be in some sense friends. Edward Grant has pointed out how the church's condemnations of Aristotelian principles in 1277 promoted the growth of science by forcing philosophers to think outside the limits of Aristotelian thought (1986, 55). Many commentators are all too casual in asserting that religion and science came into conflict in the trial of Galileo but, while this might be true in several important ways, such critics have too frequently missed the important ways in which Galileo's 1633 condemnation was also the result of 1) Galileo's scientific failures (Feyerabend 1978, 128–29) and 2) the politics of courtly life, which—regardless of the scientific opinions presented—led to Galileo's unpopularity in certain influential church circles despite his obvious piety (Biagioli 1993). Uncritical faith in the religion/science conflict in the case of Galileo has done much to maintain the incorrect assumption that interactions between religion and science are straightforward cases of harmony or, more often, conflict.

4. Some confusion remains regarding the publication date of Bacon's *New Atlantis*, which has been dated as early as 1626 and as late at 1660. The date 1627 used here comes from the version cited (Bacon 1951).

5. Clearly, for Bacon, the Christian god encourages the production of an exemplary academic college that combines the study of natural philosophy with Christian theology. The belief that scientists should and could become something of a ministerial community did not stop with Bacon. The philosopher Auguste Comte (1798–1857), for example, had a similar project, though he rejected institutional Christianity. By the 1850s, Comte had developed his Religion of Humanity, which he hoped would replace all previous religious institutions, especially Catholicism, as a way to unify society and provide people with a sense of meaning and purpose (Brooke and Cantor 1998, 48–49). In order to fulfill his goals, Comte adopted many of the traditional aspects of Catholic life for his new religion (Comte [1852] 1973). The Religion of Humanity included a divine being, rituals, a sacred calendar, even a priesthood. His calendar, designed to be "more rational" than the Gregorian calendar, included festivals honoring scientists, the dead, "Holy Women," even animistic objects of praise, such as fire, iron, and the sun. He advocated daily prayer as a way for men to better themselves. In this last, the Religion of Humanity takes a decidedly chauvinistic turn. While Comte admired women for their supposedly superior moral qualities, he proposes that they should never stray far from homemaking and that their "holy function" is to provide men with moral guidance (ibid., 24). His belief that women are the "moral providence" of the human species (ibid., 22) was, at best, a

double-edged sword that legitimated women's oppression. Men's intellects, he believed, are "stronger and of wider grasp . . . more accurate and penetrating" (ibid., 221–22) and thus "every woman . . . must be carefully secured from work away from home, so as to be able to worthily accomplish her holy mission" (ibid., 226). Thanks to their wisdom, their vows, and their separation from the mindless needs of everyday life, male engineers were the only priests who could bring about the positive scientific age (Comte [1852] 1973, passim).

6. The discovery and colonization of the Americas illustrate how eschatological expectations permeate technology. During the Age of Exploration, many people felt that the discovery of the Americas heralded the final age of human history and that God would soon inaugurate a perfect realm on Earth (Watts 1985) but in the period of American Manifest Destiny that expectation was explicitly tied to technological, as opposed to scientific, artistic, or theological progress. Early in the nation's history, the expansion of the country relied upon an ideology of Christian eschatology and technologies of land domination. Control over the land with axes, plows, irrigation, surveying, and transportation was given meaning through Christian expectations of divine purpose (Nye 2003). Human technology was a part of the divine plan: "useful improvements" (ibid., 9) allowed Americans to "complete the design latent within" nature (ibid., 10). Such eschatological technology directly parallels the ideology of the Society of Salomon's House in Bacon's New Atlantis.

7. Many authors have traced secularism considerably further back, such as the sociologists Stark and Bainbridge, who drolly write that "since the Enlightenment, most Western intellectuals have anticipated the death of religion as eagerly as ancient Israel awaited the messiah" (1985, 1). I am focused upon the twentieth century because it is during that century that the cultural powers of technoscientific researchers (qua researchers) expanded. In fact, Stark and Bainbridge themselves focus upon how secularist theories triumphed in sociology, psychology, and anthropology, all fields which came to maturity in the twentieth century.

8. Secularist theories in sociology relied upon the "crisis of credibility" (Berger [1967] 1990, 127) allegedly suffered by modern religions, which could not offer the assurances that they had prior to the "death of God," as announced by Nietzsche. The privatization of religion in modern life means that religion no longer carries the ontological or epistemic significance of its prior incarnations (ibid., 134); instead, it must compete with nonreligious institutions—such as science—in the creation of our cultural worldview (ibid., 137). According to the famed sociologist Peter Berger, modern culture—especially in its capitalistic and industrial practices—creates a space free of religion that slowly expands, taking over other sectors of the community (ibid., 129). As we shall see, however, Berger was incorrect in his belief that secularism would eliminate religious life.

9. Berger recognizes that modern religious people have two options: to privatize their religious beliefs, thus radically diminishing the significance of these beliefs, or segregate themselves into separate cultures wherein their religious beliefs retain power. Bainbridge and Stark, however, observe that the process whereby religion remains influential is considerably more complex and richer in its possibilities than is at first evident in Berger's early model.

10. Weber's argument, that rational calculation could master all forces, was later buttressed by Jaques Ellul's elaboration of technology and its role in the disenchantment of the world. Ellul (1912–1994) argues that while humankind might desire and appreciate religious mystery, technique (the rational, efficient methods of technoscientific culture) "desacralizes because it demonstrates . . . that mystery does not exist. Science brings to the light of day everything man had believed sacred. Technique takes possession of it and enslaves it. The sacred cannot resist" (Ellul [1954] 1964, 142).

11. Even as secularism theorists championed the death of religion, a modern "gnostic" trend toward spiritual transformation evolved. Where Ellul believed that the "individual who lives in the technical milieu knows very well that there is nothing spiritual anywhere" (Ellul [1954] 1964, 143), modern gnosis—a revelatory inner experience resulting in transformative spirituality—has actually grown out of nineteenth-century occultism and landed firmly in the world of digital technology (Aupers, Hautman, and Pels 2008). Aupers, Hautman, and Pels label this conflation of religion and science "cybergnosis," and see it through the public advocacy of Timothy Leary and leaders in the so-called "cyberia" movement (for a description of key intellectual leaders in "cyberia," see Dery 1996 and Rushkoff 1994). Cybergnosis is an inner experience of truth based in interaction with computers that transforms the believer, freeing him from the constraints of the body in a virtual heaven (ibid., 697). The reality of cybergnosis, both as a programming agenda and a consumer experience, reveals the difficulties inherent in secularist theories founded upon a binary differentiation of religion and science by demonstrating that these two things are neither opposites nor mutually exclusive (ibid., 702–3).

12. John Perry Barlow, a countercultural hero known for cowriting Grateful Dead songs, contributing to the *Whole Earth Catalog* and its subsequent computer network, and being cofounder and executive chair of the Electronic Frontier Foundation, offers a Religion of Humanity for the twenty-first century. Barlow considers cyberspace to be the "native home of Mind" (1994). Barlow does not argue, as do the Apocalyptic AI authors, that minds can depart the biological world to take up residence in cyberspace. He explicitly states that "the realities of the physical world will always be with us" (Barlow 1996b). Because we cannot take our bodies into cyberspace but we can communicate in other ways that allow us a certain amount of presence there, cyberspace must be a realm for our minds but not our bodies. As we shall see, Apocalyptic AI goes one step further: not only are minds "native" to cyberspace but they ought to take up permanent residence there.

13. R.U. Sirius (aka Ken Goffman), the founder of *Mondo 2000* and another of the leading figures of the digital world, has credited Brand as being *the* most important person in creating the atmosphere surrounding digital culture (Sirius 2007).

14. For thinkers such as the journalist and digerati leader Esther Dyson, for example, digitization meant freedom from the constraints of the body, a dematerialized salvation (Turner 2006, 14).

15. Modern architecture renewed this approach to creating paradise—the purification of structures through strict geometrical configuration and removal of decoration and the increased use of windows enabled by steel frames served religious aims throughout the twentieth century (M. Taylor 1993). Even steel and carbon fiber can go only so far, however. In cyberspace, no law of physics limits the height or shape of buildings. The radiance of architecture can outshine the sun. One modern architect, Frank Gehry, found out firsthand how limiting earthly life can be: His Walt Disney Concert Hall in Los Angeles was so blindingly reflective that nearby sidewalks reached 110°F and occupants of adjacent buildings complained about the painful glare. Gehry was forced to coat the building in order to diminish its radiance so that others could work and pass by in peace. Clearly, Earth is no place for transcendent architecture!

16. Second Temple Judaism is the period (sixth century BCE–first century CE) in which Jews worshipped in a rebuilt temple. Ancient Israelites worshipped God at a central temple in Jerusalem, allegedly built by Solomon, the second king of the Jews. The Temple was destroyed by Babylonian invaders in 586 BCE but was rebuilt after the Persian ruler Cyrus the Great defeated the Babylonians in 539, sent the Jews back home to Jerusalem (they had been held captive in Babylon), and ordered the Temple be reconstructed in the late sixth century.

17. Because an apocalypse is a literary work, some authors have sought to move scholarship away from the term apocalypticism, at least with regards to social ideologies. Robert Webb, for example, has argued that we should replace the term apocalypticism with "millenarian movement" (Webb 1990). Apocalypticism, Webb argues, refers to only the ideology of apocalypses (literary works), not to social groups or their ideologies. John J. Collins has argued, however, that there is little overlap between Jewish apocalyptic literature and contemporary millenarian movements, which makes Webb's position even more problematic than the one he aspires to rectify (Collins 1984, 205). Collins maintains that apocalypticism can and does refer to social ideologies as well as literary ideologies and the criticism of his position has been, so far, unconvincing.

18. I do not presume an identity between apocalyptic Judaism and apocalyptic Christianity. Joel Marcus has already shown significant differences among contemporary apocalyptic Jews (Marcus 1996, 2), thus to argue for the identity of all ancient Jewish apocalypticisms—much less the identity of all ancient Jewish and Christian apocalyptic beliefs—would be presumptuous indeed. Studies of apocalypticism have shown, however, that Jewish and Christian apocalyptic traditions are sufficiently similar to allow fruitful comparison. The entire cultural legacy of the Judeo-Christian tradition is available to modern writers, which is why I will speak of Jewish and Christian apocalyptic traditions in one breath.

19. Unfortunately, Ezra leads to a great deal of naming confusion: 1 Ezra is the canonical book of Ezra, 2 Ezra is the Book of Nehemiah, 3 Ezra is 1 Esdras, 4 Ezra is 2 Esdras 3–14, 5 Ezra is 2 Esdras 1–2, and 6 Ezra is 2 Esdras 15–16. 5 Ezra and 6 Ezra are Christian additions to 4 Ezra.

20. For translations of the various non-canonical pseudepigraphic apocrypha referenced here and below, see Charlesworth 1983.

21. For the sake of simplicity, I refer to Saul/Paul only by the name he chose after his conversion to Christianity.

22. This refuted position was advocated by Schmithals (1975).

23. Cook's dispute with the term alienation stems from an overly strict interpretation thereof; he seems to think that political and economic alienation is the only kind and distinguishes it from "cognitive dissonance" (Cook 1995, 16). Cook's use of "alienation" is exceedingly limited; there is no reason to run from the word alienation when it so clearly evokes dissatisfaction and a feeling of "not being at home" in a way that "cognitive dissonance" does not. Similar to Cook, de Boer assumes that all alienation equals political alienation, a fact disputed by Webb (1990). Moreover, Cook assumes that priestly imagery constitutes priestly authorship and never details the psychological and social outlook of Temple priests. Indeed, in his review of Cook's work, David Peterson suggests that post-exilic Temple priests may have had been subordinate to the power of *bet 'abot*, or "ancestral houses" (Peterson 1997). Cook is right, however, in pointing out that alienation does not solely cause apocalypticism (Cook 1995, 40).

24. On opposition to the Jewish elite and Roman rule, see Horsley 2000. According to Horsley, early Christian writings (e.g., the Q Gospel and the Gospel according to Mark) opposed earthly rulers and looked forward to a renewed Israel.

25. As I have already indicated, Apocalyptic AI is not revelatory in the traditional sense but it is interpretive. Not only does it regularly seek to prove its claims through recourse to prior technical achievements and historical interpretations (of the theory of natural selection, for example), but it even has the occasional interpreter enter into the narrative: in *The Age of Spiritual Machines* (Kurzweil 1999), a personality from the future converses with the author in order to clarify the

nature of the future and to confirm the author's position, while in *The Artilect War* (de Garis 2005), Hugo de Garis asks himself questions and, thus, plays the role of revelator himself. In his later work, *The Singularity is Near* (2005), Kurzweil uses myriad interpreters, including figures from the future and tech luminaries (such as Bill Gates) from the present.

26. Among apocalyptics, even more than among other people, there is always a struggle between a right way of thinking/living/seeing and a wrong way of thinking/living/seeing. Malcolm Bull focuses on the dualistic nature of apocalyptic beliefs in his definition of apocalypticism as "the revelation of excluded undifferentiation" (Bull 1999, 83). That is, the resolution to dualism comes through the understanding of fundamental undifferentiation, the understanding that our categories by which we differentiate one thing from another are problematic. According to Bull, dualistic, binary logic is widespread across human cultures but only at certain times and among certain peoples does it become the overriding principle through which the world is understood. Emphasis upon dualism and its transcendence through the apocalyptic *eschaton* are, however, key indicators of the apocalyptic imagination.

27. Bull believes that the eventual inclusion of the once excluded undifferentiation (i.e., the rectification of our presently dualistic circumstances) does not represent the victory of good over evil but, rather, a return to some state prior to the creation of both (1999, 80). I believe him to be in error in this, however, as the triumph of goodness seems presupposed in every apocalyptic text I've seen. To take one of his examples, if the apocalyptic *eschaton* restores humankind to the world of Eden, prior to the knowledge of good and evil, then it would actually restore humankind to a state of goodness. After all, in chapter one of Genesis, God pronounces the world to be good. Any reader of the Hebrew Bible would carry that concept over into his or her reading of Genesis 2 and understand Eden to be "good," not some state in which neither good nor evil exists.

28. There is no reason to believe that all apocalyptic alienation serves the same political purpose every time. For example, the apocalyptic writings of first-century Judaism before the Temple was destroyed may have been calls to war but those after the destruction of the Temple brought consolation without necessarily calling for revolution (J. Collins 2000b, 159).

29. For an alternate view, see 4 Ezra 7:88–99.

30. This, for example, opposes many Gnostic communal understandings.

31. At the premier to a film about him at the Tribeca Film Festival (Ptolemy 2009), Kurzweil, himself, acknowledged the significance of growing up under the threat of nuclear war (Kurzweil 2009b).

32. In the mid-nineteenth century, William Miller began a prophetic Christian movement in upstate New York by claiming that the Second Coming of Jesus would soon arrive. His work prompted a national movement that splintered after nothing apparent happened in October of 1844. The Seventh-Day Adventist movement emerged out of the Great Disappointment with the understanding that while no earthly event took place on October 22, a heavenly one did.

33. Although robotics and AI officially represent separate academic fields, I will generally mean intelligent robots whenever I use the term "robot." Faith in the rise of AI is inextricably intertwined with the growing presence of robots in our everyday lives and Apocalyptic AI advocates anticipate that the robots of the future will be as smart as or smarter than the people with whom they live.

34. Levy subsequently wrote an entire book on the subject of robot sex (Levy 2007).

35. Moravec, even when he was still on campus regularly, could be a difficult person to pin down. As one graduate student at Carnegie Mellon University's Robotics Institute told me, "I've been here since 1995 and I've never met him."

36. It is worth noting that many commentators stood aghast at the intellectual dishonesty of deliberately authoring a paper riddled with obscurities and incorrect statements.

37. Distaste for the body has had various levels of popularity in Judaism and Christianity, but only in exceptional cases has it reached the fervor of Apocalyptic AI.

38. Minsky's claim is reminiscent of Malcolm Bull's analysis of "hiddenness," which he considers to be a function of knowledge, in that the hidden is that which is frustrated knowledge, the difference between what we could know and what we do know (Bull 1999, 18-20). In this case, the knowledge of salvation is hidden from the traditionally religious person even though that person could, theoretically, forsake his prior commitments and awake to the soteriological truths of Apocalyptic AI. Immortality is real and knowable, but hidden. In this sense, Apocalyptic AI is, in fact, revelatory, despite my earlier claim, which applies only to divine revelations.

39. Moravec's claim that evolution is "weeding out ineffective ways of thought" is a truly extraordinary one, as it departs entirely from traditional Darwinian evolution. It is difficult to imagine what kind of competition for natural resources would lead to the supremacy of robotic over human life, which makes Moravec's claim a very clever way of circumventing traditional understandings of biology and introducing technological progress into evolution. Another author, J. Storrs Hall, argues that Darwinian evolution benefits the self-interested and aggressive (Hall 2007, 16), which might be closer to Darwin's meaning but still falls short. Aggression is not always more fit and self-interest is far too vague a concept to formulate a rigorous description of fitness. Moreover, self-interest might prove unfit: the "most" self-interested creature might prove evolutionarily unsuccessful insofar as it might not devote sufficient resources to its offspring.

40. It might be argued that this demonstrates a significant difference between Judeo-Christian apocalypticism and Apocalyptic AI. After all, history ends in the former whereas the latter leaves room for near-unlimited growth. However, upon the onset of the Mind Fire, fundamentally all the important work will have ceased. The learning that supremely intelligent machines will engage in is actually a parallel to the prayer that Jews or Christians would practice in heaven.

41. Kurzweil's faith in accelerating returns is not a widely accepted theory. Randy Isaac of IBM has directly stated that Moore's Law is—rather than a natural law—a statement of industry expectations, a successful prediction of what the industry could and should do, not what it must do. Likewise, even technology cheerleader and prognosticator Howard Rheingold has claimed that new technologies require visionaries, enabling technologies, and financial champions (Rheingold 1991, 52); in short, for technology to progress, the right people have to come together at the right time and in the right circumstances. There is, of course, a bigger problem with the connection between accelerating returns and the inevitability of intelligent machines: general progress in computer technologies may never lead to intelligent machine software in particular. Jaron Lanier, for instance, has argued that the brittleness of software (i.e., its tendency to crash as it gets too complicated) will prevent us from ever building intelligent machines no matter how fast they get (Lanier 2000).

42. The Turing Test was imagined by the famed British mathematician Alan Turing and described in his essay "Computing Machinery and Intelligence" (1950). In it, a person communicates via teletype with both an unseen computer and an unseen human being and has to figure out which one is the computer and which the human being. I will return to the Turing Test in chapter four.

43. It is important to note how the choice of "salient events" creates the allegedly exponential curve.

44. It is worth pointing out that many twentieth-century technologies have undergone decidedly little improvement over the past few decades, including transportation, energy manufacture, food production, and more.

45. The 2003 essay is an annotated version of the 1993 paper.

46. Belief in the AI apocalypse demands that the faithful combine belief in: 1) an exponential rise in computing, 2) a singularity, and 3) the ability to write software that will work despite the enormous complexity of simulating human intelligence.

47. For most researchers, robotics is a way to change the world (Gutkind 2006, 33) but in the case of Apocalyptic AI, the desire to improve the lot of human life has, obviously, taken on several additional dimensions.

48. Jewish and Christian apocalypses often anticipated a fulfillment of Hebrew scriptures in which the messiah would come and reign in peace prior to the eventual destruction of the world and creation of the new kingdom (e.g., 4 Ezra, 2 Baruch, Revelation).

49. Why the owners of companies whose robots come to perform such miracles would share ownership with the rest of humankind is left unsaid. Perhaps this faith represents a return to Karl Marx's communist philosophy, which has been shown to be religious by any number of commentators, including historians of religion (e.g., Smart [1983] 2000, 4-5) and economists (e.g., R. Nelson 2001, 24-27). Few Apocalyptic AI advocates seem sympathetic to actual Marxism, however. Quite contrary to a Marxist future, our immediate future will be a paradise of the mind, a world where intellectuals no longer need fear the tyranny of mass culture. Though not himself an Apocalyptic AI advocate (he does not believe in mind uploading), John Perry Barlow echoes the movement's sentiment when he says that we "will create a civilization of the Mind in Cyberspace. May it be more humane and fair than the world your governments have made before" (Barlow 1996a). Barlow's freedom does not apply to economic injustice, however, but to intellectual injustice. "We are creating a world that all may enter without privilege or prejudice accorded by race, economic power, military force, or station of birth. . . . We are creating a world where anyone, anywhere may express his or her beliefs, no matter how singular, without fear of being coerced into silence or conformity" (ibid.). In a similar, though more radical (and unpleasant) vein, Kurzweil argues that some members of the lower class may one day resist technological progress but in the future, the "underclass [will be] politically neutralized" (Kurzweil 1999, 196). Despite this, Kurzweil has routinely argued, both in print (e.g. 2005, 241) and in public, that technological advances will defeat poverty and environmental collapse along with ignorance and death; he is definitely concerned with the power of technology to improve life for everyone, not just the intellectual or economic elite. Blithe disregard for social consequences is unfortunately common in pop science, however, such as when roboticist Rodney Brooks (an important member of the robotics and AI community, but generally opposed to the apocalyptic agenda) describes the effects that agricultural robotics will have on the economy without giving voice to the soon-to-be impoverished ex-agriculturalists (Brooks 2004, 30). In this regard, Moravec is a very pleasant counterexample. Though his paradise seems problematic, it is among the few that explicitly give the lower classes an equal share in the future. Moravec titles an entire section of *Robot* "Consciousness Raising," which is a Marxist term (Moravec 1999, 89), and it is Moravec who first argues for the universal benefits of Apocalyptic AI.

50. It is for lack of this shift that David Levy and John Perry Barlow are not members of the apocalyptic group. Levy's and Barlow's paradises are decidedly earthly. Their utopian visions do not include the possibility of transferring consciousness to a robot (though for Levy the robots themselves will be as smart as human beings) and, therefore, preclude entrance into Moravec's Mind Fire

(see below). Thus, Levy and Barlow offer counternarratives to Apocalyptic AI just as counternarratives often accompanied the theology of technological progress in early America (Nye 2003). Levy shares many of the premises of the apocalyptic authors but draws different conclusions from them (probably because he ignores the ideas that we can or should depart our physical bodies and that evolution might lead in such a direction).

51. Kevin Warwick is the only truly apocalyptic author who casts doubt on this possibility (2004, 180–81), though he still expects human participation in the transcendent world of cyberspace. Cyborgs will use their onboard wireless Internet communication to join AIs and other cyborgs in the virtual world (2003, 133).

52. Minsky and Harrison borrow Moravec's bush robot for their "machine intelligence" in *The Turing Option*.

53. Desire for a robotic body spread outside the laboratory early in the days of Apocalyptic AI. In a brief essay for the *Whole Earth Review*, the artist Mark Pauline says, "I feel that what I'm doing now with Survival Research Labs is preparing me to *be* a machine; to me, the highest level of evolution would be to be a machine and still have your soul intact. . . . If I could actually become a machine, I wouldn't; I would become *machines*, all machines" (Pauline 1989). Similar goals exist in science fiction and among transhumanist communities, both of which will be discussed in subsequent chapters.

54. Minsky and Harrison also describe a human being with computer brain implants who can download information, including the functional ability of driving (1992).

55. For a discussion of the alleged nonexistence of a conscious mind, see chapter four.

56. At times, Moravec claims that such competition would be economically grounded (e.g., Moravec 1992a, 20) while at other times there appears to be a rather more amorphous competition over the nature of thought itself: "competitive diversity will allow a Darwinian evolution to continue, weeding out ineffective ways of thought" (Moravec 1999, 165). Both positions are troubled. Why economic competition would continue in this paradisiacal future is something of a mystery, but even *it* is more coherent than the claim that Darwinian evolution applies to "ineffective ways of thought" as opposed to the struggle over natural resources (which is closer to, though still not identical with, Moravec's economic claims).

57. We may find that there are valid aesthetic reasons for gold coins and books even if they would be less efficient than a purely binary representation of the world.

58. Precisely what would make computation meaningful is not specified. One can assume, however, that intentionality is at stake. Turning the universe into an extension of the Mind, of conscious intellect, gives it a meaningfulness that it otherwise lacks.

59. De Garis appears to lack a sophisticated approach to the Mind Fire but he expressly wishes for godhood (de Garis 2005, 97), which is surely related to Moravec's search for transcendent meaning.

60. The disdain for nationalism has been a part of apocalypticism at least as far back as the sixteenth century, when radical Protestant reformers shunned state affiliations—relics from the past—in favor of religious affiliations (Albanese 1999, 220).

61. Evolution operates in conjunction with, for Kurzweil, the Law of Accelerating Returns or, for de Garis, unnamed principles in physics to bring about the preordained future.

62. The Turing Award is given annually by the Association for Computing Machinery (ACM) for major technical contributions in computer science.

CHAPTER 2: LABORATORY APOCALYPSE

1. The term "wish fulfillment" is used here in a Freudian sense. That is, wish fulfillment does not refer to something that one cannot have but rather something that one believes in precisely because one wants to have it. For Freud, the belief that a prince will come marry a common girl is, for example, an illusion of wish fulfillment not because it is impossible—it may actually happen—but because it is believed solely out of desire for it (Freud [1927] 1989, 40).

2. The Institute of Electrical and Electronic Engineers (IEEE), a massive and well-respected professional organization in engineering, publishes the *IEEE Spectrum*.

3. Not all of the authors in the "Special Report: The Singularity" believe in a forthcoming singularity and some were even caustic about such predictions (e.g., Zorpette 2008) but the mere fact of its publication in the flagship magazine of the IEEE (circulation is approximately 380,000 individuals) shows how rapidly Apocalyptic AI ideas have become a part of the technical culture of robotics and AI and not just those fields' popular interpretation.

4. Seegrid manufactures robots to operate in factories, delivering carts, pallets, and wheeled equipment. Unlike competing inventions, the SmartCaddy (a joint project with DJ Products) uses camera vision to learn the factory and the route, so it can be taught a new route by simply driving it along rather than by installing new markings, lasers, infra-red beacons, or other easily measurable signals for the robot to detect with its sensors.

5. During my stay at the Robotics Institute, this principle applied to the various authors in Apocalyptic AI. Moravec was granted the most credence (due to his local affiliation, his contributions to mobile robotics, and also, to a much lesser extent, to the sophistication of his writing), while Kurzweil came in second based upon his own considerable accomplishments. Some people expressed reservation at the originality of Kurzweil's popular writings and the efficacy of his arguments, especially regarding the singularity, but no one doubted the quality of his technical work or the value of his intellect or inventions. Few people had much opinion of Warwick's cyborg efforts and, among the few who had heard of its author, there was no enthusiasm for de Garis's artilect theory. The local credibility of Moravec and Kurzweil can thus be traced to their impressive technical achievements and the respect they earned through them.

6. For a concise summary of the debate between Latour and the SSK school, see Latour 1999 and Bloor 1999a and 1999b. Latour has argued that there are three principles in science studies: 1) the nonhuman origin of knowledge, 2) the human origin, and 3) the separation between the first two. He argues that SSK ignores (1) by retaining (3); he would prefer to jettison (3), which he attempts through two strategies. First, he speaks of "natural objects" in the same language as he uses for "social objects." For example, in *Aramis*, which discusses a failed public transit project in France, Latour describes the "desires" of the various parts of the train (Latour [1993] 1996). Second, he creates a second axis of stabilization over time to allow a discussion of how scientific facts sometimes seem very socially constructed, sometimes very naturally constructed, sometimes a mixture of the two, etc. Each "actant" (the anthropomorphized natural object from above) moves through such categories over the history of science; as Callon puts it, "reality is a process. Like a chemical body, it passes through successive states" (Callon [1986] 1999, 70).

7. The obligatory passage point, described by Callon ([1986] 1999), is the point through which any actor must pass if he wishes for his opinions to matter in the final outcome of a scientific process. In essence, each actor seeks to make him- or herself obligatory for all the others.

8. The virtual bodies advocated in Apocalyptic AI bear little resemblance to physical bodies, which is why we can speak of both disembodied AI and virtually embodied AI. The disembodiment refers to the apocalyptic desire to escape our earthly bodies, not virtual bodies.

9. On November 3, 2007, Boss won the Urban Challenge in Victorville, Calif., finishing about twenty minutes faster than second-place Stanford over a sixty-mile course that required safe navigation through human and robot traffic.

10. In a similar vein, Howie Choset told me that he no longer spends much time "doing science." In his estimation, doing science means thinking about scientific principles, rather than worrying about funding, playing soundboard or reality check for his grad students, managing administrative tasks, or any of the other jobs that come along with academic seniority (Choset 2007). Even a cursory glance at any good work on the sociology of science demonstrates that Choset's experience mirrors that of almost every scientist in the world, but I question his belief that only "thinking about scientific principles" is doing science. Rather, all of those other tasks are integral parts of scientific research and doing them well can be as difficult—and important—as thinking about scientific principles.

11. In addition to the well-publicized triumph of the Tartan Racing Team in the 2007 DARPA Urban Challenge, Institute members frequently receive recognition. For example, the project that then occupied Touretzky—the one for which he had to find ways of cramming computer parts inside—is a robot vehicle with a camera mounted to one arm and a gripper mounted to another. It won a Technical Innovation Award for hardware/software integration at the annual meeting for the Association for the Advancement of Artificial Intelligence (AAAI) in 2007 and the completed hexapod robot (Chiara) was awarded second place in the Mobile Robots competition at the 2008 AAAI annual meeting and was featured an issue of *Robot* magazine (Atwood and Berry 2008). Similarly, Matt Mason, the director of the institute, received the IEEE Robotics and Automation Society Pioneer Award in 2009 and Adrien Treuille was named to *Technology Review* magazine's top thirty-five innovators under the age of thirty five in 2009.

12. While the RI faculty were very receptive to me, they definitely wanted to know what I meant by characterizing Moravec and his colleagues as religious and apocalyptic. It seemed that, for the Institute faculty, my approach is a novel way of discussing the ideas. Nevertheless, no one dismissed my analysis out of hand, nor did anyone object to my terminology after I had explained my meaning.

13. In fact, games might always, or nearly so, have serious ramifications but this is not the book in which to challenge the conventional usage of the word.

14. Interestingly, many science fiction authors are also popular science authors (Sterling 2007).

15. A recent review of ABC's "Masters of Science Fiction" television series states that it "is just the kind of thing that charges the imaginations of 14-year-old boys, or of older boys who sit at home on Saturday nights, phasars [sic] at the ready" (J. Schwartz 2007). I fail to see what this kind of editorialization offers, aside from allowing the author to declare himself superior to those for whom he writes.

16. In other films and novels, we also look forward to lives of leisure and plenitude enabled by robots. This dynamic appears clearly in Isaac Asimov's robot trilogy *The Caves of Steel*, *The Naked Sun*, and *The Robots of Dawn*. In each of these, Asimov presents robots as critical for human survival but his characters all too often see them as threats to their economic livelihoods.

17. The influence of science fiction at MIT led to other sci-fi work, including George Stetten's *Weissenbaum's Eye* (1989). Stetten was a student at MIT in the 1970s and is currently associate research professor at the CMU Robotics Institute.

18. Minsky has also quoted science fiction authors as authorities in his published work (see 2006, 101). Naturally, I intend no slight to Minsky by this claim (see chapter four!), I wish to point out only the significance he ascribes to science fiction.

19. Even without visiting professorships, science fiction authors have influenced the practice of computer science researchers. Minsky may have never secured a position in science fiction at the Media Lab but during the tech boom of the 1990s there were Silicon Valley companies that employed writers as innovative thinkers (e.g., Autodesk's Advanced Technology Division, which hired the cyberpunk author Rudy Rucker).

20. In his important work *Imagined Communities*, Benedict Anderson argues that nation building is a process of naturalization through time. The idea of homogenous, empty time permitted the conception of simultaneous imagined existence ([1983] 1991, 26). The nation is a "confidence of community in anonymity," which is the "hallmark of modern nations" (ibid., 36). A similar operation is at stake in the creation of a scientific community, the individuals of which recognize themselves through their simultaneous attention to similar projects. A biologist is a member of the biological sciences insofar as he or she can imagine that there is a group that attends to similar concerns via similar approaches. This power of imagination helps exclude people from the group at the same time that it allows the scientist to include others. For example, attention to the question "how did human beings arise" only situates one within the biological sciences if one uses evolutionary methods; attending to it by means of the Bible does not constitute biology.

21. Engelberger is known as the father of industrial robotics; he has received the Japan Prize, the American Society of Mechanical Engineers' Leonardo da Vinci Award, and Columbia University's Egleston Medal.

22. I am grateful to Steve Rainwater and Robots.net for advertising the survey and driving a significant number of respondents to it.

23. In fact, there is an amazing degree of coincidence between de Garis's artilect war scenario and one of Isaac Asimov stories from *I, Robot*. In both, a war takes place in which some people are apparently "for" the robots and some "against." In Asimov's postapocalyptic world, a foolish individual who did not know that the people actually fought the robots for control of the world helped put one back together, which subsequently headed off on its own to rebuild the robot army. There are shades of this in de Garis's expectation that the Terrans will outlaw the Cosmists, possibly killing many before a second wave of Cosmists secretly resurrects the program (de Garis 2005, 163–64).

24. In an interesting counter-example, when William Gibson addressed this in *Neuromancer*, the uploaded consciousness of Dixie Flatline wants the protagonist (Case) to "erase this goddam thing," referring to himself (Gibson 1984, 106).

25. While science fiction authors gave Moravec the inspiration for some of his ideas, the novelty of his approach drew wide acclaim and has provided science fiction with inspiration of its own. In Charles Stross's *Accelerando* (2005), for example, the protagonist wears a computer in his glasses that possesses much of his personality, an idea described in Moravec's *Mind Children* (1988, 112). Likewise, Stross borrows the idea of a person splitting off a second personality to travel through space and return to the original with new memories (Moravec 1988, 114). Moravec's idea of immortality through backup also appears in Cory Doctorow's *Down and Out in the Magic Kingdom* (2003). The characters reinstantiate themselves in new biological bodies whenever they desire to be young again and the deceased can be resurrected from a recent backup of his or her mind file.

26. Early in the history of computers, the success of funding seekers depended upon their ability to promise a fantastic future to granting agencies. Lab visitors saw fantastic robots and computers when visiting movie theaters so a large machine that churns out a series of incomprehensible numbers was unlikely to appear impressive; programmers made up for this by creating games on the computers that could be played by visitors and that would "look like at least a distant relative of the ones in the movies" (Castronova 2007, 23).

27. A golem is an artificial humanoid made of clay or dirt through Jewish mystical practice. For more on golems, see appendix one.

28. The preface, written by his friend and fellow Apocalyptic AI thinker Kevin Warwick, stresses that de Garis may just be "one of the major thinkers of the twenty-first century" (de Garis 2005, ii–iii). The need for sustained mutual gratification can play a key role in raising a scientist's profile. The best example of this appears in the letters of Paul Feyerabend and Imre Lakatos, two friends who, like de Garis and Warwick, took seemingly different philosophical positions though they in fact shared a great deal more than they publicly admitted (Lakatos, Feyerabend, and Motterlini 2000).

29. "Gigadeath" is de Garis's word for the billions of people who will die fighting over whether to build AIs.

30. De Garis blithely compares himself to a collection of major historical figures, including Rousseau and Marx along with several major scientists.

31. De Garis frequently tells the reader that he will dumb things down for him or her (for example, see pages 2, 54, and 74, where de Garis tells us that it is quite okay if we are not smart enough to follow his technical argument).

32. A supercollider is a high-energy particle accelerator. The SSC was to be circular, accelerating particles by use of high-energy magnets until they had reached the desired speed for collision. The hope is that by colliding particles at sufficient speeds, novel particles can be formed and studied. The SSC was to have a 54-mile circumference and was intended to discover the Higgs boson, a hypothetical elementary particle.

33. Other pop science books show similar political agendas. For example, Edward O. Wilson's most recent book, *The Creation* (2006), describes environmental concerns in biology to help religious people understand why it matters that they join the environmental movement (which is obviously political) but then moves on in its conclusion to discuss the intelligent design controversy, which bears little if at all upon the rest of his text.

34. This is not to diminish the significance of military and domestic utility offered by advanced robotics. I suspect, however, that in terms of actual value to everyday people, military applications mean little and domestic utility has yet to be proven in any powerful sense. Hyping robotics through its military or domestic possibilities is less likely to succeed than making robotics a quasi-religious endeavor.

35. Langdon Winner, Thomas Phelan Chair in the School of Humanities and Social Sciences at Rensselaer Polytechnic Institute, believes that there was a deliberate connection between posthuman pop science in the late 1990s and a search for venture capital (2002, 40). I think he is right, but that does not imply that the authors made deliberate moves in response to the real-world failures of Weinberg's advocacy.

36. Kurzweil and Moravec are not the only pop science authors to use religion as a means of gathering support. For example, much has been made of Stephen Hawking's god talk despite the fact that Hawking is, himself, an avowed atheist. "Hawking likes to connect physics with God, which is why the crowds pack his lectures" (Giberson and Artigas 2007, 88). This appears to be sufficiently

important as a marketing tool that Carl Sagan's vigorously atheistic introduction to Hawking's *A Brief History of Time* was removed from the book's tenth anniversary edition (Hawking 1998) and has been credited by the astrophysicist Peter Coles with directly producing Hawking's public prestige (quoted in Giberson and Artigas 2007, 120). One of Hawking's old schoolmates, the Royal Astronomer Sir Martin Rees, has also stated that Hawking "(or maybe his editor) judged that each mention of God would double the sales" of *A Brief History* (quoted in Giberson and Artigas 2007, 88).

37. The Bernal Prize is awarded annually by the Society for Social Studies of Science (4S) and the publisher Thomson Scientific to an individual judged to have made a distinguished contribution to the social study of science.

38. Academic articles do not generally affect the lay public. Rather, they are meant to convince other scientists that they should change their beliefs and behaviors to reflect those of the author. They are, in Latour's words, "trials of strength."

39. Kurzweil, as an independent businessman, would naturally turn toward stock market investments as his way of indicating that the public should fund the AI apocalypse. De Garis is an equal opportunity borrower, hoping that *someone* among the public and private sectors will invest.

40. I owe thanks to Sebastian Scherer of the CMU Robotics Institute for telling me about Weber's essay and an enormous debt of gratitude to my friend Alexander Ornella, of the University of Graz, for his helpful translation of it.

41. The fairy tale approach also occasionally appears in the robotics press (another form of pop science). For example, an author in the magazine *Robot* declares: "RoboCup goals reach beyond the technical advances that simply enable robots to play soccer—this global initiative is aimed at accelerating the development of integrated robotics technologies that will transform our world and benefit humanity" (Atwood 2006, 49). The split between an ideal world (in which "fairy tale promises" lack scientific standing) and the real world (in which those promises regularly appear in pop science books and funding-related materials) reflects a fundamental concern in religious life—that the real world rarely accedes to our vision of what it should be. Just as the claim that indigenous bear hunters sing for their prey and only fight them "man to man" (never using traps) should arouse our skepticism (Smith 1982, 60), so too must the claim that scientists always request grants in technical terms, dismissing futuristic promises as irrelevant to their research or its funding.

42. Apocalyptic AI could backfire over the long term. Authors ought to be careful of what kind of promises they make; after all, many promises are impossible to keep (Weiss 2007). If the population should feel deceived by apocalyptic claims and promises of infinite leisure, a backlash might remove funding altogether. This happened to biotech companies in the early 2000s, which found funding sources had gone dry when the companies failed to deliver marketable products within their own given time frames (Alexander 2003, 201–22).

43. I exercised two different strategies in my interviews and discussions: 1) I asked questions without any lead to see what my discussants would come up with on their own and 2) I gave them my opinions about various subjects and then asked the discussants for a reaction. The latter of these strategies I generally used only after I had exhausted the first. In this circumstance, the second was not required.

44. This is somewhat reminiscent of Joseph Corn's incorrect belief that technological panaceas are solely the delusion of the scientifically ignorant and cut off from the work and ideas of actual scientists (Corn 1986). The belief that politicians are behind the rhetoric of Apocalyptic AI is, I think, no more likely than Corn's position. Nevertheless, Scherer is correct to point toward the connection between political talk and pop culture interest in Apocalyptic AI.

45. Hughes is a former board member for the World Transhumanist Association and is currently executive director of the Institute for Ethics and Emerging Technologies, another transhumanist organization.

46. In a presidential press release, nanotechnology is credited with the possibility of curing human disease on a massive scale and eliminating pollution through clean manufacturing (White House: Office of the Press Secretary 2003)—both promises of the sort that Weber would call "fairy tales." Weber's fairy tale label should not be taken as indicative of the eventual success of such research; rather, she points only toward the important concern that it is the long-term promises of these technologies that leads to their encouragement and adoption, not an assessment of the immediate details involved in the research.

47. Stephen Jay Gould has offered the most well-known alternative to this position in his principle of Non-Overlapping Magisteria (NOMA). He claims that religion is the domain of morality and ethics while science is the domain of empirical problem solving (Gould 1999). Of course, science is often intertwined with morality and religions often make empirical claims. Gould's position, though admirable as an effort to help people get along, is deeply flawed.

48. Moravec has even claimed to be "less hard-core" in his atheism than he once was and recognizes some of the similarities between his own position and that of early Christian theologians (Platt 1995).

49. Moravec's simulation argument is the subject of Nick Bostrom's essay "Are You Living in a Computer Simulation?" (2003), which was recently popularized for *New Scientist* (Bostrom 2006). Somewhat shockingly, in the *New Scientist* essay Bostrom credits himself for having published the simulation argument rather than specifying that he published an essay *about* the simulation argument, which was presented by Moravec more than a decade before Bostrom. Bostrom, the director of Oxford University's Future of Humanity Institute, argues that at least one of the following propositions is true: 1) the human species is likely to go extinct before reaching the "posthuman" stage, 2) posthuman civilizations are unlikely to run computer simulations of artificial people, 3) we are almost certainly living in a computer simulation. Bostrom's assumption that a "technologically mature" society would be able to create a computer simulation that included conscious artificial intelligence is, however, circular in that it assumes what it set out to debate. Bostrom's conclusion that one of his three positions *must* be true is naive. At the *very* least, we could posit that human beings might not go extinct, that we might have the willingness to run computer simulations with artificial consciousnesses but that we find it—for any of an infinite number of reasons why—impossible. Many biologists intend to spend their entire careers studying the neural structure of simple animals like *Caenorhabditis elegans* (a one-millimeter-long roundworm that has only 302 neurons) or various lobster species; if understanding these animals is such a tremendous task, how much harder will it be to map out the human brain? Human minds are so tremendously complicated that we have no a priori reason for believing that terribly fast computers will duplicate consciousness even if we presume that consciousness is solely a product of biological processes (see chapter four).

CHAPTER 3: TRANSCENDING REALITY

1. *World of Warcraft* is a registered trademark of Blizzard Entertainment, Inc.

2. Massively multiplayer online games include massively multiplayer online role-playing games like *World of Warcraft*, online combat games and "shoot-'em-ups," among others.

3. *Mass Effect* is a registered trademark of EA International, Ltd.

4. *Ultima Online* is a registered trademark of Electronic Arts., Inc. *EverQuest* is a registered trademark of Sony Online Entertainment LLC.

5. The co-production of the world by consumers has been labeled "produsage" by the media specialist Axel Bruns (2008), who believes that MMORPGs in general, and SL in particular, are excellent examples of the shift toward produsage in modern media life (ibid., 294–299).

6. As I've said, all the MMOGs are social but games like *Second Life* might be considered "more social" in that they lack any other clear gaming objective.

7. The economic world of online games seamlessly takes advantage of online auctions to transition into the real world. Before the practice was outlawed, money, weapons, magical items, even characters could be purchased through eBay and other auction houses and then transferred in *World of Warcraft* or *EverQuest*. Some people have plenty of "real" dollars but not enough time or skill to establish powerful characters; other people have enough time and skill to establish powerful characters but need "real" money. So they exchange. In this sense, virtual money is as real as real money (Castronova 2005, 47, 148). With enough gamers, online economies could have very serious impact upon real world economics. *Second Life* maintains a financial exchange by which Linden Dollars are bought and sold. Because money can be earned and traded for earthly currency, *Second Life* has become big business. Its largest real estate mogul, Anshe Chung (real life Ailin Graff) had $250,000 worth of SL real estate in May 2006 and opened a studio and office in Wuhan, China, to help deal with the constant growth (Hof 2006). Later that same year, Chung became the first virtual millionaire, with a net worth of over one million American dollars. Chung owns land, shopping malls, and store chains, and has established several brand names in *Second Life*. Anshe Chung Studios now employs fifty people in its Wuhan office. Chung is not the only gamer to have made massive virtual real estate acquisitions. In 2005, a player in *Entropia Universe* named Jon "NEVERDIE" Jacobs paid $100,000 for a virtual asteroid; he allegedly recouped the entire cost within eight months through fees and apartment rentals. These kinds of exchanges will become all the more common as virtual living becomes ubiquitous. Chung is not the only person making an interesting living out of SL; the top ten SL entrepreneurs average $200,000 per year (*Economist* 2006). Not all SL entrepreneurs deal in real estate, however. Kermitt Quirk, for example, programmed SL's most popular game, *Tringo*, which is a combination of bingo and the video game *Tetris*. Avatars play *Tringo* at casinos across SL and it is so popular that Donnerwood Media licensed it for earthly play in cell phones and Nintendo's Game Boy Advance. In 2007, Two Way Ltd. licensed the game from Donnerwood and released it for personal computers.

8. After several criticisms of SL as a business, this has become obvious to Chris Anderson, editor in chief of *Wired*, who writes that at *Wired*, they are "bullish on SL as a consumer experience and bearish on it as a marketing vehicle" (Glaser 2007).

9. Bartle coauthored the seminal game MUD (Multi-User Dungeon) in the early 1980s.

10. Artificial Life is the field of computer programming in which programmers create artificial environments with resources and constraints that enable "evolution" to occur among the "beings" of the program.

11. Aupers and Houtman connect these religious claims to ancient Gnosticism, rather than apocalypticism, and they see the rejection of the world inherent in cyberspace apotheosis as a reflection of New Age and pagan religious traditions (2005). Ancient Gnosticism counts as among the religions most oriented toward a dualistic view of the world but Aupers and Houtman focus upon the Gnostic desire for the freedom of a divine spark from earthly life rather than upon metaphysical dualism, per se.

12. The world of J.R.R. Tolkien in particular played an important role in the rise of *Dungeons &*
Dragons and, through this, virtual reality; both fantasy and science fiction were staples of the computer gamer world (King and Borland 2003, 95)

13. Virtual reality pioneer Jaron Lanier finds it amazing that some people succeed so beautifully in
subordinating the richness of everyday life to the very poor approximation thereof in 1990s virtual
reality. He has expressly refuted the supremacy of virtual reality based upon his experiences with cut-
ting edge technology (Lanier 1996). Despite his reservations, Lanier, like plenty of residents, believes
that the benefits of SL will extend outside of virtual reality. An advisor to *Second Life*, he has claimed
that the online world "unquestionably has the potential to improve life outside" (Economist 2006).

14. I am grateful to James Wagner Au, publisher of the New World Notes blog (http://nwn.blogs.
com), Akela Talamasca of the *Second Life Insider* and *Massively.com*, Gwyneth Llewelyn of gwynethllewe-
lyn.net, Zigi Bury of *SL'ang Life Magazine*, Katt Kongo, the publisher of the *Metaverse Messenger*, a
Second Life newspaper, and Sherrie Shepherd, the *Metaverse Messenger* journalist who profiled me in
its pages, for helping me to spread word of the survey.

15. In a recent e-mail to me, Ostwald reiterated his concern that, despite improvements, virtual
communities continue to have "deep social and structural problems" but also said that the different
habits of this generation's web users "may, in time, transcend the problems even if the virtual environments do not improve" (Ostwald 2007).

16. Such results appear contradicted by Ducheneaut, Yee, Nickell, and Moore (2006), who argue
that broad social connections do not occur until relatively advanced stages of *World of Warcraft*.
However, advancement occurs rapidly at early levels before slowing at the advanced levels where
sophisticated social relationships form by necessity (tasks cannot be accomplished without them).
Therefore, any player who remains longer than a few weeks will enter into the social world of the
game. Indeed, I suspect that only those characters who discover and enjoy the social aspects of the
game will go to the trouble of continuing play after the immediate novelty has worn off; they will
then cultivate those aspects of the game on their way to higher levels of advancement where contacts
and relationships will be necessary for advancement and not just for pleasure.

17. I must admit that I wonder about the long-term viability of such a project with respect to a
neighborhood bar. In the latter, real eating and real drinking occur, which facilitates community relations. The sociability of drinking (especially alcohol) and eating will not be easily reconstructed
unless virtual food and drink somehow become essential for virtual survival (and even virtual con-
sumption may not really serve the community).

18. Admittedly, some users find the graphics restrictive and prefer the near-unlimited imaginary
potential of chat-based worlds.

19. Transhumanists and other biotech advocates largely follow a libertarian political system of
free economics and limited government.

20. A group dedicated to "the integration of Metaverse technologies" in SL.

21. Extropy is a transhumanist movement founded by More and others in the late 1980s.

22. Teilhard de Chardin (1881–1955) is particularly known for his belief that evolution moves
toward an "Omega Point" when all of life will be united with God. This evolutionary progress, as
described in *The Phenomenon of Man*, will eventually produce a "neo-humanity" ([1955] 1959, 210).

23. The Order of Cosmic Engineers asserts that it is "convictions-based" rather than "faith-based."
I confess to not understanding the distinction, especially with regard to faith/conviction in events
like human immortality and the resurrection of the dead.

24. One important exception to this is Gregory Stock, director of the Program on Medicine, Technology, and Society at UCLA's School of Medicine. Stock believes that biotechnology will prove the end-all technology for transhumanism (Stock 2003).

25. The best book on this subject is probably Hayles 1999.

26. In this area, as in many areas of the study of religion, science, and technology, we are woefully underinformed about the state of affairs in nonwestern countries. It would be profoundly useful to know whether the kinds of transhumanism that have appeared in Euro-American culture are matched by similar, different, or no transhumanist agendas in other areas of the world.

27. Durkheim is well-known for his equation that society equals the totem equals the god (Durkheim [1912] 1995, 208). A totem, loosely speaking, is a plant, animal, or—rarely—other natural feature believed by a segment of a tribal population to be the ancestor and family member of present members of that segment. Tribes were divided into systems of totems where different totems were or were not allowed access to certain people, objects, or places. Rules governing intermarriage and use of natural resources are very common to totemic peoples. Naturally, I hasten to erect my shield of *epoche* (see the endnotes to the introduction to this volume); I neither advocate nor deny Durkheim's thesis that god is nothing more than or outside of society. When Dr. Vilayanur Ramachandran and his team of neuroscientists at the University of California at San Diego associated a particular group of nerve cells in the frontal lobe with religious experience, a spokesman for Richard Harries, the bishop of Oxford, replied "it would not be surprising if God had created us with a physical facility for belief" (Connor 1997). We could likewise, if we were so inclined, assert that "it would not be surprising if God had created us with a social facility for belief." Thus, that Durkheim implicates society in the sacred does not *necessarily* preclude the ontological reality of the divine or the sacred in any form and I intend to stay well situated on top of the fence on this matter.

28. Max Weber argued that charisma dissipates when made economically routine (Weber 1968, 20–21). This has also played a role in the relationship between technology and the sacred, as when Japanese industrial robots ceased receiving Shinto blessings when they were introduced to factories (Geraci 2006, 237).

29. Similarly, Richard Bartle, comparing immersion in virtual worlds to the psychological concept of flow, argues that gamers experience a state of ecstasy when fully immersed. For Bartle (unlike Sophrosyne Stenvaag and others to be described later this chapter), immersion is about identifying with the avatar and finding one's true self-identity through play. In "virtual worlds it's almost unavoidable that the character and the player will tend toward each other. . . . Ultimately, you advance to the final level of immersion, where you and your character become one. One individual, one personal identity" (Bartle [2003] 2004, 161). In this state, the gamer ignores distractions and becomes ecstatic in his or her gaming production (ibid., 157).

30. There are far too many *EverQuest* players for them all to operate in the world together simultaneously so the game operators run the game on many different servers, which creates "parallel universes" for the game.

31. Alongside more traditional community-building exercises and even passionate expression of emotions (quite common in virtual worlds), we can even make the case for deviant sexual behavior in *Second Life*. The controversy over "child play" (wherein one individual creates and operates a "child" avatar in order to engage in sexual conduct with "adult" avatars) and the frequency of sexual activity with "furries" (avatars that have humanoid-animal forms, such as tails and cat heads and fur)

show how a substantial number of people feel that behavior that would be totally unacceptable in ordinary life is quite the opposite in virtual reality.

32. Tefillin are the phylacteries that hold small parchments of Torah writings that (mostly Orthodox) Jews tie to their left arm and forehead via leather straps as part of their morning prayer rituals in keeping with the biblical commandment to keep the words of the commandments: "Bind them as a sign on your hand, fix them as an emblem on your forehead" (Deuteronomy 11:18).

33. Online gamers already welcome robots into their virtual worlds and have formed emotional bonds with them. Even though online "robots" are very poor approximations of conscious human beings, Castronova claims they improve the emotional content of games (2005, 93) and at a Fan Faire, T. L. Taylor reports that human beings dressed up as the AIs from *EverQuest* were happily greeted by the players (T. L. Taylor 2006, 6).

34. For a summary of the role of voice chat in SL, see Boellstorff 2008, 112–16.

35. This requires that we presume a person's claims to separation between avatar and earthly person are truthful or, at any rate, meaningful. Without trying to deceive self and other, a person might believe in the separation between personalities without such separation being, in fact, true. Sophrosyne Stenvaag, for example, claims that there is absolutely no emotional carryover between herself and her Other Personality. Without having walked in her shoes, I must resort once again to *epoche*.

36. DaSilva has explicitly rejected being a transhumanist as she considers herself nonhuman (Stenvaag 2007e). Given that DaSilva remains, in many very important ways, tied to her "primary," however, the term transhumanist does apply to her; she does, after all, acknowledge that her primary "might be" a transhumanist (ibid.) and has, in fact, labeled herself among the human community using the pronoun "we" (DaSilva 2008a).

37. In 2009, Stenvaag took a (possibly permanent) hiatus from *Second Life*, "merging back into the Other Personality . . . who *needs* *sophrosyne*, and who's beginning to put it to good use" after feeling that her struggle to maintain SL as a place for the construction of identity was lost (Stenvaag 2009).

38. The name here is both illustrative and obvious. According to Greek myth, Galatea was a statue carved by Pygmalion. Aphrodite brought her to life when Pygmalion fell in love with her.

39. There are mainland continents owned and operated by Linden Lab but for a one time fee of $1,675 and a monthly maintenance fee of $295, users can purchase 65,536 virtual square meters and rent out space on their own private islands.

40. A sim (server host machine) provides the computing resources for a geographical area and the individuals within it. A given sim can hold forty or one hundred avatars, depending upon the quality of the machine, and the entire SL grid consisted of more than 2,000 sims in 2008.

41. For example, the rapid ascent to popularity of the comic "Botgirl" demonstrates this. Botgirl Questi publishes an immersionist-themed comic on her blog and after being profiled in the *New World Notes* blog became an SL celebrity, gaining wide readership and appearing (in SL) for interviews.

42. At present, Extropia is not directly connected to earthly transhumanist groups; influence upon the "atomic world" is a "third order concern" according to Stenvaag (2007e). The issue has arisen among Extropian citizens, however, and it seems only a matter of time before closer ties are formed between Extropia and earthly organizations.

43. Prisco, for example, has spoken of the need for a critical mass prior to unveiling the OCE and of his hopes for a great communicator such as Larry King or Oprah Winfrey to help pass along OCE ideas (Prisco 2008b).

44. This is a fascinating materialization of Ludwig Feuerbach's nineteenth-century thesis that we manufacture God out of our own subjectivity. Feuerbach claimed that God is the objectification of what is best in humankind. In *The Essence of Christianity*, he writes: "Such as are a man's thoughts and dispositions, such is his God; so much worth as a man has, so much and no more has his God. Consciousness of God is self-consciousness, knowledge of God is self-knowledge" (Feuerbach [1841] 1957, 12). For Feuerbach, the religious object is nothing but the human individual himself; human beings project their need for transcendence outside of themselves and therein objectify as their god the human qualities that they admire. If transhumanists hope to instantiate what they consider the authentically human into a real (if virtual) existence and call it a god then they will fully realize the Feuerbachian claim as Omer and Rosen hope.

45. In fact, rituals and messianic fervor already exist in transhumanism but Prisco's interest in making them explicit is a significant one.

46. In fact, the power of eschatological groups to remain hopeful is nothing to be taken lightly. Though the expected end of the world in 1843 became known as the "great disappointment" to William Miller's upstate New York followers, Miller's group transformed into the Seventh Day Adventists, who remain with us today.

CHAPTER 4: "IMMATERIAL" IMPACT OF THE APOCALYPSE

1. Although I will discuss only the relationship between mental states and brain states, we cannot forget the essential importance of non-brain bodily activity. As the neuroscientist Antonio Damasio points out, the brain and the body are an indissociable unity composed of endocrine, immune, autonomic, and neural components (Damasio 1994, xx). An organism's condition is directly affected by bodily activities that take place outside of the brain.

2. Nagel recognizes the connection between mind states and body states but, as any reductionist description of mental experience will necessarily eliminate its subjective experience, Nagel argues that reductionism is inappropriate as a total description of mental phenomena. A successful reduction must account for *all* features of the system to be reduced, not merely some of them. Until subjectivity itself can be reduced to body states, the mind-body problem cannot be presumed identical to other kinds of biological reductions. No matter how much we know about bat neurophysiology, we will still lack knowledge of what it is like to be the bat (Nagel 1974, 442).

3. In *The Emotion Machine* (2006), Minsky moves from the term "agent" to the term "resource" so as to avoid any personification of the mental elements.

4. A similar tack is taken by roboticist Ben Kuipers (one of Minsky's former students), who argues that consciousness is based upon a high volume of sensory and motor information (the "firehose of experience") dealt with by "trackers" that allow objects continuity through the sensory stream, laws that operationalize behavior, and correspondence between the agent's symbolic theory of the world, tracked symbols, actions, and properties of action and perception in the physical world (Kuipers 2005).

5. Moravec recognizes that this aligns him with Descartes insofar as it sets up a mind-body dualism (Moravec 1988, 119).

6. I should, perhaps, avoid referring to the computational mind model as a metaphor. Among Apocalyptic AI advocates and many philosophers of mind and AI researchers, the mind is really a computer, not simply like a computer. For example, J. Storrs Hall writes: "If the brain is an adapted organ, then . . . what is its function? The answer is simple: it is a computer" (Hall 2007, 108). It is peculiar how easily Hall leaps from the fact that the brain evolved over time to the assumption that it is a computer, an object that never experienced evolution in any biologically meaningful sense. N. Katherine Hayles explores these kinds of intellectual moves in *My Mother Was a Computer* (2005), where she maintains that not all information can be expressed in binary digits.

7. It is important to note that this is not why Apocalyptic AI advocates value the computational mind metaphor. For them, the metaphor is simply the correct way of viewing the brain. Accepting the brain as a computer helps advance the apocalyptic agenda by lending credence to the speculations of Moravec and Kurzweil: if human minds are simply intelligent computers then surely a computer can be made to be intelligent! And if that can be done, then surely computers can get extraordinarily intelligent and we can advance the apocalyptic imagination into reality.

8. It is not clear to me that this preserves the causal powers of "mind" as opposed to "brain."

9. Descartes believed that the *res cogitans* (mind) interacted with the *res extensa* (the body) through the pineal gland, which has been roundly disputed by all modern authorities on the subject, though no one is quite sure what function the pineal gland does perform (it manufactures melatonin, which has unknown properties in human brains).

10. This position is echoed by Moravec, who writes "consciousness may be primarily the continuous story we tell ourselves. . . . Viewed from the outside, the story is just a pattern of electrochemical events" (Moravec 1999, 194–95).

11. As Jerry Fodor says, there is good reason to reject the modular mind hypothesis (Fodor 2000). To be clear, Fodor supports modularity but rejects "massive modularity," the belief that the mind is nothing but a massive collection of modules or agents. In his interpretation, progress in cognitive science has failed to account for abduction, which requires a more global perspective than that allowed in massive modularity, and has—at most—shown how far cognitive scientists have yet to go before they will understand the mind.

12. Art connoisseurs would, of course, point out that modern art appreciation requires more than aesthetic analysis and that other considerations (philosophical, one might say) are relevant to an artwork's value. This does not necessarily mean, however, that only an authentic artwork would be valuable. Indeed, a few artists have become famous for their fakery, which is itself taken to be a kind of originality (e.g., J.S.G. Boggs has developed a reputation as an outstanding artist for his counterfeit bills, which he sketches and then uses to pay for things before letting his audience know who he paid with the fake so that someone can go buy the counterfeit money from its possessor). In any case, Dennett's point is simply that the physical beauty of the painting, which may have little to do with its financial or intellectual value, is not depreciated for it being painted by someone other than Cezanne.

13. Obviously, this would not apply to a human person (perhaps once blind) who sees with cameras. That individual would perhaps know better what it is like for a robot to see than a person who sees with biological eyes. Even so, however, a human being who processes camera inputs with a human brain will remain unable to understand what it would be like to process those inputs with a robotic brain. Further still, to *be* the robot in question is a far greater thing than to *see* like the robot in question.

14. Here I must ask the reader's forgiveness as I, like so many others, elide the difference between "thought" and "consciousness." I cannot defend the claim that thinking is a subset of consciousness but I claim it all the same. If a robot thinks, rather than just computes, then it is conscious. Thinking is an experience, not merely an action.

15. Established in 1990, the Loebner Prize is awarded annually to the best chatterbot program masquerading as a human person. As no entrant has come close to succeeding at a Turing Test, the best program of each year receives a $2,000–$3,000 award. Should a program ever fool the judges in a text-only Turing Test, the prize will be $25,000, and should a chatterbot be indistinguishable from a human being in a test that includes deciphering and understanding text, visual, and auditory input, the prize will be $100,000.

16. For example, Dennett disputes the Chinese Room argument on the grounds that the entire room is conscious. Given his opposition to the Cartesian Theater, the nature of his objection to Searle's argument should be obvious.

17. Some readers might find themselves wondering what a conscious robot would want to do? Watching what a robot chooses to do might, after all, help us decide whether or not it is conscious. Apparently, it would worry about surviving the end of the universe and maintaining a simulation of human beings as a way of studying biologically evolved self-awareness. These suggestions, made by Moravec and Kurzweil, have been repeated without elaboration or addition in recent years (see Watson 2007). Given that these are not the occupations of conscious human beings, however, we should probably put little faith in them. Quite frankly, robots that choose to do the sorts of things we do will have better odds of acquiring social equality.

18. Kurzweil would call this kind of argument an example of "linear thinking," which does not properly account for the power of exponential growth. Because he feels that technology progresses exponentially, there will literally be centuries of 2009-level production from 2010–2050.

19. Artificial psychology is the emerging field of understanding learning, creativity, consciousness and emotion and designing machines that possess those traits (Friedenberg 2008).

20. There may be a connection here to Moravec's belief that super-intelligent robots (and the humans who become them) might need to leave the Earth and take up residence in space, leaving only the more limited machines to remain on the planet and make it a paradise for humankind.

21. For those who wish to know how the books turn out: in *The Caves of Steel*, the murder is an accident as the killer thought he was shooting a robot (which, though illegal, would not have been murder); in *The Naked Sun* the murderess was manipulated by a human being who received all of the blame in the end; and in *The Robots of Dawn* the "murder" of a robot was performed by another robot in order to prevent a manipulative human being from getting vital information from the deceased.

22. Despite the rhetoric of equality on some Spacer colonies, there remain ways in which Spacers assert their superiority over the robots, as Baley eventually discovers (Asimov [1983] 1991, 288–89).

23. A recent essay in *PC Magazine* claims that "Americans will never overcome their cultural aversion to humanoid robots" but believes that we will not have to because robotics technology "will embed itself inside every aspect of our daily lives without our even realizing it" (Ulanoff 2007). If true, many Apocalyptic AI advocates are bound for disappointment. Ulanoff does not offer any sustained argument, however, as to why Americans could not overcome this aversion.

24. Some readers might be surprised to see the *Christian Science Monitor* endorsing radical views of technology. The CSM is one of the best newspapers in the United States. In an era of common journalistic sensationalism, the CSM is less prone to exaggeration and more likely to report news

with integrity than many news outlets. Nevertheless, says the CSM, these issues are "not the stuff of novels or movies anymore" (*Christian Science Monitor* 2007).

25. As artilects become widespread in corporate life, the value of possessing one will supposedly diminish, eliminating the material incentive for their continued enslavement.

26. Sudia is joined by the American Society for the Prevention of Cruelty to Robots (below) and several "futurists," who also anticipate awarding legal rights to robots. Sohail Inayatullah and Phil McNally, for example, believe that robots will have rights within twenty-five to fifty years, though they claim they "are not arguing that robots should have the same rights as humans" (McNally and Inayatullah 1998). Probably in response to their original digital utopian/back-to-the-land audience in the *Whole Earth Review*, Inayatullah and McNally hope to raise awareness that robots be "seen as an integral part of the known universe" (ibid.). More concretely, they argue that robots will take over much of the judicial caseload, relieving human beings of the tedious job of deciding what is right and what is wrong (or, at any rate, what is legal and what is not) and that we will give the robots some set of rights once the robots begin asking for them.

27. Asimov subsequently added a "zeroth" law: A robot may not injure humanity or, through inaction, allow humanity to come to harm.

28. Bruce Schneier is a leading figure in technological security. He is the founder of BT Counterpane, the author of several well-regarded books on cryptography, and the 2008 recipient of the Norbert Wiener Award for Social and Professional Responsibility for his outstanding contributions to social responsibility in computing technology.

29. Establishing a role for governments in a robotic future will require active participation of an informed citizenry. As the Biennial Convention of the International Bar Association's mock trial indicated, legislatures will need to play a significant part in the establishment of effective laws regulating robotic behavior (whether these favor "robot rights" or not). Members of the American government have thus also become interested in legal questions surrounding robotics and AI. Representatives Mike Doyle (D) of Pennsylvania and Zack Wamp (R) of Tennessee formed a Congressional Bi-partisan Robotics Caucus—now co-chaired by Doyle and Phil Gingrey (R-GA)—to look at "this first great technology of the twenty-first century" (Atwood and Berry 2007). It is not clear, however, that the congressional caucus will actually address the legal standing of robots anytime soon; enhancing American economic superiority seems a far likelier agenda. The American government has a tendency to avoid ethical legislation, preferring instead to allow free market economics to regulate the use of technologies. Contrary to the cheerleading from its chief proponents, this style of government has not proven overly productive in the global market. Poisonous children's toys, pet food, and toothpaste more than testify to this failure, which is often due to the political choice to place manufacturing lobbyists in charge of government offices as a form of political repayment (Lipton 2007).

30. Many of the legal problems surrounding robots will be relevant even without the existence of conscious robots. AI programs/robots have already begun managing investment portfolios and performing surgery, for example, and these may become increasingly autonomous, leading to questions about responsibility. A full spectrum of legal rights, however, will apply only if the robots are granted conscious intentions. Given that robots will be created, more or less, the way we want them to be, the question of legal rights may be irrelevant. As Moravec points out, the robots might be built to serve quite cheerfully (Moravec 1999, 139). Robots could be rather like the workers of a bee or ant colony, with no desires but to benefit the group. There is no particular reason why a robot should be built to

further its own interests or, indeed, to require that it have interests aside from the human community and whatever local human owners it contacts.

31. The 1996 version of "Should Trees Have Standing?" is a revised version of the 1972 essay.

32. Based on the physicist Roger Penrose's argument against Strong AI (1989), Allen and Widdison claim that Solum's argument bears little on contemporary debates in AI. They argue against Solum's claim that moral right entitles a self-conscious robot to legal personhood (Allen and Widdison 1996, 36). They propose that software agents, like government states, might be entitled to certain rights of legal personhood in reflection of a social reality in which they take on the roles of legal persons (ibid., 38) or as human-machine partnerships (ibid., 40) or even as a legal expediency (ibid., 41–42), though this is a far cry from what Kurzweil and others see as the rights of intelligent robots.

33. Who would have guessed that marching with an "Equal Rights for Robots" sign could land you in jail? Faced with what he considered an offensive Christian evangelical effort on his campus—which included "Jesus or hell!" signs and evangelists accosting students about their lifestyles—a humorous student made his own sign and started marching around nearby. Campus officials had him arrested, to stand trial for disorderly conduct with intent to alarm or annoy (Kline 2007).

34. This organization was originally founded (in 1992) as the Office of Science and Technology, changing names in 2006 but was then subsequently absorbed into Department for Innovation, Universities, and Skills in 2007 (Wikipedia 2009b).

35. The Ipsos MORI document was reviled by some scientists in the UK. Rightly criticizing the study for its minimal research and documentation, Owen Holand, Alan Winfield, and Noel Sharkey claim the Ipsos MORI document directs attention away from the real issues, especially military robots and responsibility for autonomous robot–incurred death or damage (Henderson 2007). The scientists gathered at the Dana Centre in London in April of 2007 to share their ideas with the public. These scientists believe that the "in principle" arguments offered by Moravec and his followers do not amount to arguments of necessity, especially after decades of research that have not led to anything that looks even remotely like machine sentience (Sharkey 2007). As such, they consider the debate over robot rights a waste of time and resources.

36. The U.K. computer scientist David Levy, on the other hand, offers a detailed and enthusiastic description of just how "sexbots" will enter into human life (Levy 2006, 347–54; Levy 2007). Levy believes that such machines will even aid marriages, by providing individuals with emotional or physical benefits lacking in their relationships (2006, 351). The EURON Roadmap raises both the possibility of social benefits due to sexbots (e.g., decreased exploitation of women and children) and the problems they might cause (lost intimacy among people).

37. Already, news articles circulate about Internet addiction, including one 2007 story about parents who neglected their children, supposedly out of an incurable addition to online gaming. Some concern is probably due for human-robot interactions as well.

38. Technologically, Lanier believes that Cybernetic Totalism will prove illusory, but his primary criticism of it is ethical. From a technical standpoint, Lanier argues that 1) computer software is brittle and will simply become more bloated and more prone to failure as we make it ever more complex (Lanier 2000, 10–11) and 2) there is absolutely no reason to believe that simply making a computer extremely fast will result in it becoming intelligent. He accuses Cybernetic Totalists who argue that the software will get smart enough to solve these problems themselves of intellectual laziness and wishful thinking (ibid., 5).

39. If, as I have argued, camouflaged apocalyptic theology is the core of what Lanier calls Cybernetic Totalism, his faith in our ability to focus on empathic relations with other human beings may be misplaced. It could well be that the dualistic mentality of apocalypticism demands that certain people be included and certain people not. Such a mindset may even make the inclusion of computers into one's "us" category rather than a "them" category easier than including some people! Note that Lanier's own circle represents a dualistic perspective; it is one, however, that does not require apocalyptic resolution. This is not to say that Lanier does not harbor his own crypto-theology, just that his position is not apocalyptic.

40. Intelligent robots will not be purely rational machines. Not only would pure rationality almost certainly prove useless—emotion is a productive engine of rational thought in human beings (Damasio 1994, xvi)—but it simply will not exist. Machines "*will* embody values, assumptions, and purposes, whether their programmers consciously intend them to or not" (Waldrop 1987, 38). The choices we make in designing and implementing our robots will circumscribe the kinds of ethics that they will possess.

41. Of course, when she finds that her ploy has been, at best, of marginal success, Rachel goes to Deckard's house and kills his living goat. Every time Dick gives us firm hold on our emotions and the reality in which his characters operate, he sweeps our certainty away in his next move.

42. Dick makes this an essential part of one of his finest books, *The Man in the High Castle* (1962), which won the Hugo Award. In *The Man in the High Castle*, the characters appear to live in a world where the Axis powers won World War II, but an author of "fiction" reveals that the Allied powers really won the war. All of the book's characters are living illusory lives.

43. Current approaches to computers and robotics show that human beings can, as Dick predicted, experience empathy for machines. Based on a series of experiments using human research subjects and interactive computers, Byron Reeves and Clifford Nass have shown that even though everyone *says* he or she knows that computers lack feelings and are just machines, study participants routinely responded to computers as though the machines were full participants in standard human social interaction (Reeves and Nass 1996, 7). They found that putting both people and computers on teams (e.g., the blue team, which would be visually obvious by the human participants' armbands and the computer monitors' colored borders) led to people responding more sympathetically to the computers on their teams. The computers were believed to be more like the human participants, friendlier, and more helpful to the human participants than were the computers of individuals not assigned a team (ibid., 157–58). As easily as computers can enter our circles of empathy, robots do so even more easily. We are "suckers for moving toys" says Matt Mason, director of the CMU Robotics Institute (Mason 2007). Although they "ought to know better," even roboticists and AI researchers ascribe personalities and intentions to robots. Some researchers profess to be immune to such emotions and try to avoid emotional attachments to their robots, but they too end up personalizing the robots and communicating with them and about them as though the robots are persons (Gutkind 2006, 31–32, 213). This helps explain the profound attachment that some users attribute to robotic vacuums and toys: see Kahney 2003, Spice 2007, and Ugobe 2007a on relationships with Roomba and Trilobyte vacuums; Garreau 2007 on military robots; and Hornyak 2006, Mitsuoka 2007, Shibata 2007, Takahashi 2007, Turkle 1999 and 2007, Ugobe 2007b, and Wada and Shibata 2006 on emotional attachments with toys.

44. MIT computer scientist Joseph Weizenbaum, most famous for his ELIZA chat program of the 1960s, long ago urged that we show a certain restraint in our ongoing computer research (Weizenbaum 1976), as had cybernetics pioneer Norbert Wiener before him (Wiener 1964).

45. Kevin Kelly, the founding editor of *Wired*, has argued that technology is alive and that we must find a way to imbue it with our ethics (Kelly 2007). He considers technology to be the seventh kingdom of life (along with archaea, protocista, monera, fungi, plantae, and anamalia) and believes that it will go out of control, eating up all available resources (this sounds amusingly like the early modern Golem stories, in which a Golem left alone eventually runs amok). The "technium," which is what he calls the living system of technology, even has its own goals, its own "inherent agenda and urges." He believes, therefore, that we must imbue our technological system, our technium, with our ethics before it becomes even more autonomous than it presently is. The influence of Moravec's *Mind Children*, which Kelly does not cite, is clear and decisive. Kelly has simply broadened Moravec's talk of the intelligent robotic children of humankind to refer to all of our technology as our children. Unlike Wolf, however, Kelly recognizes that we lack sufficient grasp upon what ethics we hope to instill in technology. Kelly's expansion of what counts as alive, however, is theoretically confusing. After all, if one human institution, technology, is alive, what about the rest? Religion? Politics? Art? What can be said of technology can quite often be said of these other institutions, including Kelly's notion that all technological inventions "still exist." That claim is, in fact, likely more true with regard to art and religion than it is with respect to technology!

46. In this, as in so many other matters, de Garis echoes the apocalyptic traditions of Christianity. Early in the twentieth century, for example, Frederick Grant wrote: "one must not be unwilling to pay any cost, however great; for the Kingdom is worth more than anything in this world, even one's life . . . one must not hesitate at any sacrifice for the sake of entrance into the Kingdom. The Kingdom must be one's absolute highest good, whole aim, completely satisfying and compensating gain" (Grant 1917, 157).

47. Charles Stross, a noted sci-fi author, has engaged the possibility that AIs might develop within the military-industrial complex and how that might affect their ethics. In *Accelerando* (2005), Stross describes a universe full of corporate super-AIs that compete with one another in a decidedly inhumane world. His human protagonists, who are themselves uploaded human minds in manufactured bodies, manage to escape the corporate AIs of their own solar system in search of other transcendent intelligences who have avoided the degeneration into *Techno economicus*.

48. Moravec's belief—that we can engineer morality directly into the robots by raising them as our "mind children"—has been influential. The science fiction author David Brin, for example, notes that when the robots become divinely intelligent there will no doubt remain quite few who "will still come home, take us out fishing, and excitedly try to explain to us what they're doing for a living" (Brin 1992, 46).

49. Early in the development of robotics and AI, preceding the Apocalyptic AI movement, Azriel Rosenfeld, a Jewish Rabbi and computer scientist at the University of Maryland, predicted that we would wonder whether robots had souls and at what point a cyborg human being would cease being human and begin to be something else (1966). Probably because he wrote so early in robotics history, Rosenfeld lumped these concerns alongside whether dolphins have the legal and religious status of human beings and concern over the cross-fertilization of human beings and apes, neither of which is still directly pertinent to the argument about robotics. Nevertheless, Rosenfeld was extraordinarily prescient, anticipating our twenty-first-century concerns and denying—as do Foerst, Furse, Levy, and others today—the a priori claim that robots are and always will be soulless (ibid., 18). Rosenfeld concludes that we must go forward with research in robotics and AI, but must do so "in the sight of God" (ibid., 26); that is, as a religious endeavor.

50. Considerable evidence exists that religious experiences are biologically based. Kurzweil rightly points toward the biological basis of religion, regardless of whether or not any religion has a supernatural basis. Many of the neurological correlations of religious practice have been preliminary identified (e.g., Newberg, D'Aquili, and Rause 2001; Tremlin 2006).

51. Anne Foerst has also claimed that robots could be baptized in the future (quoted in Levy 2006, 386).

52. Not shy of making substantive predictions, Levy believes that people will be in love with robots by 2024 (Levy 2007, 339).

53. Recent suggestions that robots might be religious are not the first claims regarding non-human religion. The eminent primatologist Jane Goodall, for example, has documented unusual behavior among chimpanzees during storms and suggested that the chimps seek to imitate the ferocity of the lightning strikes while running, tearing down tree limbs, and beating their chests in the face of the wind. She wonders if such behavior indicates that the chimps marvel at the world's mystery and stand up in challenge to the divine forces of nature in a protoreligious system (Goodall 2001). Long-standing tradition in the West denies animals the kinds of souls that human beings possess (if they are said to have them at all). But if chimpanzees could talk, would they tell us of their religious visions and their faith in the numinous powers of nature?

54. Not everyone, of course, believes that we should entertain thoughts about the religious beliefs of robots. B. Alan Wallace, a scholar of Buddhism and well-noted commentator on the study of consciousness, wrote to me that the "question as to whether [robots] could achieve enlightenment is like asking whether unicorns could breed with donkeys" (Wallace 2007). I presume that a conscious robot, not enlightenment, is the unicorn in Wallace's analogy.

55. Several authors even believe that progress in AI heralds the Christian apocalypse (i.e., the coming of Jesus) (Tamatea 2008, 150).

56. Perhaps this is due to what Tamatea considers a "sociologically uninformed" position among the opponents of AI or the fact that these opponents tend to be (unlike the theologians discussed here) members of right-wing political groups in the United States (Tamatea 2008, 157).

57. Elsewhere, Foerst has also described our relationship to humanoid robots as akin to the image of God, which she, like Herzfeld, describes in terms of relationships (Foerst 1998). She believes that the "image of God does not distinguish us qualitatively from animals and for that reason cannot distinguish us qualitatively from machines" (ibid., 108).

58. Crevier argues that Moravec's mind uploading scenario is "convincing" (Crevier 1993, 339).

59. For more on the Mormon Transhumanist Association, see http://transfigurism.org/community.

60. Herzfeld also criticizes cybernetic immortality for its failure to realize a transcendently eternal reality. Whereas Christian salvation lies outside the temporal framework, she argues, cybernetic immortality "posits a future that, while it might give us more time to work toward our destiny, cannot be everlasting" (Herzfeld 2002b, 200). In this, I think Herzfeld has missed the target. The Apocalyptic AI authors almost universally agree that time can be extended indefinitely—if not objectively, at least subjectively in a conscious engagement with Zeno's paradox as time winds down and our thoughts speed up to a subjective eternity (e.g., Kurzweil 1999, 258–60; de Garis 2005, 188). In fact, they seek an objective eternity also; as Kurzweil puts it, "the fate of the Universe is a decision yet to be made, one which we will intelligently consider when the time is right" (Kurzweil 1999, 260). The AI apocalypse, as seen by its proponents if not by Christian theologians, is eternal.

61. In a sense, the future of intelligent robots is necessarily unforeseeable even if it is soon to come. As Vinge, Kurzweil, and others have argued, a "singularity" at which point the robots become increasingly powerful at an exponential rate guarantees our inability to adequately predict what will happen beyond.

CHAPTER 5: THE INTEGRATION OF RELIGION, SCIENCE, AND TECHNOLOGY

1. Wakamaru is a 45-centimeter-tall household robot for monitoring the home and assisting people (especially the elderly) in daily tasks. Gundam is a Japanese anime comic in which human beings pilot enormous robots; it is wildly popular in Japan.

2. Although some intelligent design theorists have sought to avoid charges of religiosity by indicating that intelligent aliens—a natural force—could be the driving force rather than a god, this sleight of hand actually does nothing to change the course of the argument. After all, if aliens are responsible for human life, then who is responsible for the aliens?

3. These authors have met with serious academic criticism and have received profoundly little support among the scientific and philosophical communities. For a good criticism of Johnson, see Pennock (2001). For a scientific refutation of Behe's basic scientific claim, see Bridgham, Carroll, and Thornton (2006), which is used in a theological refutation by Putz (2006).

4. Although the teaching of creationism in public schools was not fully put to rest until *Edwards v. Aguillard* in 1987, I do not believe that it would have a substantial foothold in public opinion today. For example, when I asked my students if they think creationism should be taught in school they say "no," but when I ask if ID should be taught they often say "yes" because they think it is "fair" to show multiple sides of the argument (even if there are not multiple sides within the actual scientific community). Creationism does not have a strong scientific appearance despite the efforts of creationists, especially Whitcomb and Morris (1961).

APPENDIX ONE: THE RISE OF THE ROBOTS

1. Brad Stone traces the history of robot combat in *Gearheads: The Turbulent Rise of Robotic Sports* (B. Stone 2003).

2. FIRST (For Inspiration and Recognition of Science and Technology) was started by the award-winning inventor Dean Kamen in 1989 to help inspire young people to pursue careers in science and technology. In addition to the Lego League, FIRST sponsors the FIRST Vex Challenge and the FIRST Robotic Competition, both of which are robot competitions open to students in junior high and high school.

3. For overlapping histories of automata (both scientific and religious), see Cohen (1966), Levy (2006), and Rosheim (1994).

4. The roboticist Mark Rosheim has written an excellent work on Leonardo's designs, studying them and attempting to build modern replicas (Rosheim 2006).

5. In a brief but fascinating section of his book *Mimesis and Alterity*, Michael Taussig ties early modern automata to the practice of associating the powers of mimesis with primitivism (Taussig 1993, 213–20). As he notes, the one thing so rarely represented in eighteenth-century European automata was the one thing that was both all around the machines and instrumental in manufacturing them: the white male. Animals, children, women, and, especially, dark-skinned people were the common subjects of the automata.

6. The ideological connection between automata and homunculi existed at the time of their popularity. Jonathan Edwards, in his *Demonstration of the Existence and Providence of God*, connects the two in the year 1696 (Edwards quoted in Newman 2004, 226). As Edwards was neither an automaton engineer nor an alchemist, it seems likely that the ideological connection between the two precedes him and he borrows from preexisting traditions.

7. For example, a ninth-century bishop of Cordoba complained that while not one in 1,000 Christians there could write a decent letter in Latin, they could read and write in Arabic (Holmyard 1957, 63). Ferdinand and Isabella, who united Spain, expelled both Muslims and Jews from the nation in 1492, ending the medieval world's most pluralistic community.

8. Syriac-speaking Christians aided in the seventh- and eighth-century translation of the Greek materials (Holmyard 1957, 63, 67).

9. Muslims identified Hermes with the Qur'anic individual Idris (Stapleton, Lewis, and Sherwood 1949, 69). Hermes, often called Hermes Trismegistus ("thrice-great"), was highly regarded in alchemical circles throughout the Western world.

10. The authenticity of some or all of Khalid's poems has been disputed (see Holmyard 1957, 65–66).

11. Jābir, for his contributions to both chemistry and alchemy, marks yet another example of how religious and scientific goals can go hand in hand. His influence upon both chemistry and alchemy throughout the Western world cannot be overstated; his work directed the course of both fields in western Europe thanks to his detailed descriptions of methods and apparatuses, especially in *Kitāb al-Tajmī* (*Book of Concentration*). The concept of *takwin* (described below) is an example of how effectively medieval thinkers could integrate religion and science, especially in the search for artificial humanoids. European "recipes" for artificial life were attached to and methodologically similar to Jābir's chemical recipes. At the same time, however, there was a distinctly religious aspect to the process. Jābir's alchemical creation of life depended upon traditional Islamic themes and traditional ritual practices, especially those of liturgical prayer, supplicatory prayer, and the invocation/remembrance of the divine name (O'Connor 1994, 90).

12. For a brief summary of Jābir's life, see Holmyard 1928, vii–ix and Holmyard 1957, 68–71. We are told that Jābir's father was a pharmacist, which may help explain his interest in alchemical mixtures, but he did not know his father, who was executed for political reasons shortly after Jābir's birth. As a young man, Jābir may have studied with the sixth Shī'ī imam, Ja'far al-Sadiq, whose work was likely crucial to the occult turn in Jābir's work.

13. Apollonius of Tyana (first century CE) was a Greek Neo-Pythagorean teacher and miracle worker, known primarily through Flavius Philostratus's *Life of Apollonius of Tyana* (third century CE), wherein he is depicted as a "divine man."

14. The manufacture of bees, beetles, and wasps out of a corpse can be traced back to the Hellenistic period (O'Connor 1994, 20).

15. I am grateful to Kathleen O'Connor for confirming this suspicion through a personal e-mail (O'Connor 2007).

16. I owe the following description of the homunculus recipe to Newman 2004, 179–80.

17. Some exception in ancient Greece might be made for Galen, who believed that women contributed a sperm of their own, but even in his case the male sperm is the more important.

18. Arnald is also known as Arnaldus de Villa Nova, Arnaldus de Villanueva, Arnaldus Villanovanus, Arnaud de Ville-Neuve and Arnau de Vilanova (Wikipedia 2009a).

19. Naturally, plenty of alarmism continued to surround alchemy. Paracelsus, for example, was known to his detractors as a drunkard and a demon worshipper (Newman 2004, 111).

20. I should note that *The Chymical Wedding* appears to both sanctify marriage and the homunculus as a metaphor for Christian resurrection while Paracelsus denied the value of the former and his homunculus would surely be useless as a metaphor for the latter, as it was the product of unholy lust, i.e., spilled seed (Newman 2004, 234–35). Islamic alchemists also connected homunculi to resurrection (O'Connor 1994, 286–330), as did a few Jewish mystics with respect to the Golem.

21. Paracelsus and his followers appear to have even stronger antipathy toward women than did the Greeks, for whom women were effectively vessels (Newman 2004, 202–4). In the possibly pseudonymous *De natura rerum*, for example, the basilisk, which can kill with a glance, comes from menstrual blood.

22. For Paracelsus, the homunculus is in one sense superior (made without a woman) while in another inferior (because of the role of lust, i.e., spilled semen, in its creation) (Newman 2004).

23. The only use of the word Golem in the Bible is from the book of Psalms and in it, the word means something embryonic, something with potential. It was later that the word came to reference an artificial humanoid created through human magic.

24. On the rare occasion that Golem manufacture is discouraged, such as in the story of Jeremiah's Golem, who leaves "the Lord God is dead" written upon his own forehead when he erases the *alef* from the word *emet* (meaning "truth") to leave *met* ("dead"), it is not the manufacture of the Golem that is problematic but the possibility that subsequent human beings will cease worshipping God and begin to worship themselves, reveling in their own apotheosis. Sherwin makes the natural association to human self-glorification in modern technologies that permit the creation of artificial beings, including biotechnologies and the computer sciences, which might lead us to believe that "God is dead" (Sherwin 1985, 24–25).

25. Influenced by Pythagorean and Neoplatonic thought, alphabetical and numerical manipulation was also used by Jābir in medieval Islam (O'Connor 1994, 131–32).

26. The *Sefer Yetzirah* dates to the third through sixth centuries CE (Scholem [1974] 1978, 26–28).

27. It is presumed that Rava's Golem demonstrates his spiritual mastery because the passage in which he creates the Golem immediately follows him saying that "if the righteous wished, they could create a world" (Sanhedrin, 65b).

28. Idel believes that Golem creation also amplifies the prestige of righteous Jews over their gentile counterparts. He argues that the Talmudic story must be situated alongside pagan traditions of animating statues and acts as a polemic against these (Idel 1988, 18–19). Later Golem traditions, though prior to the flourishing of Golem mythology in the late medieval/early modern period, may not have referred to the literal creation of physical being. Scholem argues that medieval Jews sought to make Golems in a mystical trance (Scholem [1974] 1978, 352), though Idel is skeptical of this claim, which he considers to be, as yet, unverified (e.g., Idel 1990, 84). Eleazer ben Judah of Worms (c. 1160–1238 CE), for example, provided a recipe for creating a Golem out of manipulating the Hebrew alphabet but this creation appeared to last only as long as did the mystic's ecstatic trance (see Idel 1990, 59–60 for a counterargument). In Idel's analysis of the Golem, only Abraham ben Samuel Abulafia (c. 1240–after 1291 CE) and the post-Abulafia ecstatic Kabbalists fit Scholem's model (Idel 1988, 25–27; 1990, 102).

29. R. Loew's first name is occasionally given as Judah and his last name sometimes spelled Low, Lowe, and Loewe.

30. Rabbi Loew's descendent Moses Meir Perles (1666–1739 CE) wrote a biography of Rabbi Loew in 1730 that does not mention the Golem legend nor did the Jews of Prague add a golem motif to Rabbi Loew's gravestone when it was renovated in the 1720s (Kieval 1997, 7–8). It is, therefore, unlikely that Rabbi Loew had yet become the subject of Golem legends. The author of the 1841 document was not a Jew. Franz Klutschak (1814–1886 CE) was a journalist and folklorist who described Rabbi Loew and his golem in *Panorama des Universums*, a monthly paper about culture (ibid.)

31. For a modern essay in which these stories are taken as factual, see Winkler 1980.

32. Winkler takes Rosenberg's story at face value (Winkler 1980, 63–65). In fact, the library from which Rosenberg supposedly copied the text (the Royal Library in Metz) never existed and was certainly never burnt down, thereby destroying the alleged Golem manuscript (Sherwin 2004, 23).

33. The blood libel was an accusation that Jews used the blood of Christian children in preparing their Passover matzoh. Rabbi Loew and the Golem, in Rosenberg and Bloch, found ways to stop the Christians from planting false evidence against them, saving the Jews from certain doom.

34. The Golem legends were attributed to Rabbi Elijah until the mid-eighteenth century, when Rabbi Loew became the central figure of—more or less—the same tales (Scholem [1960] 1969, 202). The first written references to Rabbi Elijah's Golem come between 1630 and 1650 but may trace to the generation following Rabbi Elijah's death in 1583 (Idel 1988, 31–32).

35. The Golem first acquired its darker side in early modern folktales. Prior to this, the image of a Golem run amok was absent from Jewish mystical theology. Scholem believes that the Golem was associated with "tellurian powers" (elemental powers of the earth) during this period, which he says explains the Golem's violent nature and growing strength (Scholem [1960] 1969, 1978), a point disputed by Idel (Idel 1990, 36–37).

36. Rabbi Moses ben Jacob Cordovero, for example, felt that Golems were radically inferior to human beings. Because Cordovero did not believe that any kind of soul (lower or higher) could be etched in the Golem, Scholem uses Cordovero as an example of his theory of Tellurian powers, that is, that the Golem's power comes from the earth (Scholem [1960] 1969, 195). Idel disputes this theory. He claims that, according to Cordovero, what powers exist in the earth do so only as reflections of "supernal vitality" and do not stem from the earth, per se (Idel 1990, 197).

37. For a good summary of the Golem in twentieth-century literature, film, and popular culture, see Goldsmith 1981.

38. In fact, as she points out, several of the founders of the MIT AI Lab (now the Computer Science and Artificial Intelligence Laboratory, or CSAIL) were descended from Rabbi Loew (Foerst 2004, 39).

APPENDIX TWO: IN DEFENSE OF ROBOTICS

1. A similar argument applies to economic disenfranchisement by robots. Apocalyptic AI addresses the common fear that robotics will disenfranchise workers and further divide socioeconomic groups. Industrial robots, for example, take jobs away from factory workers, who then have few employment opportunities. Should robots continue their impressive growth, they may wreak havoc upon several sectors of the economy, including blue collar workers, retail and food service employees, and maintenance workers such as janitors and physical plant employees. Intelligent machines even threaten such professions as teaching and medicine as learning software and robotic surgical devices improve. Massive job loss would be a disastrous consequence of technological progress and could

diminish public support of robotics and AI. Fear of economic privation first arose in the industrial robot revolution of the 1980s. After Henry Scott Stokes published his article "Japan's Love Affair with the Robot" in the *New York Times* (Stokes 1982), one reader wrote a letter to the editor justifying the American resistance to robots (H. Clifford 1982). Nineteenth- and twentieth-century industrial expansion certainly did lead to lost jobs as machines replaced human workers. This could become a significant problem again in the twenty-first century. Today, we have precious few blacksmiths and glass-blowers and other tradesmen. This process of "de-skilling," whereby human technical knowledge is lost as machines take over more jobs, could lead to a blunting of our technical and intellectual powers, argues the AI researcher Daniel Crevier (Crevier 1993, 327), though he finds Moravec's vision of the future "convincing" (ibid., 339). From a subsistence perspective, if robots take over all manufacturing (and they have already absorbed much of the work in factories), many people will lose jobs. As robots become more intelligent, they will do more than just weld car parts and vacuum floors. They will increasingly replace human workers, which could lead to economic upheaval. Eventually, however, lost jobs will be inconsequential in the AI apocalypse. According to Moravec, robots will do all of our work for us and we will all own shares in the robot corporations in our new "garden of earthly delights" (Moravec 1999, 143). The short-term labor problems will become an "opportunity to recapture the comfortable pace of a tribal village while retaining the benefits of technological evolution. In the long run it marks the end of the dominance of biological humans and the beginning of the age of robots" (ibid., 131). As stockholders, we will profit from the machines' labor and thus have no need of jobs, particularly the dirty and difficult jobs that robots will take over first. As a result, Moravec argues, we need not fear the coming end; while some discomfort may arise during the earliest stages of our new society, it will be quickly replaced by a better, more leisurely life. Thus, just as the means justify the ends in military funding, they do so in economic matters.

2. I am grateful to Stuart Anderson, a PhD student at CMU, for providing me with a recording of the event.

3. Eventually, the Lab found substantial funding in private industry; corporations now pay for the privileges of having researchers work on relevant issues and of getting to tour the Lab and observe all of the projects under way.

REFERENCES

Association for the Advancement of Artificial Intelligence (AAAI). 2007. "Science Fiction." AAAI. www.aaai.org/AITopics/html/scifi.html#pontin (accessed July 3, 2007).

Abate, Tom. 2008. "If It Only Had a Heart: Can Robots Behave Humanely?" *San Francisco Chronicle*, January 29. www.sfgate.com/cgi-bin/article.cgi?f=/c/a/2008/01/29/BUF7UNM4I.DTL&hw=if +it+only+had+heart+can+robots+behave+humanely&sn=001&sc=1000 (accessed February 13, 2008).

Albanese, Catherine L. 1999. *America: Religions and Religion*. 3d ed. Belmont, Calif.: Wadsworth Publishing Company.

Alexander, Brian. 2003. *Rapture: How Biotech became the New Religion*. New York: Basic Books.

Allen, Tom, and Robin Widdison. 1996. "Can Computers Make Contracts?" *Harvard Journal of Law and Technology* 9 (1): 25–52.

Amdahl, Kate. 2007. "Better Angels." The Winged Girl Blog, July 9. kateamdahl.livejournal. com/16332.html (accessed August 2, 2007).

American Society for the Prevention of Cruelty to Robots. 2008. Web site. http://www.aspcr.com.

Anderson, Benedict. [1983] 1991. *Imagined Communities: Reflections on the Origin and Spread of Nationalism*. Rev. ed. New York: Verso.

Annas, George J., Lori B. Andrews, and Rosario M. Isasi. 2002. "Protecting the Endangered Human: Toward an International Treaty Prohibiting Cloning and Inheritable Alterations." *American Journal of Law and Medicine* 28 (2/3): 151–78.

Arkin, Ron. 2007. "Lethality and Autonomous Systems: An Ethical Stance." Paper presented at the IEEE International Conference on Robotics and Automation, Rome (April 10–14, 2007). www. roboethics.org (accessed July 3, 2007).

Asimov, Isaac. [1950] 1977. *I, Robot*. Repr. New York: Del Rey.

———. [1953] 1991. *The Caves of Steel*. Repr. New York: Bantam Books.

———. [1956] 1957. *The Naked Sun*. Repr. Garden City, N.Y.: Doubleday.

———. [1983] 1991. *The Robots of Dawn*. Repr. New York: Del Rey.

Atkeson, Chris. 2007. Personal communication with author, June 18.

Atwood, Tom. 2006. "Team Osaka Takes Humanoid RoboCup Title!: Three-time World Champions Hail from the City of Osaka Robot Cluster." *Robot* 4 (Fall): 48–53.

———. 2007. "A Talk with Bill Thomasmeyer." *Robot.* www.botmag.com/issue9/talk-bill-thomasmeyer. shtml (accessed November 27, 2007).

Atwood, Tom, and Kevin Berry. 2007. "Congressmen Doyle and Wamp Launch Congressional Caucus on Robotics." *Robot* 8 (Fall): 12.

———. 2008. "The Robotics Institute, Carnegie Mellon University, Chiara." *Robot* 13 (November/December): 12–24.

Au, Wagner James. 2009. "Ray Kurzweil to Keynote This Year's SLCC." New World Notes [weblog]. July 1. http://nwn.blogs.com/nwn/2009/07/kurzweil-at-slcc.html#comments (accessed August 10, 2009).

Aupers, Stef, and Dick Houtman. 2005. "'Reality Sucks': On Alienation and Cybergnosis." Special issue, *Concilium: International Journal of Theology* 2005/1: 81–89.

Aupers, Stef, Dick Houtman, and Peter Pels. 2008. "Cybergnosis: Technology, Religion and the Secular." In *Religion: Beyond a Concept*, edited by Hent de Vries, pp. 687–703. New York: Fordham University Press.

Bacon, Francis. 1951. *The Advancement of Learning and New Atlantis.* London: Oxford University Press.

Bailey, Lee Worth. 2005. *The Enchantments of Technology.* Urbana, Ill.: University of Illinois Press.

Bainbridge, William Sims. 2006. "Cognitive Technologies." In *Managing Nano-Bio-Info-Cogno Innovations: Converging Technologies in Society*, edited by William Sims Bainbridge and Mihail C. Roco, pp. 203–26. Dordrecht, The Netherlands: Springer.

———. 2009. "Religion for a Galactic Civilization 2.0." Posted on the Institute for Ethics & Emerging Technologies website (August 20). http://ieet.org/index.php/IEET/more/bainbridge20090820/ (accessed August 21, 2009).

Barbour, Ian G. 1997. *Religion and Science: Historical and Contemporary Issues.* San Francisco: HarperCollins Publishers.

Barfield, Woodrow. 2005. "Issues of Law for Software Agents within Virtual Environments." *Presence* 14 (6): 741–48.

Barlow, John Perry. 1994. "The Economy of Ideas." *Wired* 2.03 (March). http://www.wired.com/wired/archive/2.03/economy.ideas.html (accessed July 19, 2007).

———. 1996a. "A Declaration of the Independence of the Internet." homes.eff.org/~barlow/Declaration-Final.html (accessed July 19, 2007).

———. 1996b. "Declaring Independence." *Wired* 4.06 (June). www.wired.com/wired/archive/4.06/independence.html (accessed July 19, 2007).

Barnes, Barry, David Bloor, and John Henry. 1996. *Scientific Knowledge: A Sociological Analysis.* Chicago: University of Chicago Press.

Bartle, Richard A. [2003] 2004. *Designing Virtual Worlds.* Berkeley, Calif.: New Riders.

BBC News. 2007. "Robotic Age Poses Ethical Dilemma." *BBC News*, March 3. news.bbc.co.uk/go/pr/fr/-/2/hi/technology/6425927.stm (accessed April 11, 2007).

Behe, Michael J. 1998. "Molecular Machines: Experimental Support for the Design Inference." *Cosmic Pursuit* 1 (2): 27–35.

Bellah, Robert, and Phillip Hammond. 1980. *Varieties of Civil Religion.* San Francisco: Harper San Francisco.

Ben-David, Joseph. 1991. *Scientific Growth: Essays on the Social Organization and Ethos of Science*, edited by Gad Freudenthal. Berkeley: University of California Press.

Benedikt, Michael. 1991. Introduction to *Cyberspace: First Steps*, pp. 1–26. Cambridge, Mass.: MIT Press.

Benson, Timothy O., ed. [1993] 2001. *Expressionist Utopias: Paradise, Metropolis, Architectural Fantasy.* Repr. Los Angeles: University of California Press.

Berger, Peter L. [1967] 1990. *The Sacred Canopy: Elements of a Sociological Theory of Religion.* Repr. New York: Doubleday.

Berman, Lawrence V. 1961. "The Political Interpretation of the Maxim: The Purpose of Philosophy Is the Imitation of God." *Studia Islamica* 15 (1): 53–61.

Biagioli, Mario. 1993. *Galileo Courtier: The Practice of Science in the Culture of Absolutism.* Chicago: University of Chicago Press.

Bijker, Wiebe E. 2007. "Dikes and Dams, Thick with Politics." *Isis* 98 (1): 109–23.

Bilski, Emily D. 1998. *Golem! Danger, Deliverance and Art.* New York: The Jewish Museum.

Bloor, David. [1976] 1991. *Knowledge and Social Imagery.* 2d ed. Chicago: University of Chicago Press.

———. 1999a. "Anti-Latour." *Studies in the History and Philosophy of Science* 30 (1): 81–112.

———. 1999b. "Reply to Bruno Latour." *Studies in the History and Philosophy of Science* 30 (1): 131–36.

Boellstorff, Tom. 2008. *Coming of Age in Second Life: An Anthropologist Explores the Virtually Human.* Princeton, N.J.: Princeton University Press.

Borgmann, Albert. 2002. "On the Blessings of Calamity and the Burdens of Good Fortune." *The Hedgehog Review* 4 (3): 7–24.

Bostrom, Nick. 1998. "How Long Before Superintelligence?" *International Journal of Future Studies* 2. A revised version is available at www.nickbostrom.com/superintelligence.html (accessed July 16, 2007).

———. 2003. "Are You Living in a Computer Simulation?" *Philosophical Quarterly* 53 (211): 243–55.

———. 2005. "In Defense of Posthuman Dignity." *Bioethics* 19 (3): 202–14.

———. 2006. "Do We Live in a Computer Simulation?" *New Scientist* 192 (2579): 38–39.

Boyer, Paul. 1992. *When Time Shall Be No More: Prophecy Belief in Modern American Culture.* Cambridge, Mass.: Harvard University Press.

———. 2000. "The Growth of Fundamentalist Apocalyptic in the United States." In *The Encyclopedia of Apocalypticism*, edited by Bernard McGinn, John J. Collins, and Stephen J. Stein, vol. 3, *The Origins of Apocalypticism in Judaism and Christianity*, edited by Stephen J. Stein, pp. 140–78. New York: Continuum Press.

Brand, Stewart. 1987. *The Media Lab: Inventing the Future at MIT.* New York: Viking.

Brantlinger, Patrick. 1980. "The Gothic Origins of Science Fiction." *NOVEL: A Forum on Fiction* 14 (1): 30–43.

Breazeal, Cynthia L. 2002. *Designing Sociable Robots.* Cambridge, Mass.: MIT Press.

Bridgham, Jamie T., Sean M. Carroll, and Joseph W. Thornton. 2006. "Evolution of Hormone-Receptor Complexity by Molecular Exploitation." *Science* 312 (April 6): 97–101.

Brin, David. 1992. "Gaia, Freedom, and Human Nature—Some Ironies on the Way to Creating the Network of the Future." In *Thinking Robots, An Aware Internet, and Cyberpunk Librarians: The 1992 LITA President's Program*, edited by R. Bruce Miller and Milton T. Wolf, pp. 35–48. Chicago: Library and Information Technology Association.

Brooke, John Hedley. 1991. *Science and Religion: Some Historical Perspectives.* New York: Cambridge University Press.

Brooke, John, and Geoffrey Cantor. 1998. *Reconstructing Nature: The Engagement of Science and Religion*. New York: Oxford University Press.

Brooks, Rodney. 2002. *Flesh and Machines: How Robots Will Change Us*. New York: Pantheon Books.

———. 2004. "The Robots are Here." *Technology Review*, February.

Bruns, Axel. 2008. *Blogs, Wikipedia, Second Life, and Beyond: From Production to Produsage*. New York: Peter Lang.

Bull, Malcolm. 1999. *Seeing Things Hidden: Apocalypse, Vision and Totality*. New York: Verso.

Butrym, Alexander J. 1985. "For Suffering Humanity: The Ethics of Science in Science Fiction." In *The Transcendent Adventure: Studies of Religion in Science Fiction/Fantasy*, edited by Robert Reilly, p. 55–72. Westport, Conn.: Greenwood Press.

Callon, Michel. [1986] 1999. "Some Elements of a Sociology and Translation: Domestication of the Scallops and the Fishermen of St. Brieuc Bay." In *The Science Studies Reader*, edited by Mario Biagioli, 67–83. Abridged 1998. New York: Routledge.

Cantor, Geoffrey, and Chris Kenny. 2001. "Barbour's Fourfold Way: Problems with His Taxonomy of Science-Religion Relationships." *Zygon: Journal of Religion and Science* 36 (4): 765–81.

Castronova, Edward. 2005. *Synthetic Worlds: The Business and Culture of Online Games*. Chicago: University of Chicago Press.

———. 2007. *Exodus to the Virtual World: How Online Fun is Changing Reality*. New York: Palgrave Macmillan.

Charlesworth, James H. 1983. *The Old Testament Pseudepigraphia, vol. 1: Apocalyptic Literature and Testaments*. New York: Doubleday & Company.

Chaudhry, Lakshmi. 2000. "Valley to Bill Joy: 'Zzzzzzz.'" *Wired*, April. www.wired.com/science/discoveries/news/2000/04/35424 (accessed October 17, 2008).

Chidester, David. 2004. "Moralizing Noise." *Harvard Divinity Bulletin* 32 (3): 17.

Choset, Howie. 2007. Personal communication with author at Carnegie Mellon University, June 19.

Christian Science Monitor. 2007. "When Robots Roam the Earth." *Christian Science Monitor*, August 8. www.csmonitor.com/2007/0808/p08s01-comv.htm (accessed August 13, 2007).

Churchland, Paul. 1989. "Folk Psychology and the Explanation of Human Behavior." *Philosophical Perspectives* 3: 225–41.

Clarke, Arthur C. 1968. *2001: A Space Odyssey*. New York: New American Library.

———. 2001. *The City and the Stars and The Sands of Mars*. New York: Warner Books.

Clayton, Philip. 2000. "Neuroscience, the Person, and God: An Emergentist Account." *Zygon: Journal of Religion and Science* 35:3. 613–52.

Clifford, Harry W. 1982. "Japan's Robot Revolution." *New York Times*, February 14.

Clifford, Richard J. 2000. "The Roots of Apocalypticism in Near Eastern Myth." In *The Encyclopedia of Apocalypticism*, edited by Bernard McGinn, John J. Collins, and Stephen J. Stein, vol. 1, *The Origins of Apocalypticism in Judaism and Christianity*, edited by John J. Collins, pp. 3–38. New York: Continuum Press.

Cohen, John. 1966. *Human Robots in Myth and Science*. London: Allen & Unwin.

Coleman, Frank. 2007. *Connections: Connecting Man to Man to God*, 161 (June 17). www.geocities.com/newjoydivine/connections/070617.htm (accessed November 29, 2008).

Collins, Harry, and Trevor Pinch. [1993] 1998. *The Golem: What You Should Know about Science*. 2d ed. Cambridge: Cambridge University Press.

———. 1998. *The Golem at Large: What You Should Know about Technology*. Cambridge: Cambridge University Press.

Collins, John J. 1984. *The Apocalyptic Imagination: An Introduction to the Jewish Matrix of Christianity*. New York: Crossroad.

———. 2000a. General introduction to *The Origins of Apocalypticism in Judaism and Christianity*, vol. 1 of *The Encyclopedia of Apocalypticism*, pp. vi–xii. New York: Continuum Press.

———. 2000b. "From Prophecy to Apocalypticism: The Expectation of the End." In *The Encyclopedia of Apocalypticism*, edited by Bernard McGinn, John J. Collins, and Stephen J. Stein, vol. 1, *The Origins of Apocalypticism in Judaism and Christianity*, edited by John J. Collins, pp. 129–61. New York: Continuum Press.

Comte, Auguste. [1852] 1973. *The Catechism of Positive Religion*. Translated by Richard Congreve. London: Kegan Paul, Trench, Trübner, and Company.

Connor, Steve. 1997. "'God Spot' Is Found in Brain." *Sunday Times* (London), November 2.

Cook, Stephen L. 1995. *Prophecy and Apocalypticism: The Postexilic Social Setting*. Minneapolis: Fortress Press.

Corn, Joseph J. 1986. Epilogue to *Imagining Tomorrow: History, Technology, and the American Future*. Cambridge, Mass.: MIT Press.

Cornwall, Bob. 2007. "Robots and Religion or Can a Robot Have a Soul?" Ponderings on a Faith Journey: The Thoughts and Opinions of a Disciples of Christ Pastor and Church Historian [weblog], June 14. pastorbobcornwall.blogspot.com/2007/06/robots-and-religion-or-can-robot-have.html (accessed December 18, 2007).

Crevier, Daniel. 1993. *AI: The Tumultuous History of the Search for Artificial Intelligence*. New York: Basic Books.

Damasio, Antonio. 1994. *Descartes' Error: Emotion, Reason, and the Human Brain*. New York: Penguin.

DaSilva, Extropia. 2007. "Climbing Technological Mount Improbable." Paper presented at the Second Life Seminar on Transhumanism and Religion (April 29, 2007).

———. 2008a. "Shades of Grey: An Essay by Extropia DaSilva." Gwen's Home [weblog], August 31. gwynethllewelyn.net/2008/08/31/shades-of-grey-an-essay-by-extropia-dasilva/ (accessed October 5, 2008).

———. 2008b. "CTRL-ALT-R: Rebake Your Reality." COSMI2LE [weblog], October 6. cosmi2le. com//index.php/site/next_cosmic_engineers_meeting_in_second_life_discussion_of_ctrl_ alt_r_rebak/ (accessed October 12, 2008).

———. 2008c. "Discussion of CTRL-ALT-R: Rebake Your Reality." Order of Cosmic Engineers meeting in Extropia Core, *Second Life* (October 12).

———. 2008d. Extropia DaSilva personal profile in *Second Life*.

Davis, Eric. 1996. "Osmose." *Wired* 4.08 (August). www.wired.com/wired/archive/4.08/osmose. html (accessed February 20, 2008).

Dawkins, Richard. 2006. *The God Delusion*. Boston: Houghton Mifflin.

DeCuir, Malaquias. 2008. "Metalife." *SL'ang Life: Real Information at Home* 5: 16–17.

de Boer, Martin C. 2000. "Paul and Apocalyptic Eschatology." In *The Encyclopedia of Apocalypticism*, edited by Bernard McGinn, John J. Collins, and Stephen J. Stein, vol. 1, *The Origins of Apocalypticism in Judaism and Christianity*, edited by John J. Collins, pp. 345–83. New York: Continuum Press.

de Garis, Hugo. 2005. *The Artilect War: Cosmists vs. Terrans: A Bitter Controversy Concerning Whether Humanity Should Build Godlike Massively Intelligent Machines*. Palm Springs, Calif.: ETC Publications.

Defense Advanced Research Projects Agency (DARPA). 2003. "DARPA Over the Years." DARPA. www.arpa.mil/body/overtheyears.html (accessed July 3, 2007; no longer available).

———. 2009. www.arpa.mil/mission.html (accessed August 25, 2009).

DeLashmutt, Michael. 2006. "Perspectives on Techno-science and Human Nature: A Better Life Through Information Technology? The Techno-Theological Eschatology of Posthuman Speculative Science." *Zygon: Journal of Religion and Science* 41 (2): 267–88.

Dennett, Daniel C. 1991. *Consciousness Explained*. Boston: Little, Brown.

———. 1998. *Brainchildren: Essays on Designing Minds*. Cambridge, Mass.: MIT Press.

Derrida, Jacques. 1998. "Faith and Knowledge: The Two Sources of 'Religion' at the Limits of Reason Alone." In *Religion*, edited by Derrida and Gianni Vattimo. Cultural Memory in the Present. Stanford, Calif.: Stanford University Press. Translation of *La religion: séminaire de Capri sous la direction de Jacques Derrida et Gianni Vattimo* (Paris: Éditions du Seuil, 1996), volume of papers presented a conference in Capri February 28–March 1, 1994.

Dery, Mark. 1996. *Escape Velocity: Cyberculture at the End of the Century*. New York: Grove Press.

Dick, Philip K. 1962. *The Man in the High Castle*. New York: Putnam.

———. [1968] 1996. *Do Androids Dream of Electric Sheep?* Repr. New York: Del Rey.

———. 1975. *Confessions of a Crap Artist*. Glen Ellen, Calif.: Entwhistle.

———. 1995. "Man, Android, and Machine." In *The Shifting Realities of Philip K. Dick: Selected Literary and Philosophical Writings*, edited by Lawrence Sutin, pp. 211–32. New York: Vintage Books.

Doctorow, Cory. 2003. *Down and Out in the Magic Kingdom*. New York: Tor.

Dodds, E. R. 1947. "Theurgy and Its Relationship to Neoplatonism." *The Journal of Roman Studies* 37 (1–2): 55–69.

Drexler, Eric. [1986] 1987. *Engines of Creation: The Coming Era of Nanotechnology*. Paperback ed. New York: Anchor Press.

Dreyfus, Hubert, and Stuart Dreyfus. 1986. *Mind over Machine: The Power of Human Intuition and Expertise in the Era of the Computer*. New York: The Free Press.

Ducheneaut, Nicolas, and Robert J. Moore. 2005. "More Than Just 'XP': Learning Social Skills in Massively Multiplayer Online Games." *Interactive Technology & Smart Education* 2: 89–100.

Ducheneaut, Nicolas, Robert J. Moore, and Eric Nickell. 2007. "Virtual 'Third Places': A Case Study of Sociability in Massively Multiplayer Games." *Computer Supported Cooperative Work* 16: 129–66.

Ducheneaut, Nicolas, Nick Yee, Eric Nickell, and Robert J. Moore. 2006. "Building an MMO with Mass Appeal: A Look at Gameplay in *World of Warcraft*." *Games and Culture* 1 (4): 281–317.

Durkheim, Emile. [1893] 1933. *The Division of Labor in Society*. New York: Free Press.

———. [1912] 1995. *The Elementary Forms of Religious Life*. Translated by Karen E. Fields. New York: Free Press.

Dyson, Esther, George Gilder, George Keyworth, and Alvin Toffler. 1994. "A Magna Carta for the Knowledge Age." Release 1.2, August 22. Alamut: Bastion of Peace and Information. www.alamut.com/subj/ideologies/manifestos/magnaCarta.html (accessed July 20, 2007).

Eamon, William. 1994. *Science and the Secrets of Nature: Books of Secrets in Medieval and Early Modern Culture*. Princeton, N.J.: Princeton University Press.

Economist. 2006. "Living a Second Life." September 28. www.economist.com/displaystory.cfm? story_id=7963538 (accessed October 31, 2006).

Eliade, Mircea. 1985. *Symbolism, the Sacred, and the Arts*. Edited by Diane Apostolos-Cappadona. New York: Crossroad.

Ellul, Jacques. [1954] 1964. *The Technological Society*. Translated by John Wilkinson. New York: Alfred A. Knopf.

European Robotics Research Network (EURON). 2006. "EURON Roboethics Roadmap 1.1." Project coordinator, Gianmarco Veruggio.

Extropia Core Network. 2007. "Extropia." Extropia. core.extropiacore.net (accessed November 27, 2007).

Feuerbach, Ludwig. [1841] 1957. *The Essence of Christianity*. Translated by George Eliot. New York: Harper Torchbooks.

Feyerabend, Paul. 1978. *Against Method: Outline of an Anarchistic Method of Knowledge*. London: Verso.

Feynman, Richard. 1959. "There's Plenty of Room Left at the Bottom." Lecture presented to the American Physical Society at California Institute of Technology, December 29. www.its.caltech. edu/~feynman/plenty.html (accessed August 28, 2007).

Fodor, Jerry. 2000. *The Mind Doesn't Work that Way: The Scope and Limits of Computational Psychology*. Cambridge, Mass.: MIT Press.

Foerst, Anne. 1998. "Cog, a Humanoid Robot, and the Question of the Image of God." *Zygon: Journal of Religion and Science* 33 (1): 91–111.

———. 2004. *God in the Machine: What Robots Teach Us About Humanity and God*. New York: Dutton.

Foulk, Emie. 2007. "Robots Turn Off Senior Citizens in Aging Japan." *Reuters*, September 20. www.reuters.com/article/inDepthNews/idUST29547120070920?sp=true (accessed September 23, 2007).

Freud, Sigmund. [1927] 1989. *Future of an Illusion*. Translated by James Strachey. Repr. of 1961 translation published by Hogarth. New York: W.W. Norton.

Friedenberg, Jay. 2008. *Artificial Psychology: The Quest for What It Means To Be Human*. New York: Psychology Press.

Fuerth, Leon. 2009a. "Foresight and Anticipatory Governance." Paper circulated to the Rockefeller Foundation's meeting on Smart Globalization and Pro-Poor Foresight in Bellagio, Italy. www.forwardengagement.org/storage/forwardengagement/documents/leon_fuerth_foresight_anticipatory_governance.pdf (accessed August 22, 2009).

———. 2009b. "Forward Engagement: The Study of Long-Range Developments as Factors in Contemporary National Policy." Syllabus for IAFF 290.14. Available: www.forwardengagement.org/index.php?option=com_content&task=view&id=16&Itemid=45 (accessed August 22, 2009).

Fukuyama, Francis. 2002. *Our Posthuman Future: Consequences of the Biotechnology Revolution*. New York: Farrar, Straus, and Giroux.

Furse, Edmund. 1996a. "A Theology of Robots." Paper presented at the University of Glamorgan (May 14). www.comp.glam.ac.uk/pages/staff/efurse/Theology-of-Robots/A-Theology-of-Robots.html (accessed May 23, 2007).

———. 1996b. "Towards the First Catholic Robot?" *The Independent*, October 26. Available at www.comp.glam.ac.uk/pages/staff/efurse/Catholic-Robot/First-Catholic-Robot.html (accessed May 23, 2007).

Garreau, Joel. 2005. *Radical Evolution: The Promise and Peril of Enhancing Our Minds, Our Bodies—and What It Means to be Human.* New York: Doubleday.

———. 2007. "Bots on The Ground: In the Field of Battle (Or Even Above It), Robots Are a Soldier's Best Friend." *Washington Post*, May 6. www.washingtonpost.com/wp-dyn/content/article/2007/05/05/AR2007050501009_pf.html (accessed May 11, 2007).

Gartner Group. 2007. "Gartner Says 80 Percent of Active Internet Users Will Have a 'Second Life' in the Virtual World by the End of 2011." Press release, April 24. Gartner. www.gartner.com/it/page.jsp?id=503861 (accessed January 10, 2008).

Gelernter, David. 1994. *The Muse in the Machine: Computerizing the Poetry of Human Thought.* New York: The Free Press.

———. 2007. "Artificial Intelligence Is Lost in the Woods." *Technology Review*, July/August. www.technologyreview.com/Infotech/18867/?a=f (accessed July 5, 2007).

Geraci, Robert M. 2006. "Spiritual Robots: Religion and Our Scientific View of the Natural World." *Theology and Science* 4 (3): 229–46.

———. 2007a. "Cultural Prestige: Popular Science Robotics as Religion-Science Hybrid." In *Reconfigurations: Interdisciplinary Perspectives on Religion in a Post-secular Society*, edited by Stefanie Knauss and Alexander D. Ornella, pp. 43–58. Vienna: LIT Press.

———. 2007b. "Robots and the Sacred in Science and Science Fiction: Theological Implications of Artificial Intelligence." *Zygon: Journal of Religion and Science* 42(4): 961–80.

———. 2007c. "Apocalyptic AI." Seminar held for the Philosophy of Robotics Group at the Robotics Institute at Carnegie Mellon University, June 21.

———. 2007d. "Religion for the Robots." *Sightings*, June 14. divinity.uchicago.edu/martycenter/publications/sightings/archive_2007/0614.shtml (accessed December 18, 2007).

———. 2008a. "Apocalyptic AI: Religion and the Promise of Artificial Intelligence." *Journal of the American Academy of Religion* 76 (1): 138–66.

———. 2008b. *Human Nature and the Ethics of Progress: Power and Purpose in Twentieth-century Religion, Science and Art.* Saarbrücken: VDM Verlag.

———. 2010. "Popular Appeal of Apocalypse AI." *Zygon Journal of Religion and Science* 45 (4) 1: 1003–20.

Giberson, Karl, and Mariano Artigas. 2007. *Oracles of Science: Celebrity Scientists versus God and Religion.* New York: Oxford University Press.

Gibson, William. 1984. *Neuromancer.* New York: Ace Books.

Gilbert, James. 1997. *Redeeming Culture: American Religion in an Age of Science.* Chicago: University of Chicago Press.

Gips, James. 1995. "Towards the Ethical Robot." In *Android Epistemology*, edited by Kenneth M. Ford, Clark Glymour, and Patrick J. Hayes, pp. 243–52. MIT Press.

Glaser, Mark. 2007. "Hype and Backlash for *Second Life* Miss the Bigger Picture." *MediaShift*, December 5. www.pbs.org/mediashift/2007/12/digging_deeperhype_and_backlas.html (accessed December 21, 2007).

Goldsmith, Arnold L. 1981. *The Golem Remembered, 1909–1980.* Detroit: Wayne State University Press.

Goodall, Jane. 2001. "Rain Dance." *Science and Spirit*, May/June. www.science-spirit.org/article_detail.php?article_id=229 (accessed August 26, 2009).

Gould, Stephen Jay. 1999. *Rocks of Ages: Science and Religion in the Fullness of Life.* New York: The Library of Contemporary Thought.

Grant, Edward S. 1986. "Science and Theology in the Middle Ages." In *God and Nature: Historical Essays on the Encounter between Christianity and Science*, edited by David C. Lindberg and Ronald L. Numbers, pp. 49–75. Berkeley, Calif.: University of California Press.

———. 1996. *The Foundations of Modern Science in the Middle Ages: Their Religious, Institutional and Intellectual Contexts*. Cambridge, U.K.: University of Cambridge Press.

Grant, Frederick. 1917. "The Gospel Kingdom." *The Biblical World* 50 (3): 129–91.

Greenberg, David S. [1967] 1999. *The Politics of Pure Science*. Rev. ed. Chicago: University of Chicago Press.

Gumbs, Ken. 2007. *Building Gods* (rough cut). Four Door Films.

Gutkind, Lee. 2006. *Almost Human: Making Robots Think*. New York: W.W. Norton.

Hadaway, C. Kirk, and P. L. Marler. 1998. "Did You Really Go to Church This Week? Behind the Poll Data." *Christian Century*, May 6: 472–75. www.religion-online.org/showarticle.asp?title=237 (accessed August 12, 2007).

Hall, J. Storrs. 2007. *Beyond AI: Creating the Conscious of the Machine*. Amherst, N.Y.: Prometheus Books.

Hanson, Paul D. [1975] 1979. *The Dawn of Apocalyptic: The Historical and Sociological Roots of Jewish Apocalyptic Eschatology*. Rev. ed. Philadelphia: Fortress Press.

Haq, Syed Nomanul. 1994. *Names, Natures and Things: The Alchemist Jābir ibn Hayyān and his Kitāb al-Ahjār (Book of Stones)*. Boston: Kluwer.

Haraway, Donna J. 1997. *Modest_Witness@Second_Millennium.FemaleMan©_Meets_Oncomouse™: Feminism and Technoscience*. New York: Routledge.

Harding, Sandra. 1998. *Is Science Multicultural? Postcolonialisms, Feminisms, and Epistemologies*. Bloomington: Indiana University Press.

Harris, Sam. 2004. *The End of Faith: Religion, Terror and the Future of Reason*. New York: W. W. Norton.

Harrison, Harry, and Marvin Minsky. 1992. *The Turing Option*. New York: Warner Books.

Hawking, Stephen. 1998. *A Brief History of Time*. Updated 10th Anniversary ed. New York: Bantam.

Hayles, N. Katherine. 1999. *How We Became Posthuman: Virtual Bodies in Cybernetics, Literature, and Informatics*. Chicago: University of Chicago Press.

———. 2005. *My Mother Was a Computer: Digital Subjects and Literary Texts*. Chicago: University of Chicago Press.

Hayward, Jeremy W., and Francisco J. Varela, eds. 1992. *Gentle Bridges: Conversations with the Dalai Lama on the Sciences of the Mind*. Boston: Shambhala.

Hefner, Philip. 2009. "The Animal that Aspires to be an Angel: The Challenge of Transhumanism." *Dialog: A Journal of Theology* 48:2: 164–73.

Helmreich, Stefan. [1998] 2000. *Silicon Second Nature: Culturing Artificial Life in a Digital World*. Paperback ed. Los Angeles: University of California Press.

Henderson, Mark. 2007. "Human Rights for Robots? We're Getting Carried Away." *Times* (London), April 24. www.timesonline.co.uk/tol/news/uk/science/article1695546.ece (accessed June 4, 2007).

Herzfeld, Noreen. 2002a. "Creating in Our Own Image: Artificial Intelligence and the Image of God." *Zygon: Journal of Religion and Science* 37 (4): 303–16.

———. 2002b. "Cybernetic Immortality versus Christian Resurrection." In *Resurrection: Theological and Scientific Arguments*, edited by Ted Peters, Robert John Russell, and Michael Welker, pp. 192–201. Grand Rapids, Mich.: William B. Eerdmans.

Hillis, Danny. 2001. "A Time of Transition/The Human Connection." In *True Names and the Opening of the Cyberspace Frontier*, edited by James Frenkel. pp. 27–32. New York: Tor.

Himmelfarb, Martha. 1993. *Ascent to Heaven in Jewish and Christian Apocalypses*. New York: Oxford University Press.

Hof, Robert D. 2006. "My Virtual Life." *Business Week* 3982 (May 1): 72–75.

Hollinger, Geoff. 2007. Interview with author at Carnegie Mellon University, June 13.

Holmyard, E. J., ed. 1928. *The Works of Geber*. Translated by Richard Russell. New York: E. P. Dutton and Company.

———. 1957. *Alchemy*. New York: Penguin.

Hornyak, Timothy N. 2006. *Loving the Machine: The Art and Science of Japanese Robots*. New York: Kodansha International.

Horsley, Richard A. 1993. *Jesus and the Spiral of Violence: Popular Jewish Resistance in Roman Palestine*. Minneapolis: Fortress Press.

———. 2000. "The Kingdom of God and the Renewal of Israel: Synoptic Gospels, Jesus Movements, and Apocalypticism." In *The Encyclopedia of Apocalypticism*, edited by Bernard McGinn, John J. Collins, and Stephen J. Stein, vol. 1, *The Origins of Apocalypticism in Judaism and Christianity*, edited by John J. Collins, pp. 303–44. New York: Continuum Press.

Hughes, James J. 2006. "Human Enhancement and the Emergent Technopolitics of the Twenty-first Century." In *Managing Nano-Bio-Info-Cogno Innovations: Converging Technologies in Society*, edited by William Sims Bainbridge and Mihail C. Roco, pp. 285–307. Dordrecht, The Netherlands: Springer.

Huntington, John. 1991. "Newness, *Neuromancer*, and the End of Narrative." In *Fictional Space: Essays on Contemporary Science Fiction*, edited by Tom Shippey, pp. 59–75. Atlantic Highlands, N.J.: Humanities Press International.

Idel, Moshe. 1988. "The Golem in Jewish Magic and Mysticism." In *Golem! Danger, Deliverance and Art*, edited by Emily D. Bilski, pp. 15–35. New York: The Jewish Museum.

———. 1990. *Golem: Jewish Magical and Mystical Traditions on the Artificial Anthropoid*. Albany: SUNY Press.

Ipsos MORI. 2006. "Robo-rights: Utopian Dream or Rise of the Machines?" www.sigmascan.org//ViewIssue.aspx?IssueId=53 (accessed June 4, 2007, no longer available).

Iqbal, Muzaffar. 2002. *Islam and Science*. Burlington, Vt.: Ashgate.

Jackelén, Antje. 2002. "The Image of God as *Techno Sapiens*." *Zygon: Journal of Religion and Science* 37 (2): 289–302.

Jakobsson, Mikael, and T. L. Taylor. 2003. "The Sopranos Meets *EverQuest*: Social Networking in Massively Multiplayer Online Games." Paper presented at MelbourneDAC: the Fifth International Digital Arts and Culture Conference, May 19–23.

John Mark Ministries. 2007. "Religion for the Robots." By Robert M. Geraci. John Mark Ministries weblog, June 14. jmm.aaa.net.au/articles/19887.htm (accessed November 29, 2008).

Johnson, Phillip E. 1990. "Evolution as Dogma: The Establishment of Naturalism." *First Things* 6 (October): 15–22.

Joy, Bill. 2000. "Why the Future Doesn't Need Us." *Wired* 8.04 (April). www.wired.com/wired/archive/8.04/joy.html (accessed June 2007).

Kahney, Leander. 2003. "The New Pet Craze: Robovacs." *Wired* 11.06 (June). www.wired.com/science/discoveries/news/2003/06/59249 (accessed July 2007).

Karakuriya. 2007. "Karakuriya Doll." UNIX Co., Ltd. karakuriya.com/english/doll/karakurizui.htm (accessed July 25, 2007).

Kass, Leon. 2003. "Letter of Transmittal to the President." *Beyond Therapy: Biotechnology and the Pursuit of Happiness—A Report of the President's Council on Bioethics.* Washington, D.C.: The President's Council on Bioethics.

Keiper, Adam. 2006. "The Age of Neuroelectronics." *The New Atlantis: A Journal of Technology and Society* (Winter): 4–41.

Kelly, Kevin. 1999. "Nerd Theology." *Technology in Society* 21 (4): 387–92.

———. 2007. "The Technium and the Seventh Kingdom of Life: A Talk with Kevin Kelly." *Edge* 217 (July 18). www.edge.org/3rd_culture/kelly07/kelly07_index.html (accessed July 19, 2007).

Ketterer, David. 1974. *New Worlds for Old: The Apocalyptic Imagination, Science Fiction, and American Literature.* Bloomington: Indiana University Press.

Kieval, Hillel J. 1997. "Pursuing the Golem of Prague: Jewish Culture and the Invention of a Tradition." *Modern Judaism* 17 (1): 1–23.

Kim, Yoon-mi. 2007. "Korea Drafts 'Robot Ethics Charter.'" *Korea Herald*, April 28. www.koreaherald.co.kr/SITE/data/html_dir/2007/04/28/200704280033.asp (accessed May 8, 2007).

King, Brad, and John Borland. 2003. *Dungeons and Dreamers: The Rise of Computer Game Culture from Geek to Chic.* New York: McGraw-Hill/Osborne.

King, Mary. 2007. "Robots & AI in Japan and the West." Robots and AI [weblog], April 21. robotandai.blogspot.com/2007/04/abstract-this-research-project-explores.html (accessed May 24, 2007).

Kline, Charles. 2007. "Arrested." From the Mind of Charles [weblog], June 8. hngkong.wordpress.com/2007/06/08/arrested/ (accessed June 10, 2007).

Kruk, Remke. 1990. "A Frothy Bubble: Spontaneous Generation in the Medieval Islamic Tradition." *Journal of Semitic Studies* 35 (2): 265–82.

Kuhn, Thomas. [1962] 1996. *The Structure of Scientific Revolutions.* 3d ed. Chicago: University of Chicago Press.

Kuipers, Benjamin. 2005. "Consciousness: Drinking from the Firehose of Experience." Paper presented at the National Conference on Artificial Intelligence. Revised version. www.cs.utexas.edu/~qr/papers/Kuipers-aaai-05.html (accessed August 16, 2007).

Kurzweil, Ray. 1990. *The Age of Intelligent Machines.* Cambridge, Mass.: MIT Press.

———. 1999. *The Age of Spiritual Machines: When Computers Exceed Human Intelligence.* New York: Viking.

———. 2005. *The Singularity Is Near: When Humans Transcend Biology.* New York: Penguin Books.

———. 2007. Acceptance speech, HG Wells Award for Outstanding Contributions to Transhumanism. www.transhumanism.org/index.php/WTA/more/wells2007/ (accessed August 11, 2007).

———. 2009a. Keynote address at the *Second Life* Community Convention, August 14.

———. 2009b. Question and answer session after the premier of *Transcendent Man.* Tribeca Film Festival, NY (August 28).

Kushner, David. 2009. "When Man and Machine Merge." *Rolling Stone* 1072. 56–61.

Lakatos, Imre, Paul Feyerabend, and Mateo Motterlini, eds. 2000. *For and Against Method: Including Lakatos's Lectures on Scientific Method and the Lakatos-Feyerabend Correspondence.* Chicago: University of Chicago Press.

Lanier, Jaron. 1996. "Jaron Lanier: Interviewed by Lynn Hershmann Leeson." In *Clicking In: Hot Links to a Digital Culture,* edited by Lynn Hershman Leeson, pp. 43–53. Seattle: Bay Press.

———. 2000. "One Half of a Manifesto." *Edge* 74 (September 25). www.edge.org/documents/archive/edge74.html (accessed September 12, 2006).

———. 2006. "Digital Maoism." *Edge* 183 (May 30). www.edge.org/documents/archive/edge183.html (accessed September 12, 2006).

Larson, Edward. 1997. *Summer for the Gods: The Scopes Trial and America's Continuing Debate over Science and Religion.* Cambridge, Mass.: Harvard University Press.

Lasswell, Harold D. 1956. "The Political Science of Science: An Inquiry into the Possible Reconciliation of Mastery and Freedom." *The American Political Science Review* 50 (4): 961–79.

Latour, Bruno. 1983. "Give Me a Laboratory and I Will Raise the World." In *Science Observed: Perspectives on the Social Study of Science,* edited by Karin Knorr-Cetina and Michael Mulkay, pp. 141–70. Beverley Hills, Calif.: SAGE Publications.

———. 1987. *Science in Action: How to Follow Scientists and Engineers through Society.* Cambridge, Mass.: Harvard University Press.

———. 1988. *The Pasteurization of France.* Translated by Alan Sheridan and John Law. Cambridge, Mass.: Harvard University Press.

———. [1992] 1999. "One More Turn After the Social Turn . . ." In *The Science Studies Reader,* edited by Mario Biagioli, pp. 276–89. New York: Routledge.

———. 1993. *We Have Never Been Modern.* Translated by Catherine Porter. Cambridge, Mass.: Harvard University Press.

———. [1993] 1996. *Aramis: Or, the Love of Technology.* Translated by Catherine Porter. Cambridge, Mass.: Harvard University Press.

———. 1999. "For David Bloor . . . and Beyond: A Reply to David Bloor's 'Anti-Latour.'" *Studies in the History and Philosophy of Science* 30 (1): 113–29.

———. 2002. "What is Iconoclash? Or Is There a World Beyond the Image Wars?" *Iconoclash: Beyond the Image Wars in Science, Religion, and Art.* Karlsruhe and Cambridge, MA: ZKM Center for Art and Media and MIT Press. 14–37.

———. 2007. "Can We Get Our Materialism Back, Please?" *Isis* 98 (1): 138–42.

Latour, Bruno, and Steve Woolgar. [1979] 1986. *Laboratory Life: The Construction of Scientific Facts.* Repr. Princeton: Princeton University Press.

Lee, James. 2007. "Sci-Fi's Next Empire: *Mass Effect* Does for Games what *Star Wars* Did for Films." *Wired* 15:06 (June), p. 96.

Levy, David. 2006. *Robots Unlimited: Life in a Virtual Age.* Wellesley, Mass.: A.K. Peters.

———. 2007. *Love and Sex with Robots: The Evolution of Human-Robot Relationships.* New York: HarperCollins Publishers.

———. 2009. E-mail correspondence with author. March 6.

Lewis, Leo. 2007. "The Robots Are Running Riot! Quick, Bring Out the Red Tape." *Times* (London), April 6. www.timesonline.co.uk/tol/news/world/asia/article1620558.ece (accessed April 11, 2007).

Lincoln, Bruce. 1989. *Discourse and the Construction of Society: Comparative Studies of Myth, Ritual, and Classification.* New York: Oxford University Press.

———. 1995. *Authority: Construction and Corrosion.* Chicago: University of Chicago Press.

———. 2003. *Holy Terrors: Rethinking Religion after September 11th.* Chicago: University of Chicago Press.

Lindberg, David C., and Ronald L. Numbers. 1986. *God and Nature: Historical Essays on the Encounter between Christianity and Science.* Berkeley: University of California Press.

Lipton, Eric. 2007. "Safety Agency Faces Scrutiny amid Charges." *New York Times*, September 2. www.nytimes.com/2007/09/02/business/02consumer.html?pagewanted=1&ei=5089&en=576 a57b1f5d64d08&ex=1346385600&partner=rssyahoo&emc=rss (accessed September 3, 2007).

Luo, Michael. 2006. "Seeking Entry-Level Prophet: Burning Bush and Tablets Not Required." *New York Times*, August 28. *Republished by WorldWide Religious News.* www.wwrn.org/article.php?idd=22541&sec=55&cont=6 (accessed October 2, 2007).

Marcus, Joel. 1996. "Modern and Ancient Jewish Apocalypticism." *The Journal of Religion* 76(1): 1–27.

Mason, Matt. 2007. Personal communication with author at Carnegie Mellon University, June 26.

Mattia, Joan P. 2007. "Pharisee & Tax Collector." Sermon notes. St. Peter's in the Woods: A Mission of the Episcopal Church. www.spiw.org/apps/articles/default.asp?articleid=39893&columnid=438 (accessed November 29, 2008).

McKnight, Stephen A. 2006. *The Religious Foundations of Francis Bacon's Thought.* Columbia, Mo.: University of Missouri Press.

McNally, Phil, and Sohail Inayatullah. 1988. "The Rights of Robots: Technology, Culture and Law in the Twenty-first Century." Republished by KurzweilAI.net, August 6, 2001. www.kurzweilai.net./meme/frame.html?main=/articles/art0265.html? (accessed May 2, 2007).

Meeks, Wayne. 2000. "Apocalyptic Discourse and Strategies of Goodness." *The Journal of Religion* 80(3): 461–75.

Menzel, Peter, and Faith D'Aluisio. 2000. *Robo sapiens: Evolution of a New Species.* Cambridge, Mass.: MIT Press.

Merlin, Qyxxql. 2007. Blog comment, May 20, on "A Crisis of Faith," by W. James Au, New World Notes [weblog], May 18. nwn.blogs.com/nwn/2007/05/avatars_of_unch.html (accessed June 5, 2007).

Metz, Cade. 2007. "*Second Life* Will Dwarf the Web in Ten Years: So Says Linden Lab CEO." *The Register*, August 1. www.theregister.co.uk/2007/08/01/second_life_to_dwarf_web_in_ten_years/ (accessed August 14, 2007).

Metz, Rachel. 2009. "At Singularity University, Tech Is Seen as Savior." AP News (August 28). Available at: www.physorg.com/news170697852.html (accessed August 30, 2009).

Miller, David M. 1985. "Toward a Structural Metaphysic: Religion in the Novels of Frank Herbert." In *The Transcendent Adventure: Studies of Religion in Science Fiction/Fantasy*, edited by Robert Reilly, pp. 145–56. Westport, Conn.: Greenwood Press.

Minsky, Marvin. [1968] 1995. "Matter, Mind and Models." Reprinted from *Semantic Information Processing*, edited by Minsky (MIT Press). groups.csail.mit.edu/medg/people/doyle/gallery/minsky/mmm.html (accessed June 14, 2007).

———. 1985. *Society of Mind.* New York: Simon and Schuster.

———. 1994. "Will Robots Inherit the Earth?" *Scientific American*, October. Reposted by the MIT Media Lab. web.media.mit.edu/~minsky/papers/sciam.inherit.html (accessed June 14, 2007).

———. 2006. *The Emotion Machine: Commonsense Thinking, Artificial Intelligence, and the Future of the Human Mind.* New York: Simon and Schuster.

Mitsuoka, George. 2007. "2007 CES Roundup." *Robot* 7: 64–68.

Moelwyn-Hughes, E.A. 1964. Introduction to *The Sceptical Chymist*, by Robert Boyle. pp. v–xii. New York: Dutton.

Moravec, Hans. 1978. "Today's Computers, Intelligent Machines and Our Future." *Analog* 99(2): 59–84. Reposted by the Field Robotics Center at Carnegie Mellon University's Robotics Institute.

www.frc.ri.cmu.edu/~hpm/project.archive/general.articles/1978/analog.1978.html (accessed August 5, 2007).

———. 1988. *Mind Children: The Future of Robot and Human Intelligence*. Cambridge, Mass.: Harvard University Press.

———. 1992a. "Letter from Moravec to Penrose." E-mail correspondence published in *Thinking Robots, An Aware Internet, and Cyberpunk Librarians: The 1992 LITA President's Program*, edited by R. Bruce Miller and Milton T. Wolf, pp. 51–58. Chicago: Library and Information Technology Association.

———. 1992. "Pigs in Cyberspace." In *Thinking Robots, An Aware Internet, and Cyberpunk Librarians: The 1992 LITA President's Program*, edited by R. Bruce Miller and Milton T. Wolf, pp. 15–21. Chicago: Library and Information Technology Association.

———. 1999. *Robot: Mere Machine to Transcendent Mind*. New York: Oxford University Press.

———. 2007. E-mail correspondence with author, June 25.

More, Max. 2003. "Principles of Extropy: Version 3.11." Extropy Institute. www.extropy.org/principles.htm (accessed October 4, 2008).

Mori, Masahiro. 1970. "The Uncanny Valley." Translated by Karl F. MacDorman and Takashi Minato. *Energy* 7(4): 33–35.

———. [1981] 1999. *The Buddha in the Robot: A Robot Engineer's Thoughts on Science and Religion*. Translated by Charles S. Terry. Tokyo: Kosei.

Mormon Transhumanist Association. 2009. http://transfigurism.org/community/.

Nagel, Thomas. 1974. "What It's Like To Be a Bat." *The Philosophical Review* 83(4): 435–50.

Nelson, Robert H. 2001. *Economics as Religion: From Samuelson to Chicago and Beyond*. University Park, Pa.: Pennsylvania State University Press.

Nelson, Victoria. 2001. *The Secret Life of Puppets*. Cambridge, Mass.: Harvard University Press.

New Oxford Annotated Bible(New Revised Standard Version). 1991. Edited by Bruce M. Metzger and Roland E. Murphey. New York: Oxford University Press.

Newberg, Andrew, Eugene D'Aquili, and Vince Rause. 2001. *Why God Won't Go Away: Brain Science and the Biology of Belief*. New York: Ballantine Books.

Newell, Allen. 1990. "Fairy Tales." In *The Age of Intelligent Machines*, edited by Raymond Kurzweil, pp. 420–23. Cambridge, Mass.: MIT Press.

Newitz, Annalee. 2006. "Your Second Life is Ready." *Popular Science*, September. www.popsci.com/popsci/technology/7ba1af8f3812d01ovgnvcm1000004eecbccdrcrd.html (accessed November 27, 2006).

Newman, William R. 2004. *Promethean Ambitions: Alchemy and the Quest to Perfect Nature*. Chicago: University of Chicago Press.

Noble, David F. 1999. *The Religion of Technology: The Divinity of Man and the Spirit of Invention*. New York: Penguin.

Nordmann, Alfred. 2006. "Ignorance at the Heart of Science? Incredible Narratives on Brain-Machine Interfaces." Workshop presented by NanoBio-RAISE. www.unibielefeld.de/ZIF/FG/2006Application/PDF/Nordmann_essay.pdf (accessed July 15, 2007).

Novak, Marcos. 1991. "Liquid Architectures in Cyberspace." In *Cyberspace: First Steps*, edited by Michael Benedikt, pp. 225–54. Cambridge, Mass.: MIT Press.

Nye, David E. 2003. *America as Second Creation: Technology and Narratives of a New Beginning*. Cambridge, Mass.: MIT University Press.

O'Connor, Kathleen. 1994. *The Alchemical Creation of Life (Takwin) and Other Concepts of Genesis in Medieval Islam.* PhD diss., University of Pennsylvania.

——. 2007. E-mail correspondence with author, August 26.

O'Leary, Stephen D. 2000. "Apocalypticism in American Popular Culture." In *The Encyclopedia of Apocalypticism*, edited by Bernard McGinn, John J. Collins, and Stephen J. Stein, vol. 3, *Apocalypticism in the Modern World and the Contemporary Age*, edited by Stephen J. Stein, pp. 392–426. New York: Continuum Press.

Oldenberg, Ray. 1989. *The Great Good Place: Cafés, Coffee Shops, Community Centers, Beauty Parlors, General Stores, Bars, Hangouts, and How They Get You Through the Day.* New York: Paragon House.

Omer, Mordechai, and Avi Rosen. 2007. "The Ultimate Cathedral." Translated by Sonia Dantziger. Reposted by NewmediaFIX. newmediafix.net/daily/?p=1064 (accessed August 11, 2007).

Onishi, Norimitsu. 2006. "In a Wired South Korea, Robots Will Feel Right at Home." *New York Times*, April 2. www.nytimes.com/2006/04/02/world/asia/02robot.html?ex=1177819200&en=62ae972429357fe1&ei=5070 (accessed April 11, 2007).

Order of Cosmic Engineers (OCE). 2008. "Prospectus—Order of Cosmic Engineers." Order of Cosmic Engineers [wiki]. cosmeng.org/index.php/ Prospectus (accessed October 4, 2008).

Ostwald, Michael. 2000. "Virtual Urban Futures." In *The Cybercultures Reader*, edited by David Bell and Barbara M. Kennedy, pp. 658–75. New York: Routledge.

——. 2007. E-mail correspondence with author, May 30.

Otto, Rudolph. [1917] 1958. *The Idea of the Holy: An Inquiry into the Non-rational Factor in the Idea of the Divine and Its Relation to the Rational.* Translated by John Harvey. London: Oxford University Press.

Pauline, Mark. 1989. "Is the Body Obsolete?" *Whole Earth Review* 33.

Pausch, Randy. 2007. Personal communication with author at Carnegie Mellon University, June 22.

Pennock, Robert T. 2001. "Naturalism, Evidence, and Creationism: The Case of Phillip Johnson." In *Intelligent Design Creationism and Its Critics: Philosophical, Theological, and Scientific Perspectives*, edited by Pennock, pp. 77–98. Cambridge, Mass.: MIT Press.

Penrose, Roger. 1989. *The Emperor's New Mind: Concerning Computers, Minds, and the Laws of Physics.* New York: Oxford University Press.

Peralta, Eyder. 2006. "In Second Life, the World Is Virtual. But the Emotions Are Real." *Houston Chronicle*, May 26. www.chron.com/disp/story.mpl/ent/3899538.html (accessed October 31, 2006).

Peters, Ted. 2008. "Transhumanism and the Posthuman Future: Will Technological Progress Get Us There?" *Metanexus*, June 5. www.metanexus.net/magazine/ArticleDetail/tabid/68/id/10546/Default.aspx (accessed December 16, 2008).

Peterson, David L. 1997. Review of *Prophecy and Apocalypticism: The Postexilic Social Setting*, by Stephen L. Cook. *The Journal of Religion* 77(4): 655–56.

Peterson, Gregory R. 2004. "What Does Silicon Valley Have to Do with Jerusalem?" *Zygon: Journal of Religion and Science* 39(3): 541–54.

Philipse, Herman. 1998. "Review: Shifting Position?" *Philosophy and Phenomenological Research* 58(4): 885–92.

Philosophy of Robotics Group, Carnegie Mellon University Robotics Institute. 2006 "The Ethics of Defense Funding." February 17.

Pickler, Nedra. 2007. "Candidates Seek Votes in Cyberspace." *Yahoo! News*, April 19.

Platt, Charles. 1995. "Superhumanism." *Wired* 3.10 (October). www.wired.com/wired/archive/3.10/moravec.html?pg=1&topic= (accessed October 17, 2008).

Pohl, Frederik. 1975. "The Tunnel under the World." In *The Best of Frederik Pohl*, edited by Lester del Rey, pp. 8–35. Garden City, N.Y.: Nelson Doubleday.

Pontin, Jason. 2007. "On Science Fiction: How it Influences the Imaginations of Technologists." *Technology Review*, March/April.

Postrel, Virginia. 1998. *The Future and Its Enemies: The Growing Conflict over Creativity, Enterprise, and Progress.* New York: Touchstone

Proctor, James D., ed. 2005. *Science, Religion, and the Human Experience.* New York: Oxford University Press.

Prisco, Giulio. [2004] 2007a. "Engineering Transcendence." COSMI2LE [weblog], December 1. Revised 2007. cosmi2le.com//index.php/site/more/engineering_transcendence (accessed April 26, 2007).

———. 2007b. "Transcendent Engineering." Presented at the Second Life Seminar on Transhumanism and Religion (April 29, 2007).

———. 2007c. "Soft Tiplerianism." COSMI2LE [weblog], May 27. cosmi2le.com//index.php/site/soft_tiplerianism (accessed June 5, 2007).

———. 2007d. "Life 2.0: Augmentationists in *Second Life* and Beyond." COSMI2LE [weblog], August 8. cosmi2le.com//index.php/site/life_20_augmentationists_in_second_life_and_beyond/ (accessed August 11, 2007).

———. 2007e. "New Transhumanist Meeting Place at Extropia Core in *Second Life*." COSMI2LE [weblog], December 8. cosmi2le.com//index.php/site/new_transhumanist_meeting_place_at_extrapia_core_in_second_life/ (accessed December 22, 2007).

———. 2008a. "Parallels and Convergences: Mormon Thought and Engineering Vision." COSMI2LE [weblog], September 6. cosmi2le.com//index.php/site/parallels_and_convergences_mormon_thought_and_engineering_vision/ (accessed October 4, 2008).

———. 2008b. Interview with author, August 19.

———. 2008c. "My Talk at In Nano Veritas." COSMI2LE [weblog], September 2. cosmi2le.com//index.php/site/my_talk_at_in_nano_veritas (accessed November 27, 2008).

Ptolemy, Barry (director). 2009. *Transcendent Man: The Life and Ideas of Ray Kurzweil.* Ptolemaic Productions. Film.

Putnam, Robert D. 2000. *Bowling Alone: The Collapse and Revival of American Community.* New York: Simon and Schuster.

Putz, Oliver. 2006. "Hormone-Receptors and Complexity: Putting to Rest Another God of the Gaps?" *Theology and Science* 4(3): 209–14.

Reader, Ian, and Tanabe, George J. 1991. *Practically Religious: Worldly Benefits and the Common Religion of Japan.* Honolulu: University of Hawaii.

Reeves, Byron, and Clifford Nass. 1996. *The Media Equation: How People Treat Computers, Television, and New Media Like Real People and Places.* New York: Cambridge University Press.

Reiji, Asakura. 2003. "The Androids Are Coming." *Japan Echo* 30(4): 13–18.

Rheingold, Howard. 1991. *Virtual Reality: The Revolutionary Technology of Computer-Generated Artificial Worlds—and How It Promises to Transform Society.* New York: Touchstone Books.

Rifkin, Jeremy. 1983. *Algeny.* In collaboration with Nicanor Perlas. New York: Viking.

Roco, Mihail C., and William Sims Bainbridge, eds. 2003. *Converging Technologies for Improving Human Performance: Nanotechnology, Biotechnology, Information Technology and Cognitive Science.* Boston: Kluwer.

———, eds. 2006. *Managing Nano-Bio-Info-Cogno Innovations: Converging Technologies in Society.* Dordrecht, The Netherlands: Springer.

Rolston, Holmes III. 1990. "Joining Science and Religion." *John Paul II on Science and Religion: Reflections on the New View from Rome,* edited by Robert J. Russell, William R. Stoeger, and George V. Coyne, pp. 83–94. Notre Dame, Ind.: Vatican Observatory Publications and the University of Notre Dame Press.

Roof, Wade Clark. 1999. *Spiritual Marketplace: Baby Boomers and the Remaking of American Religion.* Princeton, N.J.: Princeton University Press.

Rose, Frank. 2007. "Lonely Planet." *Wired* 15.08 (August): 140–144.

Rosenfeld, Azriel. 1966. "Religion and the Robot." *TRADITION: A Journal of Orthodox Thought* 8(3): 15–26.

Rosheim, Mark E. 1994. *Robot Evolution: The Development of Anthrobotics.* New York: John Wiley and Sons.

———. 2006. *Leonardo's Lost Robots.* New York: Springer.

Rosmarin, Rachel. 2007. "Virtual Fun and Games." *Forbes.com,* November 8. www.forbes.com/technology/2007/11/08/virtual-world-games-technology-cx_rr_1108world.html (accessed December 21, 2007).

Royal Academy of Engineering. 2009. "Autonomous Systems: Social, Legal and Ethical Issues." London: The Royal Academy of Engineering. Available at: www.raeng.org.uk/autonomoussystems.

Rubin, Charles. 2003. "Artificial Intelligence and Human Nature." *The New Atlantis: A Journal of Technology and Society* 1 (Spring): 88–100.

Rushkoff, Douglas. 1994. *Cyberia: Life in the Trenches of Cyberspace.* New York: HarperCollins.

Russell, D.S. 1964. *The Method and Message of Jewish Apocalyptic: 200 BC–100 AD.* Philadelphia: Westminster Press.

———. 1978. *Apocalyptic: Ancient and Modern.* Philadelphia: Fortress Press.

Russell, Robert John. 2002. "Bodily Resurrection, Eschatology, and Scientific Cosmology: The Mutual Interaction of Christian Theology and Science." In *Resurrection: Theological and Scientific Arguments,* edited by Ted Peters, Robert John Russell, and Michael Welker, pp. 3–30. Grand Rapids, Mich.: William B. Eerdmans.

Schaffer, Simon. 2002. "The Devices of Iconoclasm." In *Iconoclash: Beyond the Image Wars in Science, Religion, and Art,* edited by Bruno Latour and Peter Weibel, pp. 498–515. Cambridge, Mass.: MIT University Press and ZKM Center for Art and Media.

Schmithals, Walter. 1975. *The Apocalyptic Movement: Introduction and Interpretation.* Translated by John E. Steely. New York: Abingdon Press.

Schneier, Bruce. 2006. "A Robotic Bill of Rights." Schneier on Security: A Blog Covering Security and Security Technology, May 26.

Schodt, Frederick L. 1988. *Inside the Robot Kingdom: Japan, Mechatronics, and the Coming Robotopia.* New York: Kodansha International.

Schoepflin, Rennie B. 2000. "Apocalypticism in an Age of Science." In *The Encyclopedia of Apocalypticism,* edited by Bernard McGinn, John J. Collins, and Stephen J. Stein, vol. 3, *Apocalypticism in the Modern World and the Contemporary Age,* pp. 427–41. New York: Continuum Press.

Scholem, Gershom. [1960] 1969. "The Idea of the Golem." *On the Kabbalah and Its Symbolism.* Translated by Ralph Manheim. First English translation published by Schocken Books in 1965. New York: Schocken Books.

———. 1971. "The Golem of Prague and the Golem of Rehovot." In *The Messianic Idea in Judaism: And Other Essays on Jewish Spirituality*, pp. 335–40. New York: Schocken Books.

———. [1974] 1978. *Kabbalah.* New York: Meridian.

Schultz, Daniel. 2007. "Iron Man." Street Prophets [weblog], June 14. www.streetprophets.com/ story/2007/6/14/12520/7784 (accessed November 29, 2008).

Schwartz, Jerry. 2007. "ABC Offers 'Masters of Science Fiction.'" *Associated Press News Wire*, July 31. news.yahoo.com/s/ap/20070731/ap_en_ot/ap_on_tv_scifi_2 (accessed July 31, 2007, now available at www.bookrags.com/news/abc-offers-masters-of-science-moc).

Schwartz, Sheila. 1971. "Science Fiction: Bridge Between the Two Cultures." *English Journal* 60(8): 1043–51.

Searle, John. 1980. "Minds, Brains and Programs." *Behavioral and Brain Sciences* 3: 417–24.

Setzer, Claudia. 2004. *Resurrection of the Body in Early Judaism and Early Christianity: Doctrine, Community, and Self-Definition.* Boston: Brill Academic Publishers.

Sharkey, Noel. 2007. E-mail correspondence with author, August 17.

Shea, William. 1986. "Galileo and the Church." In *God and Nature: Historical Essays on the Encounter between Christianity and Science*, edited by David C. Lindberg and Ronald L. Numbers, pp. 114–35. Los Angeles: University of California Press.

Sheehan, Charles. 2004. "Robotics' Research Gaining in Prestige." *Associated Press*, April 11.

Sherwin, Byron. 1985. *The Golem Legend: Origins and Implications.* New York: University Press of America.

———. 2004. *Golems among Us: How a Jewish Legend Can Help Us Navigate the Biotech Century.* Chicago: Ivan R. Dee.

———. 2007. "Golems in the Biotech Century." *Zygon: Journal of Religion and Science* 42(1): 133–43.

Shibata, Takanori. 2007. *Most Therapeutic Robot: PARO.* DVD.

Shivers, Olin. 1999. "Stunning Achievement." Review of *True Names and the Opening of the Cyberspace Frontier*, by Vernor Vinge. Amazon.com, March 23. www.amazon.com/True-Names-Opening-Cyberspace-Frontier/dp/0312862075/ref=cm_cr-mr-title/103–0096591–9331054 (accessed April 17, 2007).

Singer, Isaac Bashevis. 1988. Foreword to *Golem! Danger, Deliverance and Art*, edited by Emily D. Bilski, pp. 6–9. New York: The Jewish Museum.

Singularity University. 2009. http://singularityu.org/overview/.

Sirius, R.U. 2007. Public presentation for the Leiden University and Erasmus University Rotterdam Science Fiction Science Faction program, April 11. www.cyberspacesalvations.nl/ (accessed July 5, 2007, video no longer available).

Slagle, Matt. 2007. "Robot Maker Builds Artificial Boy." *Associated Press*, September 13. www.msnbc. msn.com/id/20754739 (accessed September 13, 2007, no longer available).

SLidentity. 2007. "Voice and the Crisis of RL Identity in SL." Identity in the Digital Age [weblog], June 23. slidentity.wordpress.com/2007/06/23/voice-and-the-crisis-of-rl-identity-in-sl/ (accessed August 11, 2007).

Smart, Ninian. [1983] 2000. *Worldviews: Crosscultural Explorations of Human Beliefs.* 3d ed. Upper Saddle River, N.J.: Prentice Hall.

Smith, Jonathan Z. 1982. *Imagining Religion: From Babylon to Jonestown*. Chicago: University of Chicago Press.

Snodgrass, Melinda. 1989. "The Measure of a Man." Original airdate February 11. Season 2, episode 9 of *Star Trek: The Next Generation*. Produced by Paramount Television.

Society for Universal Immortalism (SfUI). 2008. "Society for University Immortalism." www.universalimmortalism.org/ (accessed March 16, 2008).

Sokal, Alan D. 1996a. "Transgressing the Boundaries: Toward a Transformative Hermeneutics of Quantum Gravity." *Social Text* 46/47: 217–52.

———. 1996b. "A Physicist Experiments with Cultural Studies." *Lingua Franca*. May/June: 62–64.

Solum, Lawrence B. 1992. "Legal Personhood for Artificial Intelligences." *North Carolina Law Review* 70: 1231–87.

Soskis, Benjamin. 2005. "Man and the Machines: It's Time to Start Thinking about How We Might Grant Legal Rights to Computers." *Legal Affairs: The Magazine at the Intersection of Law and Life*, Jan/Feb. www.legalaffairs.org/issues/january-february-2005/feature_soskis_janfeb05.html (accessed April 16, 2007).

Spark, Alasdair. 1991. "The Art of Future War: *Starship Troopers, The Forever War* and Vietnam." In *Fictional Space: Essays on Contemporary Science Fiction*, edited by Tom Shippey, pp. 113–65. Atlantic Highlands, N.J.: Humanities Press International.

Spice, Byron. 2007. "Helpful Robot Alters Family Life." *Live Science*, June 8. www.livescience.com/technology/070608_bts_robot_manners.html (accessed June 19, 2007).

Stapleton, H.E., G.L. Lewis, and Taylor F. Sherwood. 1949. "The Sayings of Hermes Quoted in the Mā' Al-Waraqī of Ibn Umail." *Ambix: The Journal of the Society for the Study of Alchemy and Early Chemistry* 3(3–4): 69–90.

Star, Susan Leigh, and James R. Griesemer. 1989. "Institutional Ecology, 'Translations,' and Boundary Objects: Amateurs and Professionals in Berkeley's Museum of Vertebrate Zoology, 1907–39." *Social Studies of Science* 19(3): 387–420.

Stark, Rodney, and William S. Bainbridge. 1985. *The Future of Religion: Secularization, Revival, and Cult Formation*. Los Angeles: University of California Press.

Steinhart, Eric. 2008. "Teilhard and Transhumanism." *Journal of Evolution and Technology* 20(1): 1–22.

Stengers, Nicole. 1991. "Mind is a Leaking Rainbow." In *Cyberspace: First Steps*, edited by Michael Benedikt, pp. 49–58. Cambridge, Mass.: MIT Press.

Stenvaag, Sophrosyne. 2007a. "What Makes a Person: Personality, Identity and Physiology, Part 1." Finding Sophrosyne [weblog], July 9. sophrosyne-sl.livejournal.com/11456.html (accessed August 2, 2007).

———. 2007b. "What Makes a Person: Personality, Identity and Physiology, Part 2." Finding Sophrosyne [weblog], July 11. sophrosyne-sl.livejournal.com/12352.html (accessed August 2, 2007).

———. 2007c. Personal communication in *Second Life*, November 23.

———. 2007d. "Extropia at +1 Month." Finding Sophrosyne [weblog], December 10. sophrosyne-sl.livejournal.com/46734.html (accessed December 19, 2007).

———. 2007e. "The Future of Extropia." Sophrosyne's Saturday Salon meeting in Second Life (December 29).

———. 2008a. E-mail correspondence with author, March 6.

———. 2008b. E-mail correspondence with author, October 6.

————. 2009. "Our Revels Are Now Ended." Sophtopia [weblog], June 24. http://sophtopia.blog-spot.com/2009/06/our-revels-now-are-ended.html (accessed August 1, 2009).

Stephenson, Neal. 1992. *Snow Crash*. New York: Bantam.

Sterling, Bruce, ed. 1986. *Mirrorshades: The Definitive Cyberpunk Anthology*. New York: Arbor House.

————. 2007. Public presentation at Pakhuis de Zwijger for the Leiden University and Erasmus University Rotterdam Science Fiction Science Faction program, March 21. www.cyberspacesalva-tions.nl/ (accessed July 5, 2007).

Stetten, George. 1989. *Weissenbaum's Eye*. Syracuse, N.Y.: Zwitter Press.

Stock, Gregory. 2003. *Redesigning Humans: Choosing Our Genes, Changing Our Future*. New York: Houghton Mifflin Company.

Stokes, Henry Scott. 1982. "Japan's Love Affair with the Robot." New York Times, January 10.

Stone, Allucquere Rosanne. 1991. "Will the Real Body Please Stand Up?: Boundary Stories about Virtual Cultures." In *Cyberspace: First Steps*, edited by Michael Benedikt pp. 81–118. Cambridge, Mass.: MIT Press.

Stone, Brad. 2003. *Gearheads: The Turbulent Rise of Robotic Sports*. New York: Simon and Schuster.

Stone, Christopher. 1987. *Earth and Other Ethics: The Case for Moral Pluralism*. New York: Harper and Row.

————. 1996. *Should Trees Have Standing? And Other Essays on Law, Morals and the Environment*. Dobbs Ferry, N.Y.: Oceana Publications.

Stout, Jeffrey. 2008. "2007 Presidential Address: The Folly of Secularism." *Journal of the American Academy of Religion* 76(3): 533–44.

Stross, Charles. 2005. *Accelerando*. New York: Penguin.

————. 2007. *Halting State*. New York: Ace Books.

Sudia, Frank W. 2004. "A Jurisprudence of Artilects: Blueprint for a Synthetic Citizen." *Law Update* 161: 11–18.

Sutin, Lawrence, ed. [1989] 1991. *Divine Invasions: A Life of Philip K. Dick*. Repr. New York: Citadel Twilight.

————, ed. 1995. *The Shifting Realities of Philip K. Dick: Selected Literary and Philosophical Writings*. New York: Vintage Books.

Tabuchi, Hiroko. 2008. "Japan Looks to a Robot Future." *AP News*, March 2. www.msnbc.msn.com/id/23438322/ (accessed March 3, 2008).

Takahashi, Tomotaka. 2007. Demonstration of Chroino and FT at Human Interaction: Vision 2020, hosted by the Japan Society, New York (June 6).

Takanishi, Atsuo. 2007. "*Mottaninai* Thought and Social Acceptability of Robots in Japan." Paper presented at the IEEE International Conference on Robotics and Automation, Rome (April 10–14).

Tamatea, Laurence. 2008. "If Robots R-Us, Who am I: Online 'Christian' Responses to Artificial Intelligence." *Culture and Religion* 9(2): 141–60.

Taussig, Michael. 1993. *Mimesis and Alterity: A Particular History of the Senses*. New York: Routledge.

Taylor, Mark C. 1993. *Disfiguring: Art, Architecture, Religion*. Chicago: University of Chicago Press.

Taylor, T.L. 2006. *Play between Worlds: Exploring Online Game Culture*. Cambridge, Mass.: MIT Press.

Teilhard de Chardin, Pierre. [1955] 1959. *The Phenomenon of Man*. Translated by Bernard Wall. New York: Harper & Brothers.

Thompson, Dick. 1989. "The Most Hated Man in Science." *Time*, December 4. www.time.com/time/magazine/article/0,9171,959181,00.html (accessed September 15, 2007).

Thomsen, Christian W. 1982. "Robot Ethics and Robot Parody: Remarks on Isaac Asimov's I, *Robot* and Some Critical Essays and Short Stories by Stanislaw Lem." In *The Mechanical God: Machines in Science Fiction*, edited by Thomas P. Dunn and Richard D. Erlich, pp. 27–39. Westport, Conn.: Greenwood Press.

Tirosh-Samuelson, Hava. 2007. "Facing the Challenges of Transhumanism: Philosophical, Religious, and Ethical Considerations." *The Global Spiral: A Publication of the Metanexus Institute*, October 5. www.metanexus.net/magazine/tabid/68/id/10169/Default.aspx (accessed November 6, 2007).

Tomas, David. 1991. "Old Rituals for New Space: Rites de Passage and William Gibson's Cultural Model of Cyberspace." In *Cyberspace: First Steps*, edited by Michael Benedikt, pp. 31–47. Cambridge, Mass.: MIT Press.

Touretzky, Dave. 2007a. Personal communication with author at Carnegie Mellon University, June 25.

———. 2007b. Personal communication with author at Carnegie Mellon University, June 28.

———. 2007c. E-mail correspondence with author, citing an August 31 e-mail from himself to Bruce Klein (September 11).

Townes, Charles H. 1990. "Response to the Message of John Paul II." In *John Paul II on Science and Religion: Reflections on the New View from Rome*, edited by Robert J. Russell, William R. Stoeger, and George V. Coyne, pp. 113–17. Notre Dame, Ind.: Vatican Observatory Publications and the University of Notre Dame Press.

Translook (the SL Transhumanists wiki). 2008. translook.com/index.php/Main_Page (accessed March 16, 2008, no longer available).

Tremlin, Todd. 2006. *Minds and Gods: The Cognitive Foundations of Religion*. New York: Oxford University Press.

Turing, Alan. 1950. "Computing Machinery and Intelligence." *Mind* 59(236): 433–60.

Turkle, Sherry. 1996. "Rethinking Identity Through Virtual Community." In *Clicking In: Hot Links to a Digital Culture*, edited by Lynn Hershman Leeson, pp. 116–22. Seattle: Bay Press.

———. 1999. "What Are We Thinking About When We Are Thinking About Computers?" In *The Science Studies Reader*, edited by Mario Biagioli, pp. 543–52. New York: Routledge.

———, ed. 2007. *Evocative Objects: Things We Think With*. Cambridge, Mass.: MIT Press.

Turner, Fred. 2006. *From Counterculture to Cyberculture: Stewart Brand, the Whole Earth Network, and the Rise of Digital Utopianism*. Chicago: University of Chicago Press.

U.S. Congress. Senate. 2003. *Twenty-first Century Nanotechnology Research and Development Act*. 108th Cong., 1st sess. S 189. 108–153.

Ugobe. 2007a. "Top Ten Essays from March 2007 Contest." Ugobe. www.ugobe.com/essay_contest/essay_winners.html (accessed on May 22, 2007, no longer available).

———. 2007b. "Behind the Scenes: The Making of Pleo." Ugobe. www.pleoworld.com/home/videos (accessed August 13, 2007, no longer available).

Ulanoff, Lance. 2007. "Robot Consumers, Grow Up." *PC Magazine*, November 7. www.pcmag.com/article2/0,2704,2212839,00.asp (accessed December 25, 2007).

van Gennep, Arnold. [1909] 2004. *Les Rites de Passages*. New York: Routledge

Veeser, H. Aram, ed. 1994. *The New Historicism Reader*. New York: Routledge.

Veruggio, Gianmarco. 2007. "The Roboethics Roadmap." Paper presented by Bruno Siciliano at the IEEE International Conference on Robotics and Automation, Rome (April 10–14). www.roboethics.org (accessed May 2, 2007).

Vinge, Vernor. [1981] 2001. *True Names.* In *True Names and the Opening of the Cyberspace Frontier,* edited by James Frenkel. New York: Tor Books.

———. [1993] 2003. "Technological Singularity." Rev. ed. available at www-rohan.sdsu.edu/faculty/ vinge/misc/WER2.html (accessed August 29, 2009).

Virtual Temple, The. 2007a. "Virtual Reality and Religion at the Virtual Temple." Online discussion in *Second Life,* February 1.

———. 2007b. "Avatars as Persons at the Virtual Temple." Online discussion in *Second Life,* July 19.

von Rad, G. 1965. *Theologie des Alten Testaments.* Munich: Kaiser.

Wada, Kazuyoshi, and Takanori Shibata. 2006. "Robot Therapy in a Care House: Its Sociopsycholog- ical and Physiological Effects on the Residents." *Proceedings of the 2006 IEEE International Con- ference on Robotics and Automation,* May. pp. 3966–71.

Waldrop, M. Mitchell. 1987. "A Question of Responsibility." *AI Magazine* 8(1): 29–39.

Wallace, B. Alan. 2000. *The Taboo of Subjectivity: Toward a New Science of Consciousness.* New York: Oxford University Press.

———. 2003. *Buddhism and Science: Breaking New Ground.* New York: Columbia University Press.

———. 2007. E-mail correspondence with author, May 20.

Walter, Chip. 2005. "You, Robot." *Scientific American* 292: 1, 36–37.

Warwick, Kevin. [1997] 2004. *March of the Machines: The Breakthrough in Artificial Intelligence.* Origi- nally published as *March of the Machines: Why the New Race of Robots Will Rule the World,* London (Century). Chicago: University of Illinois Press.

———. 2003. "Cyborg Morals, Cyborg Values, Cyborg Ethics." *Ethics and Information Technology* 5(3): 131–37.

———. 2007. "Upgrading Humans: Why Not?" Public presentation at Uvvy Island in *Second Life.* April 23.

Watson, Ian. 2007. "The Aims of Artificial Intelligence: A Science Fiction View." *IEEE Intelligent Systems* 18(2): 78–80.

Watts, Pauline Moffitt. 1985. "Prophecy and Discovery: On the Spiritual Origins of Christopher Columbus's 'Enterprise of the Indies.'" *The American Historical Review* 90(1): 73–102.

Webb, Robert L. 1990. "'Apocalyptic': Observations on a Slippery Term." *Journal of Near Eastern Studies* 49(2): 115–26.

Weber, Jutta. 2007. "Das Märchen vom digitalen Schlaraffenland." *C't* 7(March 19): 84–93.

Weber, Max. 1958. "Science as a Vocation." *From Max Weber: Essays in Sociology,* edited by Hans Gerth and C. Wright Mills, pp. 129–56. Oxford: Oxford University Press.

———. 1968. *On Charisma and Institution Building: Selected Papers.* Chicago: University of Chicago Press.

Weinberg, Steven. 1992. *Dreams of a Final Theory: The Scientist's Search for the Ultimate Laws of Nature.* New York: Vintage Books.

Weiss, Lee. 2007. Personal communication with author at Carnegie Mellon University, June 29.

Weizenbaum, Joseph. 1976. *Computer Power and Human Reason: From Judgment to Calculation.* San Francisco: W. H. Freeman.

Wertheim, Margaret. 1999. *The Pearly Gates of Cyberspace: A History of Space from Dante to the Inter- net.* New York: W.W. Norton and Company.

Whitcomb, John C., and Henry M. Morris. 1961. *The Genesis Flood: The Biblical Record and Its Scientific Implications*. Grand Rapids, Mich.: Baker Book House, The Presbyterian and Reformed Publishing Company.

White, Andrew. 1923. *The History of the Warfare of Science with Theology in Christendom*. Repr. New York: D. Appleton and Company.

White House: Office of the Press Secretary. 2003. "President Bush Signs Nanotechnology Research and Development Act." Press release, December 3. White House.www.whitehouse.gov/news/ releases/2003/12/20031203–7.html (accessed November 10, 2007).

Wiener, Norbert. 1964. *God and Golem, Inc.: A Comment on Certain Points where Cybernetics Impinges on Religion*. Cambridge, Mass.: MIT Press.

Wikipedia. 2009a. "Arnaldus de Villa Nova." http://en.wikipedia.org/wiki/Arnaldus_de_Villa_Nova (accessed August 24, 2009).

———. 2009b. "Office of Science and Innovation." http://en.wikipedia.org/wiki/Office_of_ Science_and_Innovation (accessed August 22, 2009).

Wilson, Daniel. 2005. *How to Survive a Robot Uprising: Tips on Defending Yourself Against the Coming Rebellion*. New York: Bloomsbury USA.

Wilson, Edward O. 2006. *The Creation: An Appeal to Save Life on Earth*. New York: W.W. Norton.

Winkler, Gershon. 1980. *The Golem of Prague: A New Adaptation of the Documented Stories of the Golem of Prague with an Introductory Overview*. New York: Judaica Press.

Winner, Langdon. 2002. "Are Humans Obsolete?" *Hedgehog Review* 4(3): 25–44.

Wolf, Milton T. 1992. "The Interface: Slouching Toward the Future—or—Guess Who's Coming to Dinner?" In *Thinking Robots, An Aware Internet, and Cyberpunk Librarians: The 1992 LITA President's Program*, edited by R. Bruce Miller and Milton T. Wolf, pp. 71–81. Chicago: Library and Information Technology Association.

Wright, Robert. 1997. "The Man Who Invented the Web: Tim Berners-Lee Started a Revolution, but It Didn't Go Exactly as Planned." *Time*, May 19. www.time.com/time/magazine/article/ 0,9171,986354,00.html?iid=chix-sphere (accessed July 3, 2007).

Yamaguchi, Yuzo. 2002. "All Too Human: Honda's Walking, Talking Robot, Asimo, Leads Automaker into Uncharted Territory, Engineers Ponder Potential for Sharing Technology." *Automotive News* 76 (5968, January 28): 100–103.

Zelazny, Roger. 1967. *Lord of Light*. Garden City, N.Y.: Doubleday.

Zorpette, Glenn. 2008. "Waiting for the Rapture." *IEEE Spectrum*, June. www.spectrum.ieee.org/ jun08/6311 (accessed June 3, 2008).

CPSIA information can be obtained
at www.ICGtesting.com
Printed in the USA
BVOW06s0306060817

491226BV00002B/6/P

9 780199 964000